preacher of the Word, and a leader in the work of Christ's Kingdom. In his role as chaplain and then president, he has been used by the Lord to deepen the commitment of Geneva College to the truths of the Reformed Faith, and to impact the lives of thousands of students. He has also been an effective spokesman for the College and the Reformed Faith in the wider evangelical community. This volume is a fitting tribute to a man who has sought to honor his Savior in a long life of service.

Wayne R. Spear, Professor-Emeritus, Reformed Presbyterian Seminary

For the 50 plus years that I have known him as my teacher, colleague, and friend, Jack's relentless passion to proclaim the Word of God, to teach, preach, and live the call to submit every area of our lives to the Lordship of Christ has continued unabated. That passion is reflected in the breadth and depth of the chapters of this book. I heartily recommend it to all who seek to daily live out the implications of the Gospel of the Kingdom.

Ralph Phillips, Portage Learning

I am so delighted to learn of the creation of this Festschrift to honor the faithful ministry of Dr. Jack White. He has evidenced such remarkable academic leadership in the cause of the Kingdom and the defense of the faith, once for all delivered to the saints. May this book inspire all who read it to follow in Dr. White's footsteps and to use their skills to promote and contend for the Truth.

Rev. Jonathan Gerstner, Ph.D.

I0220515

We learn the truest truths over the shoulder and through the heart, and that is why I am glad to commend this collection of essays in honor of Jack White. His teaching about the Great Story of God's work in history transformed the hearts and minds of a generation, giving us eyes to see that the biblical vision of life and the world was coherent from beginning to end, making a promise of redemption worthy of our lives, helping us to see the signposts of the world that someday will be.

Steven Garber, Professor of Marketplace Theology and Director of the Program in Leadership, Theology and Society, Regent College, author of *Visions of Vocation: Common Grace for the Common Good*

I have known Jack as an editor's ideal board member, supportive but asking hard questions. Later, when he chaired the accrediting committee for The King's College, where I was provost, he was the ideal accreditor, checking the plumbing and electrical connections but more concerned with the synapses of student brains. In both efforts he showed the grace, humor, and perseverance that would come as no surprise to those blessed to have known Jack as a pastor, urban seminary pioneer, and college president.

Marvin Olasky, Editor-in-Chief, *World* Magazine

It is with unalloyed pleasure and passion that I commend this Festschrift for Jack White, my mentor, colleague, dear friend, and co-laborer for Christ (to use a phrase of Jack's). I rejoiced as a colleague in hearing Jack's inaugural address and during more than 40 years of friendship have seen him exuberantly serve Christ in advancing His kingdom with eloquence, grace, and godly zeal. This volume is a worthy tribute to a prince of a man – a well done effort, indeed!

Timothy L. Russell, Pastor to Middle Adults, Second Presbyterian Church, Memphis

Jack White was the kind of professor who commanded a student's attention, even when students weren't quite sure why or how he did so. In his classes, God didn't "speak," he "carved his words in stone." And people didn't "listen" to God, he "emblazoned the truth on their minds." As teacher and preacher, Jack was a man to be reckoned with, a man who made claims on God's behalf. He knew the Bible, the world, the English language, and the human spirit, and he devoted himself, mind and body, to bring God's word to bear on all of it. This, he declared, would be good for us and, more importantly, satisfying to the Lord God who made and kept covenants. Jack conveyed, with startling force and endearing conviction, the great truth: The Triune God is the Savior and the Lord of every inch of life. He was the same man in each of his roles – preacher, college president, friend – so that he deserves every honor conveyed through this book.

Dan Doriani, Professor of Theology and Vice President, Covenant Seminary

For over a half century, Dr. John "Jack" White has been a leader among leaders when it comes to "Advancing the Vision" and building the Kingdom for our Lord. Having had the privilege to work alongside Jack for eight years at Geneva College, I can attest to the fact that he is the consummate Servant-Leader. Who else but Jack is equally comfortable speaking to a delegation of international higher education officials at a formal dinner *and* cheering for his favorite horse and rider at the Darlington (PA) Polo grounds? I am thrilled that this volume is being published so that others can experience the practical and biblical wisdom from his life, which I experienced on a daily basis while serving at Geneva. I am also glad that Jack gets to hear on this side of Heaven those special words, "Well done, thou good and faithful servant..."

Bill Katip, President, Grace College and Seminary

It has been my privilege to know Jack White as a friend since our days together as students at Geneva College and, subsequently, the Reformed Presbyterian Seminary. It was already evident then that the Lord was equipping Jack to be a strong

Advancing the Vision

Advancing the Vision

Essays in Honor of John H. White

Edited By
Jonathan M. Watt
Bruce R. Backensto

FALLS CITY PRESS

Beaver Falls, Pennsylvania
www.fallscitypress.com

Published by Falls City Press

2108 Seventh Avenue
Beaver Falls, PA 15010
www.fallscitypress.com

All websites listed herein are accurate as of the date of publication, but may change in the future. The inclusion of a website does not indicate the promotion of the entirety of the website's content.

Cover Design by Rafetto Creative
www.rafettocreative.com

Publisher's Cataloging-in-Publication Data

Backensto, Bruce R., 1947—
Watt, Jonathan M., 1957—

p. cm.
Includes bibliographical references.
ISBN: (paper) 978-0-9864051-5-0

1. Reformed Church—Doctrines
BR50.w36 2019

Contents

Dedication

This volume is affectionately dedicated
to John H. "Jack" White:
Our friend, exemplar, pastor, mentor, and teacher.

FOREWORD

The contributors to this *Festschrift* gladly acknowledge that Jack White has deeply influenced their lives—for some, over more than six decades—and have chosen to express that heartfelt appreciation through this volume. His influence has, in fact, been more than individual and personal; it has taken on institutional and international dimensions as well. The three sections of the volume have been arranged to reflect this.

Part 1 (Biography and Reminiscence) includes a glimpse into Jack's life and involvements by Dean Smith (Ch.1), along with focused accounts of his leadership in diversity at Geneva College, by Bradshaw Frey (Ch.2), at the Center for Urban Biblical Ministry, by Karla Byrd and John Stanko (Ch.3), and in the course of his training years and lifelong friendship with Ed Robson (Ch.4).

Part 2 (History, Theology, and Exegesis) offers studies in church history, systematics and exegesis by Byron Curtis (Ch.5), Scott Shidemantle (Ch.6), Calvin Troup (Ch.7), Barry York (Ch.8), Bruce Backensto (Ch.9), Jeff Stivason (Ch.10), and Sharon Sampson (Ch.11). They reflect the encouragement Jack has so consistently extended to others for the development of our understanding of the Word and our need to apply that life of the mind toward advancing the body of Christ.

Part 3 (Pastoral Theology and Networking) further explores the presence of Christian minds and lives to the world at large, with essays on leadership by Robert Frazier (Ch.12) and Maureen Vanterpool (Ch.13), and on how this looks in our rapidly globalizing world, as seen through the eyes of Jonathan Watt (Ch.14), Esther Meek (Ch.15), and Ken Smith (Ch.16). The final piece (Ch.17) by Jim Gidley represents the developing relationship of Geneva College across the globe today.

Jonathan M. Watt & Bruce R. Backensto
Winter Commencement, Geneva College
December 14, 2019

CHAPTER ONE

A Brief Biography of John H. "Jack" White

Dean R. Smith

John H. "Jack" White was born in Newburgh, New York on June 14, 1936, the son of John and Ethel White. The Whites were members of the Newburgh Reformed Presbyterian Church. Jack attended that church where he made a public profession of his faith. During the summers he would attend White Lake Covenanter Camp, where he met John Russell. He later roomed with John at Geneva College. It was through John's influence that Jack came to a full saving knowledge of and commitment to Jesus Christ as his Lord and Savior.

At Geneva, Jack met Norma Woods from Clarinda, Iowa, whom he married following graduation. They had two children: Natalie (now Mrs. Ray Austin) and Stephanie. Norma went to be with the Lord in 2011. In God's providence, He brought Mary Tait into Jack's life. They were married on October 19, 2013. Within their combined families, now considered "theirs," they have five children and eleven grandchildren. Jack's education included: a B.A. in History from Geneva College in 1958 (where he was listed in "Who's Who in Colleges and Universities"); an M.A. in History from the University of Pittsburgh in 1962; and finally, a D. Min. from the Pittsburgh Theological Seminary in 1977.

In 1962, Jack became pastor of the College Hill Reformed Presbyterian Church in Beaver Falls, Pennsylvania. His dynamic preaching produced a very fruitful ministry at this church, impacting college students and seeing a number of men go on to enter ministry. In 1970, he was invited to Geneva College to serve as Dean of Religious Services and Assistant Professor of Biblical Studies. His duties and title changed in 1978 to Director of Church Relations, and in 1985 he was named Associate Vice President for Religious Services before being promoted to Associate Professor of Biblical Studies the following year. In 1991, Jack was elected President of Geneva, a position he held until his retirement in 2004. During that time, Jack played a key role in developing the Masters in Counseling for Geneva College and also helped facilitate the development of the Degree Completion Program (DCP) at Geneva.

Preaching and Teaching

When Jack became pastor at College Hill, it quickly became evident that he was a gifted preacher and teacher. His preaching quickly attracted many college students, and along with the aid of Woody Woods, Jack established a strong college ministry. A number of those who were attracted as students later settled in Beaver Falls and became members and then leaders in the congregation. His preaching and teaching opened up a number of opportunities: commencement and opening convocation addresses at Covenant Theological Seminary, Westminster Theological Seminary, and Covenant College; additionally, there were Chapel and Spiritual Emphasis Week messages delivered at Biola College, Wheaton College, Westmont College, Sterling College, Gordon-Conwell Divinity School, Messiah College, Grove City College, Reformed Presbyterian Theological Seminary, Reformed Theological Seminary, Jackson, Mississippi, and Reformed Episcopal Seminary. Jack has preached frequently at churches of many denominations: Presbyterian, Christian and Missionary Alliance, Lutheran, Methodist, and many others. He also preached at First Presbyterian Church in Pittsburgh and was an interim preacher at Peter's Creek Baptist Church, the largest Baptist Church in the Pittsburgh Baptist Conference.

Community Service

One of the marks of Jack's ministry through the years was his vision for laboring with others. In a time when many Reformed people work in isolation from other Christian denominations and groups, Jack worked closely with other believers and Christian organizations. Jack has indicated that he received this vision from the RPCNA Covenant of 1871, Section 4:

> That, believing the church to be *one*, and that all the saints have communion with God and with one another in the same Covenant; believing, moreover, that schism and sectarianism are sinful in themselves; and inimical to true religion, and trusting that divisions shall cease, and the people of God become one Catholic church over all the earth, we will pray and labor for the visible oneness of the Church of God in our own land and throughout the world, on the basis of truth and of Scriptural order. Considering it a principal duty of our profession to cultivate a holy brotherhood, we will strive to maintain Christian friendship with pious men of every name, and to feel and act as one with all in every land who pursue this grand end. And, as a means of securing this great result, we will by dissemination and application of the principles of truth herein professed, and by cultivating and exercising Christian charity, labor to remove stumbling-blocks, and to gather into one the scattered and divided friends of truth and righteousness.

While this statement has sometimes been forgotten or ignored, Jack has faithfully practiced it throughout his ministry. I have listed some examples of Jack's influence, although almost any list is incomplete. Some products of this are listed here.

In the Beaver Falls Community & Region

Jack was one of the founders of the Beaver County Christian School in the 1960s. In 1978, he helped start the Tiger Pause Youth Ministry. Most recently, he has served on the Beaver Falls Ministry Collaboration which has brought a street minister to Beaver Falls. Jack has served on the governing boards of both the New Castle City Rescue Mission and Ellwood City Hospital.

In the Greater Pittsburgh Area

Coalition for Christian Outreach (CCO)—Jack united with others in the founding of the CCO in 1971 in Pittsburgh. It now ministers on 104 college campuses. Its annual Jubilee Conference attracts over 2,000 students each year and brings nationally known Christian figures to speak. Jack was recognized by the CCO board for his leadership in 2014.

Center for Urban Biblical Ministry (CUBM)—As President of Geneva College, Jack worked with Dr. Bruce Stewart of Reformed Presbyterian Theological Seminary (RPTS) and others to obtain a grant to develop a Community Ministry major in the Degree Completion program. This enabled students with an associate's degree to complete their undergraduate work and be eligible for seminary. A number of students have gone through CUBM and DCP to obtain their M.Div. from RPTS. Over these years, he additionally served as a board member of the Urban Impact ministry in Pittsburgh.

Nationwide

National Association of Evangelicals (NAE)—Jack served as a member of the Executive Committee of the Board of Administration of the NAE since 1975. He was second Vice-President between 1985 and 1986, First Vice-President from 1986 to 1988, and finally President from 1988 to 1990. He was also a member of the NAE Higher Education Commission, which he chaired from 1991–1996. NAE is a cooperative ecumenical organization with 54-member denominations and over 200 schools and para-ministry organizations with a service constituency of 15 million.

World Relief Corporation (WRC)—WRC is the relief and development arm of the NAE, now serving in some 50 nations around the world. From 1994–97, Jack was Chairman of the Board.

Westminster Theological Seminary (WTS)—Jack served on the Board of WTS from 1989–2015 and was chairman from 1990–2006.

Center for Urban Theological Studies (CUTS)—In conjunction with his service on the WTS Board, Jack, along with others, saw the need to help equip minority pastors who often were bi-vocational and needed more biblical training. Together they worked to establish the CUTS program in Philadelphia as an adjunct program with Geneva College.

Scholarship

Jack has been a preacher, a pastor, and an administrator. Throughout all of this, he has always had a scholar's heart and mind in both his preparation for sermons and classes, and in his study and writing. He served as publisher of the *Christian's Scholar Review* from 1991–1994. He is the author of *The Book of Books* (P&R Pub. Co., 1978), a study on the nature and character of biblical revelation; and *Slavery to Servanthood* (Great Commission Publications, 1987), a study of the Exodus theme in the Bible. He was also a contributor of the following articles: "The Pastor - His Identity and Authority" to *Soli Deo Gloria: A Festschrift for John Gerstner* (R.C. Sproul, Presbyterian & Reformed Pub. Co., 1976); *A Society in Peril* (Blattner & Perrotta, Servant Press, 1989); and *Come to the Banquet: Meditations for the Lord's Table* (Bodey & Holmes, Baker Books, 1998).

Additionally, Jack has contributed articles to *Christianity Today*, *Decision*, *Eternity*, and *Table Talk*, and has had reviews and articles published in *Christianity Today*, *Presbyterian Journal*, *Westminster Theological Journal*, *Presbyterian Guardian*, *Covenanter Witness*, *Renaissance and Reformation*, *Christian Scholar's Review*, and *Christian Herald*. His article on the "Relevance of Calvinism" has been listed in the "International Bibliography on Calvin and Calvinism" published in *Calvin Theological Journal* and also in the Netherlands and Japan in the fall of 1974. He contributed chapters on "Rapture and the Great Tribulation" to *A Study of the Revelation* (1976); "Worship in the Pentateuch—a Biblical Theological Overview" in *The Biblical Doctrine of Worship* (1974); and presented on "Calvinism and the Sovereignty of God" and "Calvin—The Man" at The Second Reformed Presbyterian International Youth Convention (1964). Jack's periodical articles include: "Decision" (Publication of Billy Graham Evangelistic Association, April 1990); "God our Redeemer," "Interview: Cross Cultural Journal of Christian Leadership," "The Children of the Convener" (also editor), and "Study on Church and Society," (Reformed Ecumenical Synod, 1975–77).

He edited *The Book of Books* (Presbyterian and Reformed Pub. Co., 1978/2019) and contributed a chapter entitled "How to Approach the Bible for Study." Recently studying the late Johannes G. Vos's correspondence from China, Jack concluded that the renewal of the evangelical church in China today has its roots in the writings and teaching of Vos and other Reformed Presbyterian missionaries who served there in the latter nineteenth and early- to mid-twentieth centuries.

In March 2019, Jack was recognized with the "Faithful Servant Award" by the Reformed Presbyterian Theological Seminary in Pittsburgh. At that recognition, Jack was clear to say *Soli Deo Gloria* —"To God Be the Glory."

And in response, we say "Amen!"

CHAPTER TWO

Holding a Heritage: The White Years

Bradshaw Frey

In his inaugural address as Geneva's eighteenth president on October 9, 1992, John H. "Jack" White chose the theme of *remembering* in order to cast a vision for the future of the college. As a former pastor who is deeply immersed in the biblical drama, White described the faithful functioning of a college as dependent on its ability to place itself in its historical heritage the way Israel had been called to remember God's faithfulness throughout its history. Before coming to the college, White had significantly contributed to the lynchpin moment of calling the college back to its faith moorings. Along with colleagues Dr. Jim Carson, Dr. Ken Smith, Sr., and Mrs. Jean Hemphill (and with significant input from Dr. J.G. Vos), they drafted the document known as "The Foundational Concepts of Christian Education" still in use today. It was an act of remembering the founders' intent as they launched Geneva.

Upon becoming President of Geneva, White called on the college to "remember" another part of its heritage. He knew the college had been founded by people who were not only staunch Presbyterians but also staunch abolitionists. He believed it was clear that the founders intended Geneva to reflect their counter-cultural posture on issues of race. His charge to students at his inauguration was that we honor our heroic past that included:

> ...our first African-American graduate, Aphelia Hall Nesbit, class of 1866, who became a teacher in Cincinnati. Also, James McCartney, William George, and John Johnson, who were active conductors on the Underground Railroad in the 1850s and 60s. Our Geneva forefathers believed that slavery was such a heinous sin that it led them to a reasoned but vigorous civil disobedience. May we so teach that we send a continuing and growing number of students out into this society as servant-leaders to transform it for the Kingdom of God.[1]

The White years at Geneva would be marked by a robust attempt to channel this nineteenth-century heritage to the college at the end of the twentieth century. But White's charge was to what he called a commitment to a particular understanding of diversity that was biblically sensitive, not politically correct.[2]

This commitment to diversity had a deep history for White. While a graduate student at the University of Pittsburgh in 1964, he had volunteered to drive to Selma, Alabama, during the civil rights battle being waged there. The Reformed Presbyterian Church of North American (RPCNA) had a congregation in Selma that was predominantly African-American and which also had (at that time) a black pastor, the Rev. Claude Brown. Denominational leaders wanted to give the congregation and pastor tangible support, so White volunteered. While forbidden by the denomination from marching, White was at many meetings with Brown, even historic meetings where Dr. Martin Luther King, Jr. was addressing marchers and others in the famous Brown AME Chapel.

While serving as Vice President for Religious Affairs at the college, White had assisted Dr. Bill Krispin and Westminster Theological Seminary to establish a theological training center for urban pastors and laypeople in Philadelphia that they called the Center for Urban Theological Studies (CUTS). CUTS was a remarkable partnership between urban pastors and academics with traditionally white institutions that provided White a constant barometer on how Geneva was progressing with regards to diversity. Eventually, the CUTS model was brought to Pittsburgh in the Center for Urban Biblical Ministry (CUBM) in conjunction with the Reformed Presbyterian Seminary. In addition, while serving in leadership of the National Association of Evangelicals (NAE), he eventually become the organization's president and worked hard to establish increased synergy between NAE and the National Black Evangelical Association.

Geneva College's interest in and movement toward a more diverse campus moved at a slower pace. By the end of the tumultuous 1960s, Geneva had developed an active Black Student Union (BSU). The organization had petitioned the college to offer more options for studying black culture and history. In response the college invited three sociologists from the University of Pittsburgh to offer a course titled "Black Culture in the US" on campus. The BSU also worked with the campus to bring various programs to campus highlighting issues of race and culture. However, by the mid-1980s, it was clear that Geneva was languishing in its attempts to be more intentionally diverse as a college.[3]

White was disappointed that Geneva had failed to make more headway on these issues because he believed Geneva's Reformed theological heritage gave it a particularly strong resource. White had hired Irving "Bucky" Waldron and Henry "Tuna" Hansard, former star athletes at the college who were African-American, to do campus ministry through the regional organization, the Coalition for Christian Outreach (CCO). Though Geneva was rooted in and taught primarily the Western cultural tradition, White realized all cultures were tarnished by human sin. No culture measured up to God's expectations; therefore, a college in the Reformed tradition ought not to baptize any single culture without critique.

In a similar vein, White believed that because of what the Calvinistic tradition called "common grace," all cultures had some vestige of what God had created cultures to be. This meant all cultures had something to contribute to Christian learning and all cultures needed to be put under the scrutiny of biblical critique. Finally, White affirmed that institutions and not just individuals could respond in faithfulness or disobedience. In particular, a college could be judged in the same way as a culture. He referenced Calvin's contention that not just individuals but their "callings" were formed by sinful human beings and thus needed the redirection offered by the scripture.

This theological foundation was very timely. The diversity movement itself had moved from a focus on justice and equity with an aim at inclusion to a focus on multiculturalism.[4] White was unable to affirm the idea that all cultures were equal and that their merit was relative. But his theology allowed him to affirm the partial goodness of all cultures while likewise critiquing the problems all cultures had. While not a perfect fit for the multicultural thrust of the diversity movement, it gave White and Geneva the possibility of interfacing with the movement in a useful way.

During the presidency of Dr. Joseph McFarland, a catalyzing moment occurred in the late 1980s. Two strong African-American trustees launched an initiative at the Board level. Mr. Clarence Farmer and Dr. Donald Sheffield both had extensive backgrounds in diversity initiatives. Farmer had been a champion of civil rights in Philadelphia and one of the businesses he owned had done a good deal of the diversity training for city employees in Philadelphia. Sheffield had been part of an initiative by Penn State University to address the failure of public education in Pennsylvania to prepare minority and under resourced children for higher education. (There may well have been a number of others at the Board level who championed this new direction. This narrative is limited to what was reflected in Board minutes and by those interviewed.)

On January 25, 1991 the Geneva College Board of Trustees adopted what was titled a "Statement of Affirmation." This affirmation had been the result of a task force that had been appointed by Dr. McFarland and chaired by Farmer. Named the "Minority Issues Task Force," the group included: Todd Allen, Kristi Dolch, Elizabeth Douglas, Joy Jewell, William Katip, Bill Krispin, Donald Sheffield, Brad Frey, Fanny Farmer, William Harris, and also McFarland (*Ex Officio*). Board minutes referencing this meeting include, "The consensus of the Board is that we must send an immediate strong message to Geneva's publics [*sic*] that, as an institution, Geneva is committed to dealing with minority issues and to promoting cultural diversity on campus."[5]

In addition to this strong, counter cultural language, the Board adopted the remarkable "Statement of Affirmation" document. The preamble of the document drew heavily on the theology of diversity that White had articulated merged with the forceful leadership of Clarence Farmer and Donald Sheffield. It reads:

> The Geneva College community professes a commitment to the reconciling message of the Gospel. This message represents both our greatest challenge and our highest hope. Geneva College has historically opposed acts of human injustice and has, from its earliest history, endeavored to provide aid, shelter, and educational opportunity for students regardless of background. By means of this statement, we commit ourselves to a renewed effort to develop policies that will promote cultural diversity and foster an appreciation of all persons among Geneva's students, faculty, staff, alumni and other connectional activities consistent with the Christian character of Geneva College.[6]

There is no question that Geneva had a mixed history in the attention it paid to issues of race. While there were courageous moments in our early history, there was also the reality that black students weren't allowed to live on campus until the early 1950s and that the College Hill community that surrounds Geneva was a *de facto* segregated community until the 1980s. Unfortunately, the Christian church in America has had a long history of failing to seize the moment when it could have provided a biblical voice for justice as deep atrocities were done to people of color.[7] At Geneva this reality is played out in the continuing frustration over the fact that its early history is often celebrated in the absence of much attention being paid to parallel issues of our the present time.

Nonetheless, the Board of Trustees, sensing the importance of the moment spelled out in detail what they intended with an eight-part affirmation:

1. A commitment to equity and justice among all persons created in the image of God.
2. A commitment to bring the critique and standard of the Bible to bear upon all cultures.
3. A commitment to provide an academic program which introduces students to the issues of living and serving in a multicultural society consonant with our Evangelical and Reformed faith.
4. A commitment to aggressively recruit minority and women candidates for job openings in staff, faculty, and administrative positions and measure progress annually.
5. A commitment to recruit a culturally diverse student population and seek scholarship aid for these students.
6. A commitment to create campus wide programs which foster an atmosphere of appreciation for cultural diversity.
7. A commitment to provide staff support services and budget support for this multicultural initiative.
8. A commitment to review progress towards the goals and recommendations of this plan on a regular basis and hold all persons charged with the plan's implementation and assessment accountable (Board Minutes, Jan. 25, 1991).

This "Affirmation" became "marching orders" for White. Upon becoming president, he affirmed his intention to make this a central part of his presidency.

Several observations about the Board's actions. First, for a conservative, Christian college like Geneva, this was quite a forward-looking step. Second, the Board clearly intended that whatever initiatives taken should be consistent with the sponsoring denomination's theological commitments. And, third, it is a very concrete document. There could be little question that the Board intended an aggressive response to its directives.

That this initiative was gaining momentum at the beginning of White's presidency was reflected in the college newspaper, *The Cabinet*. An October 1992 article questioned White about "this new push for diversity." He noted that Geneva had long been a religiously diverse campus with only about 7% of the student body being from the RPCNA. However, he said, this initiative was about ethnicity not religion. "We have a very poor record with African-American representation," White claimed. He noted that recently the number of African-American students and international students had increased but that he intended those numbers to continue to grow. He went on to explain that it was critical for the college to prepare students to be change agents in their society and that this initiative was critical for that end.[8]

Nearly a year later, Doug Barnes, Editor of the Cabinet, followed up with White to see what progress had been made. White reported that two important steps had been taken. Todd Allen had been appointed as the Assistant to the President for Multicultural Affairs. White emphasized the importance of how this position was administratively placed. "Todd is not just a director but has immediate access to me for the needs of students of color."[9] A month later White clarified further. He said that the newly created Multicultural Office, directed by Mr. Allen, would plan a few programs but was mainly intended to act in an advisory capacity on college policies and existing programs.[10]

The second step was the appointment of Ann Burkhead as Director of Specialized Enrollment. White intended that parallel tracks would develop, and that Geneva would be the great beneficiary of seeing the number of African-American students increase while at the same time seeing internationals increase as well. In the June 1995 issue of the *Geneva Alumnus* publication White outlined how both initiatives were progressing. He noted that both the mission statement and the strategic themes the college had adopted intended to foster diversity.[11] The international student initiative also gave the college a place to affirm the role of children of missionaries ("missionary kids," or MKs). Often characterized as "third culture kids" who do not neatly fit in their host culture or here in US culture, this attention to the variety of cultures could enhance the college's service to MKs.

An additional piece was necessary if the college was to thoroughly implement this new-found momentum for diversity. Farmer had counseled early on that the college needed to generate a document that would guide it. White directed Allen to put together a committee to develop such a document.[12] The plan was to be directed by the eight affirmations that the Board had already passed. Other colleges had developed documents such as this that were to be used as guides. One document that was particularly useful was an extensive plan developed by Calvin College in Grand Rapids, Michigan. As a sister college, it was believed that there would be similar sensibilities as they had navigated their way to develop a guidance-giving document that was also consonant with their standing as an institution of faith. Committee members were drawn from faculty, staff and administration. Once the document was complete the intention was to take it to the faculty for approval before sending it to the Board for final approval.

The Committee charged each vice president to come up with a plan for their area of the college that they believed was keeping with the spirit of the "Affirmations" but that also seemed currently reasonable. Each plan was submitted to the committee that translated it into areas of assessment, affirmations of good developments, and concrete plans for the future. As the work of the committee and the responses of the various areas of the college were developed it became apparent that there was significant discontent with the direction of the plan especially amongst the faculty. One of the most oft-cited concerns was that the college was too aggressively capitulating to the secular multicultural initiatives sweeping the country. The committee was confused by this critique, since virtually every statement its president had made on the college's posture both distanced the current cultural movement and tried to place the college's work in its historic commitments.

The committee decided that if such a misunderstanding was believed that they should do what they could to convince colleagues that the document was appropriate for the college. Professor of Biblical Studies, Dr. Byron Curtis, was recruited to write a preamble to the document that outlined the biblical teaching on diversity. The committee believed that everything in the document would be filtered through the preamble if there was any uncertainty on what was intended.

The "preamble strategy" failed. When the document was distributed to the faculty it was met with staunch resistance. By the October, 1995 meeting of the Board, it was reported that there was strong resistance to the document. Sheffield pleaded with the Board to help the college understand the urgency of the plan.[13] But the opposition to the document did not subside so a year later White decided to postpone approval of the document so the concerns of various members of the college community could be addressed.[14] White later confided that he believed that if he set the document aside for a while, the intensity of the controversy would die down some.

Vice President for Enrollment William Katip and Provost James Boelkins were both strong supporters of these initiatives. Boelkin's efforts to hire women and minority faculty were praised by White to the Board during its April, 1995 meeting. While work on the diversity document stalled, good progress was being made on the international student front. In an article in the *Geneva Alumnus,* Katip described the progress. Burkhead was not only functioning well as the Director of Specialized Enrollment, but was also commended for the role she was playing in advising international students. She was also exemplary at hospitality. Geneva had a good functioning relationship with Christ College in Taipei, Taiwan, and a regular flow of 7–10 students a year had begun from that country. In reciprocation, Geneva provided faculty support for Christ College. Dr. Norman and Beverly Carson spent a year at Christ College, and were replaced by retired president McFarland and his wife, Roberta. Finally, Mr. Phil Breeding went for a longer stay.[15]

The same issue of the magazine described the things being done at the college for international students to flourish. In addition to Burkhead's role, support was given for English as a Second Language (ESL) classes, cultural training, and an international student organization. The college had a recruiter actively traveling to Asia and other locales to find students. English and Linguistics professor, Dr. Paul Kilpatrick, along with Burkhead, were also able to renew the sister-college relationship with Kosin College in Pusan, Korea. The article noted that Geneva had about 30 international students, though that number would swell to 110 during the White years.

In White's and the college's theology of diversity, the most frequently quoted Bible reference was Revelation 5:9. In the issue of the *Geneva Alumnus* devoted to this new direction White commented on the passage by saying, "Christians are called to win people from all races and cultures, furthermore to seek to bring those cultures into submission to Christ's standards."[16] White and his supporters thought this theology was a mandate for the direction he was taking the college.

After nearly a year of "cooling off," committee members pressed White to move the document forward. One issue White had with the document was that he believed it needed a good edit. He thought it was unclear at points, was awkward at others, and in some places was just plain sloppy. He thought before he introduced a version for approval it needed a good cleaning up. White had a close friend who was a good editor and was both interested in and knowledgeable about diversity. White sent the document to him to be fixed.

Unfortunately, somewhere in the request, a misunderstanding took place. White thought he was simply asking for a thorough edit. His friend heard his request to fix the document to be one that "put more teeth" into it. The edit took longer than White thought and he was under intense pressure to get the document out to the faculty from the committee. Succumbing to the pressure when it was finally returned, White had it printed and distributed without reviewing the changes that had been made.

When faculty who opposed the document, and those who were cautious of it now read it they were very frustrated. Since the "action plan" had been intensified they assumed their previous hesitations had not only not been heard but ignored. This version of the document seemed to intentionally oppose their problems with it. The showdown came at a faculty meeting where most of the meeting was to be for discussion of the document. The committee had scrambled to have the changes put back to the original language but, by then, the damage was done.

After a representative of the committee gave a brief review of the document the microphone was opened to any who wished to speak. One faculty member, whose frustration had been brewing for months, stepped to the microphone and read a seven-page document. His frustrations centered around three issues and, to a large extent, these three issues summarized much of the opposition to the document.

First, he feared that this document signaled a move on the part of the college away from its historic commitment to Western culture and its European antecedents. The multicultural movement, from his perspective, denigrated that heritage or at least relativized it. Second, he feared the document was simply Geneva's way of caving into the general drift of American culture. Instead of maintaining our distinctive call as a college we were capitulating to cultural pressure. We were being politically correct. And, finally, that the administration generally and White in particular was being heavy handed and "Gestapo-like" in their approach. The critique was so intense that when he was finished no one else went to the microphone. Finally, the committee representative countered that they obviously disagreed but that disagreement was so thorough it seemed it could not be accommodated in the time remaining at the meeting. Several other faculty members then spoke of their problems with the document. Other than the committee members no one spoke for it. The faculty chair then acknowledged that time had run out and that there would have to be a special meeting called to continue the conversation and take a vote.

At the special meeting the following week a compromise was struck. The document would be approved but only after the action points were removed. Many faculty members were willing to consider the action items but wanted more time and debate before ratifying that part of the document. The committee was quite frustrated because they had regularly announced when they were meeting and invited faculty members to come and voice concern or give critique. Since no colleagues had acted on the invitation to meet with them, the committee believed there was more support than there was.

One committee member hastily prepared a letter chastising his colleagues for what he thought was an obstructionist stance. The letter brought a rebuke from the faculty, many who found it offensive. A special meeting was called to both listen to, question, and rebuke the committee member. White also visited the committee member to express his displeasure with the letter.

The document, now titled "Blueprint for Excellence Through Diversity," also faced some problems with the Board. Board minutes contain no record of the discussions that took place, but at two different times (January 1997 and April 1998), the Board reaffirmed its commitment to the eight affirmations it had passed in 1991. They also passed the version of the document that had been passed by the faculty.

The follow-up discussion to develop an action plan that would operationalize the commitments made in the document never took place. The community seemed exhausted from the battles over the document. However, because the college had both a multicultural office and an office to recruit and care for international students, it seemed a foundation had been laid by White and his administration to change the course of the college.

By the end of the White years, things began to unravel. In an austerity move, new vice president for enrollment, Murray Evans, scrapped much of the apparatus to recruit and acculturate international students. Student recruitment became much more generalized and with it both the number of international students and American minority students plummeted. By the time Dr. Kenneth A. Smith became the new president, the "Blueprint for Excellence Through Diversity" had become largely overlooked. At one point, the newly appointed provost, Dr. Stanley Clark, announced he was going to do a diversity audit of each of the departments. Even though such a practice was suggested in the document and the "Affirmations," there was significant resistance. In his first year as president, Smith called the remaining committee members together for a quick meeting, saying he was told that no one on campus really paid attention to the document and he did not intend to be held accountable to it. He said that at his previous university, "diversity" was simply a code word for LGBTQ issues, with which he disagreed. He said he intended to give attention to diversity issues but not in conjunction with the document. Smith's pronouncement was telling, and a focus on students of color and international students have eroded since the White years.

Most of the initiatives taken during the White years were significantly dialed back or eliminated. What had been a "direct report" position when first established, the head of the multicultural office was downgraded, first to director then to coordinator; it is a part-time position at the time of this writing. In a recent graduate student project, students of color were interviewed in depth about their experience at Geneva. Their responses were alarming, as they suggested a campus culture that is uncomfortable at best and hostile at worst.

President White framed his inauguration in the biblical idea to "remember." During his presidency he worked hard to put in place structures that would allow Geneva to remember the part of its heritage deeply embedded in issues of race and diversity in its history. White's hope was that by "remembering" we would be able to "advance the vision." Great progress was made during his tenure toward that goal. Much of that progress has eroded in the intervening years. There is little left of the concrete advances tied to the eight "Affirmations" of the Board and a campus climate that has left students of color feeling remarkably marginalized. If the vision of the college's founders channeled through White and the college's Trustees of the 1990s is to be viable into the twenty-first century, urgent action is needed.

There is still a substantial foundation remaining. Three times the Board of Trustees voted on, and approved, the eight affirmations. Those affirmations, if attended to, would reinvigorate much of the activity of the White years. Though tremendously diminished, there is still the apparatus to reclaim a commitment to students of color and international students. Those are legacies of the White years.

Through the initiatives to make Geneva a richly diverse campus, White saw himself as holding a heritage that had been set by the college founders. His work was significant enough to leave the framework for that heritage to be reclaimed. The college now needs some of White's courage to once again hold its heritage.

Notes

[1]John H. "Jack" White, "*Remember: And Thus Advance the Vision*," Inaugural Address, October 9, 1992, pp. 6 – 7.

[2]*Geneva Alumnus*, June 1995, p. 1.

[3]*Geneva Alumnus*, June 1995, p. 1.

[4]For a discussion of this topic see Damon A. Williams, *Strategic Diversity Leadership: Activating Change and Transformation in Higher Education* (Herndon, VA: Stylus Publishing L.L.C., 2013).

[5]Board of Trustees, *Minutes* January 25, 1991.

[6]*Minutes*, January 25, 1991.

[7]For further discussion on this issue see Jemar Tisby, *The Color of Compromise: The Truth About American Church's Complicity in Racism*

(Grand Rapids, MI: HarperCollins Christian Publishing, 2019).

[8]*The Cabinet*, October 9, 1992, p. 6.

[9]*The Cabinet*, September 17, 1993, p. 6.

[10]*The Cabinet*, November 19, 1993, p. 5.

[11]*The Geneva Alumnus*, June 1995, p. 1.

[12]Board *Minutes*, January 25, 1995.

[13]Board *Minutes*, October 27, 1995.

[14]Board *Minutes*, October 25, 1996.

[15]*Geneva Alumnus*, June 1995, p. 4.

[16]*Geneva Alumnus*, June 1995, p. 1.

References

Geneva College Board of Trustee Minutes, References to Diversity, 1990–2004. [This project was helped immeasurably by College Archivist, Mrs. Kae Kirkwood, who searched archival material for various resources. She was also given permission to extract Trustee material useful for this project.]

Geneva College Student Newspaper *The Cabinet*, Oct. 9, 1992; Sept. 17, 1993; and, Nov. 19, 1993. *Geneva Alumnus*, June 1995.

John H. White. "Remember: And Thus Advance the Vision." Inaugural Address Oct. 9, 1992.

James McGeary. "Black Student Experiences with Campus Climate: A Phenomenological Study on Racialized Experience." Nov. 29, 2018.

CHAPTER THREE

John H. "Jack" White's Work Toward Racial Reconciliation

Karla Threadgill Byrd & John W. Stanko

The idea of accredited biblical training in ministry for African-Americans in Pittsburgh goes back many years, but it began to crystallize in the mid-1980s when a group of African-American church leaders met to consider how they could organize an institution which would help to develop the gifts for ministry of those who were serving in the church.

At the same time, a significant number of African-American church leaders (45 in 1988) were enrolled as students in the Reformed Presbyterian Theological Seminary (RPTS) for instruction and training. The Seminary felt committed to help these students, but a great majority of them did not have a college degree, and since the Seminary was becoming fully accredited, it needed to limit the number of students who did not have a baccalaureate degree.

As leaders in the African-American churches met together with the President of the Reformed Presbyterian Theological Seminary as well as representatives of Geneva College and of the Pittsburgh Leadership Foundation, it was decided to consider a program in Pittsburgh similar to the Center for Urban Theological Studies (CUTS) in Philadelphia, which had developed an undergraduate degree program for African-American students which is affiliated with Geneva College in Beaver Falls, Pennsylvania.

The first meetings of an Ad Hoc Committee were held in the Bethany Baptist Church in 1987 and were led by Richard Farmer. Subsequent meetings of the Pittsburgh CUTS Committee were held at the Monumental Baptist Church and at the Ebenezer Baptist Church. When Richard Farmer left Pittsburgh, LeRoy Walker replaced him as Chairman of the committee. Other members of the committee included: James Sims, Edna Tollivar, Thomas Smith, John Leftwich, Yvonne Thornton and John Hart of the Pittsburgh Leadership Foundation, John White of Geneva College, and Bruce Stewart of the Reformed Presbyterian Theological Seminary.

The first classes were held informally at the Bethany Baptist Church and the Monumental Baptist Church. As more church and community leaders became involved and more students enrolled, most of the classes were held at the Reformed Presbyterian Theological Seminary, though occasional classes were held in Canonsburg and Beaver Falls.

On July 5, 1989, the name was changed to the Center for Urban Biblical Ministry (CUBM). A charter and by-laws were adopted, and a fully accredited Associate of Arts (AA) degree through Geneva College was offered. The program emphasized commitment to service, preaching, teaching, community development, and counseling. In addition to classes and an academic curriculum, CUBM also provides seminars on culture, community development, and church management in the African-American church.

John White, known to his friends as Jack, was on staff at Geneva when talks began with CUBM and became president shortly thereafter. He was instrumental in establishing the partnership between the two organizations, and then played a key role in obtaining a federal grant, naming CUBM as a partner, for The Marriage Works and TwoGether Pittsburgh initiatives to strengthen relationships in the urban community. Dr. White still serves on the CUBM board but has long since retired from any role at Geneva College. Here is an interview he gave that is included in *The CUBM Story: Celebrating 25 Years at the Center for Urban Biblical Ministry 1988–2013.*[1]

Q: What is your current position at Geneva College, and how did your work with CUBM and racial reconciliation get started?

> *JW: My current position is president emeritus of Geneva College. I was the president from 1991–2004. Previous to that I was what was called Vice President for Religious Services and Church Relations. I started that position in 1970. The title of Church Relations wasn't added until the '80s, approximately. And that's where the connection with the beginnings of CUBM come in. One of things that I did was contact Evangelical and Reformed churches throughout the east, Pennsylvania, Maryland, Ohio, and so forth.*
>
> *I'll just tell it anecdotally. One day, I'm in Philadelphia, and I got a phone call the old-fashioned way from a Geneva grad by the name of Wilson Cummings. Wilson was the pastor, a white guy, of an inner-city church. And he was working in team with a man named William Crispin. One day, as he told the story, a black man came to the door and introduced himself as the pastor of the church in the area. And he asked, "Are you going to do the usual thing that white people do when they come to plant a church? Are you going to do your own thing? Or are you going to find out what God is doing in the African-American church?"*
>
> *And Bill had enough grace to say, "Well, up until now I was going to do my own thing. But beginning now, it makes a lot of sense."*
>
> *And the man said, "I tell you what, give me two months, and you just hang out with me. And then we'll talk." Bill did that. This guy's name, I don't remember. This is all*

background to how CUTS got started. At the end of the time, with the help of a lot of the other African-American pastors, Bill discovered that there was a great sense of need for more biblical and theological education.

At that time in Philadelphia, 85% of the African-American church leaders were not college graduates, and they were bi-vocational. So he went to his alma mater, Westminster Theological Seminary, started a weekend theological institute, and the pastors loved it. I mean, you're talking about what for white folks in the Reformed community were the theological stars, Cornelius Van Til, John Murray, Edward J. Young.

The pastors loved it and then wanted to go to seminary, but they didn't have their undergraduate degrees. So Wilson called me and asked, "What do you think? Can Geneva help?" I responded, "I don't know, I have no power in these things, although I do report directly to the president and I know Geneva has a history of concern and education for the African-American communities."

Most people don't know that Geneva was an abolitionist institution. After the Civil War, they had a lot of freedmen, as they were called at that time, as students of Geneva. Geneva's got a rich history. Therefore, I went to the president, who was a close friend but a cautious man. He finally said, "Let's try to start something and let it run for a couple of years." The result of that was the Center for Urban Theological Studies in Philadelphia.

Fast-forward to Pittsburgh. I would say it was about '87 or '88. Bruce Stewart, who was the president at Reformed Presbyterian Theological Seminary, called me one day and said, "A bunch of people are getting together at Tom Smith's church," which was a key church in the Hill District. I went to that meeting, and there was a discussion about the need for biblical education in the Pittsburgh urban community.

At that time, there was a Bible institute in the Hill that had existed for years and was like an advanced Sunday School (that was not my judgment, but the judgment of the leaders on the Hill), and they really didn't have anything else. One of the guys there looked at me and asked, "Why did you do it in Philadelphia and not in Pittsburgh?" I hemmed and hawed around with my answer, and I don't even remember what I said, because I thought I said, "That's a great question." We then started meeting regularly to give birth to what became the Center for Urban Biblical Ministry.

Q: Let's go back to the early days. You wanted to present accredited education that was biblically based. Would you say in relation to that that there is too much unaccredited education?

JW: I would say there is, sadly. During this experience, the wonderful privilege that I've had is to cross paths, to be preaching and living close to the African-American church community. One of the saddest things I remember, and it was heartbreaking, that African-American men would come to my office with a big folder of certificates from various educational institutions. I would ask them to leave it and make an arrangement for them to come back. These were sometimes pastors from Pittsburgh, but mostly pastors from New Castle, Sharon, Beaver Falls, and so forth.

I would look [the places] up where they earned the certificates, and they weren't even listed. Maybe I shouldn't say that none of them were, but 90% of them weren't. I tried to find a way to break the news graciously to these leaders. One man said to me, "You're telling me I just have a bunch of pieces of paper?" I said, "My brother, it grieves me, but that's exactly right." I mean, he said it so well: "All I've got is a piece of paper." It had no value for anything else. I just cried. These leaders thought they were getting bachelor's degrees, sometimes doctorates, and it was just scandalous.

Q: Was that heavy in everyone's minds to make this as legitimate as possible, not wanting to be providing anything people can poke holes in?

JW: Exactly. Here was a community that was educationally deprived. And by in large it was white folks, I'm confident, who took terrible advantage of them. I can still remember that man in my office like it were yesterday, and he must have had invested thousands of dollars in that folder.

Q: Was it easy to establish an accredited system in Philadelphia and Pittsburgh? What's the process for that since CUBM is not physically attached to Geneva?

JW: It was not easy to do. One of the blessings that Geneva has is that it has a very early charter in the state of Pennsylvania, which gives it special authority that a lot of institutions don't have. We don't have to get state approval for offering a new degree or doing a new thing or something like that. However, Geneva does have an accrediting agency, and that agency has to have what's called a site visit that can sometimes be onerous.

I would say it was a blessing to Geneva, because what happened was we became kind of an example of an institution doing something to address a need for adult and urban education back in the 60s, the 70s, the 80s, and so forth. CUTS goes all the way back into the late 70s. This became the thing that educational institutions ought to do, if they had any conscience about this community that really has been educationally deprived.

Even back in the beginning, we gave life experience credit. It wasn't easy, but why should somebody take speech 101 when that person had been preaching for 15 years? And Middle States was tremendously helpful. I'll never forget being stunned when the general secretary of Middle States got up off his chair and pulled down two books from his bookshelf and showed me the things that were being written on what we were trying to establish. He assured me that Geneva would have Middle States' blessing.

Q: Was CUTS (Center for Urban Theological Studies) the model that you were building CUBM off of?

JW: Yes. It wasn't exactly reproduced here. There was a zeal for it in Philly among the large enough African-American community churches, so they could really pull it off. There were a couple of models, because the model in Philadelphia was never really reproduced here, because it was an association of white churches. There though I don't think we called them white, but non-urban and urban churches coming together to do this together. It wasn't the mentality that "we white folks are doing something for you." And the structure of the board right now at CUBM is 50-50 white and black, and that's exactly what worked so well at CUTS.

That was no wonderful thinking or strategic thinking. It was just something we stumbled into. Lots of white pastors in Philadelphia, some of them right in the city, had a real heart to see this happen, and supported it financially, which never really happened in Pittsburgh, unfortunately. We haven't gotten that sort of synergy. It has a lot to do both with the size, and maybe the parochialism of western Pennsylvania versus Philadelphia.

Q: What do you remember from the early times? What were some of the challenges?

JW: The challenges were financial. There were times when we would meet together as the board and we were deeply in the red for a small place. And I can still hear the vice president for business, my chief financial officer at Geneva, coming to my office to show me the numbers and saying to me, "Boss, close it down."

Q: And what was your response?

JW: I'd tell him, "We can't do it."

Q: Then what did they say?

JW: "Well, you're the president, fortunately. If you were going to make a decision purely on a financial basis, you'd close it down." One thing that needs to be said to Geneva's credit, Geneva hasn't always been a friendly participant, there's been some tension there. But Geneva has funded a substantial amount over the years. I wouldn't want to guess how much it was. I think if we really knew, we (being Geneva), it might startle us a little bit.

Q: Would you say, when Geneva said we have to step in, that was the point where things were better.

JW: Candidly, it wasn't until we got the right leadership. Namely, somebody like Karla. I don't know how you say that tactfully, I really don't. We never had the right leadership in terms of energy, the right kind of vision, understanding of education, and frankly, respect in the African-American community. We're naïve about the politics of the African-American community. That doesn't need to go anywhere except to make big kudos to Karla. I would say, and you can quote me on this, Karla Byrd's leadership has turned the place around—along with chairman of the board Bill Glaze. Bill was a new guy in town back then; he's no longer a new guy in town. So the combination of Bill Glaze and Karla, that's the sort of thing that we didn't have.

Q: I suppose that's something you have to work towards in any new venture.

JW: Yes, in Philadelphia, we had the right guys from the beginning, and God's providence. They were the people who when they connected with CUTS, they were serving little tiny churches that were really church plants. Then they became the big churches. They were the underground, fundamentally unknown churches to the white, evangelical community.

In 1988, '89, if you had asked, "What's the largest evangelical church in Philadelphia," somebody would have said Church of the Savior out in Wayne. In reality, it was Deliverance Evangelistic Temple, right in the heart of downtown. They actually built a beautiful building where Connie Mack stadium used to be, on one of the main streets, just off Broad Street in Philadelphia.

But, the pastor of that church was very much involved in CUTS, and his associate pastor was deeply involved. The associate pastor of that church graduated from Geneva, one of the first ones in the 1980s, then got an M. Div. from Westminster Theological Seminary and a D. Min. from Westminster Theological Seminary. And a lot of people from that church, and the pastor never took the thing, but he was always blessing it. I had the privilege of preaching there and being introduced. It was embarrassing, because you know how they are in the African-American community, how they praise you and all that sort of thing. But that was the dynamic that we had in Philadelphia that we didn't have in Pittsburgh. At least in the beginning.

Q: For the city of Pittsburgh, why do you think CUBM is a vital and important institution? Why do you think it's something that needs to be?

JW: My sense is that the need has not changed. There needs to be institutions and movements that bring together Christian people across race lines, and CUBM does that. Second, I think that the educational deprivation of the African-American community is as serious as it was back in those days. As a matter of fact, I think it's gotten worse statistically.

There's a tremendous need. Education doesn't solve everything, but it is a big tool. I could tell story after story of bi-vocational pastors in Philadelphia who were basically doing assembly line jobs, and then they got a degree. Then suddenly they became managers or were promoted to other positions. It had the economic development dynamic and the reconciliation dynamic. It is about people in the African-American church becoming biblically informed, theologically sensitive in their preaching and teaching. Those needs are still there.

Q: What would you like to see the future hold?

JW: Well, dream is the dream. Is it possible, this is what Philadelphia is doing, now without Geneva College? Dreaming the dream of a fully independent African-American educational institution in the city. I think that would be the wonderful dream come true, something owned by, controlled by the Bible-believing African-American community. That's the vision in Philadelphia, and they're still moving towards that.

Q: Do you have any other interesting memories, or funny stories, that you remember from the time of development to fruition? Anything from the early board days? Anything you were personally surprised by?

JW: I used to come to board meetings and one of the persons at the board meeting would regularly ask me this question, "Why does Geneva have to collect the tuition?" I would drive down from Beaver Falls and pray fervently that that guy wouldn't ask the question again because I didn't know how long I could be patient. I'd give this explanation: "Well, students can't get financial aid unless it's an accredited" and so on.

You do understand that what happens is the tuition comes right back. Geneva takes, I think in those days it was 10%, for registrar's fees and financial aid, but 90%

of it came back to CUBM to use as they saw fit. And I do that every month. I was patient, but I could stand it no longer. I called the leader at Philadelphia, a guy named Verley Sangster; African-American guy. And I said, "Verley, what's going on? Here's what's happening and what this man keeps asking me." And he laughed and he said, "Jack, when the white man collects the money, the white man controls." I said, "Verley, I missed it." Now, I had been in this community, having the privilege of interjecting myself in this community for, by that time, at least 15, if not 20 years, but I missed it.

Q: I guess that was alluding to the ultimate goal for CUTS and CUBM.

JW: And it's true, isn't it? It's just a general principle. The man who said that you are telling me all I have is a bunch of pieces of paper. White-run entities had so pulled the wool over the eyes of people. The leaders thought they were getting some kind of degree that was worth something, and it wasn't worth anything. I say that to say, it shows you how insensitive and naïve we white folk can be, in seeking this big vision of ministering. Part of my frustration was that we've been coming here for how many years. Well, think of yourself as a servant. Think of yourself as responding to their needs and missing that very fundamental point.

Q: So for you has it been an educational experience?

JW: It's not so much the white community coming to provide an education for these dear deprived folks down there, or some attitude like that. It's a mutuality of learning. I would fly out and teach at CUTS, and it was always a rich experience. I could give illustration after illustration of how most of the time I was being taught by the students.

The interviewer did not ask Dr. White what his theological or biblical motivation was to be part of the CUBM community partnership. It is up to us to piece together circumstantial evidence to justify and identify the initiative called CUBM. That is not difficult to do. First, let's look at the Geneva College website, where it says this about Geneva's early history: Geneva College has been providing academically excellent, Christ-centered and affordable education to students for nearly 170 years. Since opening its doors on Thursday, April 20, 1848, the college's dedication to educating students—traditional, adult learners and graduate—without regard to gender, race, or creed has earned Geneva a well-deserved reputation for accessibility.

Some historical highlights include:

- Established a Female Seminary just three years after opening and became fully co-educational in 1865—praised for providing an equivalent education for both genders
- Opened its doors to freed southern slaves around 1865, an uncommon practice during the post-Civil War period
- A leader in providing adult learners a path to earning a degree, Geneva initiated its Extension Program in the early 1900s, which laid the foundation for the Adult Degree Programs[2]

This mission involving CUBM is consistent with the Reformed Presbyterian theological worldview of the kingdom of God, again as found on Geneva College's website: "The Kingdom of God: Jesus Christ reigns as the mediatorial King over all nations and peoples; He is Lord in every aspect of life." [3]

Every aspect of life is just that: all spheres of human endeavor, life, and culture that includes business, government, and education. The latter has been Geneva College's focus since 1848, and since then it has pioneered many creative educational initiatives that are consistent with its Kingdom values, especially in the area of adult, non-traditional education.

Having established the general theological heritage and framework upon which Dr. White drew, let us spend a bit of time looking at the biblical mandate, not for his educational endeavors, but for the biblical motivation and instruction that would have caused him to cross racial and economic barriers to work with the African American community.

The situation in the early church was not so different than modern American society. There were many ethnic groups, and the Jews did not have contact with any of them unless they had to. The Romans were the occupying force in Palestine, and the Jews loathed them and anyone who served their needs, like the hated publicans or tax gatherers who were Jews who made money off their own people while collecting taxes for Rome. The Jews expressed their hatred and animosity for Gentiles and Romans, as well as apostate Jews, on many occasions. This bias carried over into the early church as we can see in this familiar story as reported in Acts 6:1–7:

> In those days when the number of disciples was increasing, the Hellenistic Jews[a] among them complained against the Hebraic Jews because their widows were being overlooked in the daily distribution of food.[2] So the Twelve gathered all the disciples together and said, "It would not be right for us to neglect the ministry of the word of God in order to wait on tables.[3] Brothers and sisters, choose seven men from among you who are known to be full of the Spirit and wisdom. We will turn this responsibility over to them [4] and will give our attention to prayer and the ministry of the word." [5] This proposal pleased the whole group. They chose Stephen, a man full of faith and of the Holy Spirit; also Philip, Procorus, Nicanor, Timon, Parmenas, and Nicolas from Antioch, a convert to Judaism. [6] They presented these men to the apostles, who prayed and laid their hands on them. [7] So the word of God spread. The number of disciples in Jerusalem increased rapidly, and a large number of priests became obedient to the faith.

In this passage we see a problem in the early church, and Luke seems to indicate that it was an ethnic problem. Those closest to the power, identified as the Hebraic Jews, were not eager to share their resources for whatever reason. Perhaps they did not have many relationships with believing Grecian Jews. We know that they were suspect of that group because they had such close proximity to Gentiles and thus were unclean.

Whatever the reason, there was a divide in the church, and when it was brought to the attention of leadership, they did not ignore it or wait for it to go away. They dealt with it by involving themselves to formulate a plan that involved the people who brought the complaint. The people elected seven men of Grecian background (who we now identify as deacons) to oversee the problem in conjunction with the Hebraic leaders. The apostles said, "We will turn this responsibility over to them." They gave those deacons the power and authority to access the resources that could help the widows who were in need.

Whether consciously or not, White applied a solution for a modern problem following the principles found in Acts 6:

- He heard the cry that there were inequities in how educational opportunities and resources were being distributed.
- He did not ignore the problem but rather helped formulate a plan to correct the inequity.
- He involved those who were deprived and allowed them to have a say and a governing role in the distribution of the opportunities.
- He made the resources of the dominant, established entity available to those who were without.

The results of the Geneva/CUTS/CUBM partnerships were the same as those in Acts 6: the plan worked and the "word of God spread." To date, CUBM has graduated more than 100 students and many more than that have graduated from CUTS. God has blessed the union and it has produced the fruit of students in the urban community who have had access to degrees that they would not have had a chance to obtain without Geneva College's assistance.

One only need visit the non-traditional Geneva College graduation on Saturday afternoons of graduation day to see the impact Geneva College has had on the African American community. There are many people of color who are included in the Degree Completion Program, the graduate programs, and the Center for Urban Biblical Ministry. The composition of the graduating classes has resembled the view of heaven John described in Revelation:

> After this I looked, and there before me was a great multitude that no one could count, from every nation, tribe, people and language, standing before the throne and before the Lamb. They were wearing white robes and were holding palm branches in their hands (Revelation 7:9).

This reflects the global mission of the church, which was founded on the principle of reconciliation produced by the cross of Christ. This reconciliation is to manifest itself through the church to the world, and to principalities and powers:

> Although I am less than the least of all the Lord's people, this grace was given me: to preach to the Gentiles the boundless riches of Christ, and to make plain to everyone the administration of this mystery, which for ages past was kept hidden in God, who created all things. His intent was that now, through the church, the manifold wisdom of God should be made known to the rulers and authorities in the heavenly realms, according to his eternal purpose that he accomplished in Christ Jesus our Lord. In him and through faith in him we may approach God with freedom and confidence (Ephesians 3:8–12).

In a day when people are discussing terms like white supremacy, diversity, and reconciliation, Dr. White has proved to be a pioneer, addressing these issues decades before it was common. He was truly a biblical leader who was true to his calling as an educator and his Reformed theological disposition. Many lives were impacted and transformed because of Dr. White's presence and work.

In his book, *White Awake: An Honest Look at What It Means to Be White*, Pastor Daniel Hill makes many recommendations at the end of his book in his chapter "Active Participation" for white people and churches asking how they can be involved in the work of reconciliation. One of his points is "find a place to serve consistently." Hill writes,

> [We] need not only to find a place where we can serve consistently but also to do so without expecting to lead or be in charge. People eagerly volunteer and, in an attempt to be helpful, try to employ their ideas. We need a different posture in our service—one of waiting to be invited in... This is consistent with the posture of Jesus Himself, who reminded his disciples that 'the Son of Man did not come to be served, but to serve" (Mark 10:45). The path of wisdom chooses humility over pride and service over ego. When we serve consistently and humbly, it positions us to see new things and build trust with the organization. This creates a unique opportunity to go deeper in our cultural identity journey.[4]

As we close, we include another quote from Daniel Hill's book that epitomizes the posture of White as he has served the Pittsburgh and Philadelphia urban communities for nearly 30 years:

> To be theologically awake is to take these words of Jesus seriously: "No one can see the kingdom of God unless they are born again" (John 3:3). It is also to embrace the fact that a spiritual rebirth ushers in both the salvation of our souls and our participation in the redemption of this world. It is also to hold together activism and evangelism; protest and prayer; personal piety and social justice; intimacy with Jesus and proximity to the poor.[5]

We at CUBM are grateful that a leader like Dr. John H. "Jack" White is part of our journey and history. We thank God for his leadership and for the cooperation of Geneva College that has made such a difference in both of Pennsylvania's largest cities. We honor Dr. White in this publication with the honor that is his due, and we commit to continue his legacy of reconciliation and transformation through education made available to all citizens through creative, God-honoring partnerships.

Notes

[1]John W. Stanko, editor; The CUBM Story: Celebrating 25 Years at the Center for Urban Biblical Ministry 1988–2013 (Mobile, AL: Gazelle Press, 2013), pages 21–37).

[2]Retrieved from https://www.geneva.edu/about-geneva/identity/history-heritage.

[3]Retrieved from https://www.geneva.edu/about-geneva/identity/history-heritage.

[4]Daniel Hill, *White Awake: An Honest Look at What It Means to Be White* (Downers Grove, IL: InterVarsity Press, 2017), page 170).

[5]*Ibid.*, page 144.

CHAPTER FOUR

The Man Who Took Him Down

Edward A. Robson

The degradation of execution by crucifixion did not end with the death of the hanging one. The corpse was left on the cursed tree as a feast for beasts and birds, and as a public warning to rebels, murderers, and insurrectionists that you too could become such a spectacle. The steps in execution by crucifixion were prescribed, but the steps for the removal of the corpse after crucifixion were not.[1]

His name was Joseph of Arimathea. The task before him was invidious for he was a prominent member of the Jewish Council, a man of wealth and political prestige. Fearful of the consequences of being associated with Jesus while He was living, with boldness and conviction he now requested from Pilate the body of Jesus at His death.

The narratives concerning Joseph of Arimathea appear in the Gospels of Matthew, Mark, Luke, and John. Each narrative records the details of the same events from a different perspective. The Greek text of all four Gospels involving Joseph of Arimathea is well attested and reliable.

The location of Arimathea is no longer known but the remarkable actions of two old men are. Both Joseph of Arimathea and Nicodemus were members of the Council/Sanhedrin. This essay considers the brief interval of time between the 14th -17th of Nisan in 30 A.D, between the hours of 3–6 p.m. on the 15th of Nisan[2] during which time Joseph of Arimathea and Nicodemus transferred the body of Jesus from the contempt of the cross to the tomb fit for their King.

The narratives in the Gospels pertaining to Joseph are only part of the revelations surrounding Jesus's Crucifixion. Many critics of the narratives in the Gospels seem to be unaware of or discount the prophecies from the Hebrew Scriptures which preceded the events of these narratives. Giving credence to both the Gospel narratives and the prophecies of the Hebrew Scriptures, let us consider in detail *The Man Who Took Him Down.*

Based upon the simultaneous and independent testimonies appearing in the Synoptic Gospels and John, we know that Joseph of Arimathea was a rich old man and a disciple of Jesus, but his allegiance was secret because he feared his colleagues. He was born in Arimathea but planned to be buried in a garden in Jerusalem.[3] Although fearful of the Jews, he nevertheless opposed the decision of the Sanhedrin to condemn Jesus to death. Joseph of Arimathea was an honorable and righteous man, and recognized that Jesus was innocent of the crimes of blasphemy against the Temple and insurrection against Roman rule because His Kingdom was not of this world.[4] Joseph dissented from the proceedings of the Council and observed the crucifixion of Jesus from afar.

Because Joseph of Arimathea is referred to in all Four Gospels,[5] it is useful here to make a few more comments about the relationship between the Synoptic Gospels and John. When these four Gospels record the same events in the life and ministry of Jesus, they do so as independent, simultaneous witnesses.[6] Among the pieces of evidence that demonstrates this independence is the use of the Greek word, *kai*, in the respective narratives. [7]

At first, Joseph of Arimathea was reluctant to openly identify himself as a follower of Jesus. While Jesus lived, Joseph lacked the courage to make known that he was His disciple. However, after Jesus's Crucifixion, Joseph changed. With both courage and boldness, Joseph of Arimathea, using his personal prestige measured by his wealth, by his character, and by his standing in the society of 30 A.D. gained an audience with Pilate to ask for the body of Jesus for burial. The circumstances surrounding Jesus's Crucifixion demanded that Joseph act quickly.

From a distance, Joseph observed that Jesus was the first to be crucified on Friday, 15th Nisan, 30 A.D. Even from a distance, Joseph was able to read the accusation placed above Jesus, summarizing His crimes:

Jesus of Nazareth King of the Jews

This placard of accusation brought protests from Joseph's colleagues in the Sanhedrin, but their request to have the placard of accusation changed was rebuffed by Pilate with the words:

What I have written I have written.[8]

The Apostle John, not at a distance, also witnessed these events, and at the foot of the cross where Jesus still hanged, swore an oath that what he would record in the Gospel bearing his name as an eye-witness is true: Jesus is the Christ, the Son of the Living God, crucified to save him and us from Eternal Judgment.[9]

The requests of Joseph's colleagues to have the legs of the malefactors and the Deceiver broken was granted; but it was unnecessary to break the legs of Jesus because He was already dead.[10] The process of crucifixion was grizzly from beginning until death, which was absolutely certain to occur. No one left a cross alive. As noted earlier, those crucified were only three or four feet off the ground. Usually mildly drugged, the criminals were seated upon a wooden or metal spike support at the level of the testicles. Their hands and feet were nailed or strapped to the cross-beam and the upright of this instrument of torture made of wood. Under the supervision of a Roman guard, the body of the one crucified hanged until death and remained on the cross until consumed by creatures or by natural decomposition. How ironic that the Carpenter from Nazareth should be brought to death by hammers and nails and the wood of a tree, the instruments of his childhood craft and occupation.

Between 3–6 p.m. Roman time, on the 15th Nisan, 30 A.D., Joseph requested the body of Jesus. To show his magnanimity,

Pilate granted Joseph's request but not without verifying that Jesus was dead. A Centurion testified that Jesus's heart was pierced and that what was left of His blood and body fluids flowed from his left side. Certain that Jesus was dead, Pilate then granted the corpse to Joseph who took Him down from the cross. How, we do not know. One wonders if Pilate gave any credence to the testimony of perhaps the same Centurion: *Truly this Man was the Son of God.*[11]

There were several time-constraints hovering over the entire narrative from Jesus's prayer before Gethsemane (John 17) to His Crucifixion which required that Jesus be dispensed with without delay. His struggles in Gethsemane were followed in quick succession by Judas's betrayal, apprehension by the soldiers, trials before Caiaphas and Pilate, scourging, nailing, and death. It was now the time between the evening (Jewish time) before the High Holy Day[12] of the Passover in A.D. 30. About how the corpses of the other two criminals were taken down from their crosses, we know nothing. About what happened to the corpses of the two criminals executed on either side of Jesus, we know nothing. We do know that the soul of one of those young men was now in the presence of the glory of the Lord.[13] About the other, we know nothing.

Between the evenings, Joseph of Arimathea bought a linen cloth valued at about 20 days' wages. Nicodemus bought about 75 pounds avoirdupois of myrrh and aloes.[14] Together these two old men wrapped the body of Jesus in the linen cloth[15] with the spices for a rapid burial. It was the custom of the Jews to bury the dead quickly. They placed the body of Jesus in what was to be Joseph's tomb, and closed the entrance with a great stone in the shape of a grinding wheel.

The deed was done and the Deceiver was dead. But just to make certain that His body was not removed by stealth from the grave in the cave, Caiaphas made the first of his two last requests recorded in the Gospels. He asked Pilate for a guard to make certain that the body of Jesus remained in the tomb for the next three days.[16] Magnanimity again prevailed with a degree of contempt for the Jews. Pilate granted Caiaphas's request that a Roman guard be placed at the tomb and that the Roman seal be placed upon the large stone at the tomb's entrance, prohibiting its opening.

Rome's mandate notwithstanding, an angel of the LORD rolled back the stone and sat upon it. The men of warfare and arms guarding the tomb lifted no weapon in opposition to the divine summons, Ephphatha! The responses of the guards were understandable:

> *Matt. 28:2–4*
> *And behold, a severe earthquake had occurred, for an angel of the Lord descended from heaven and came and rolled away the stone and sat upon it....and the guards shook for fear of him, and became like dead men.*

The women who had come to anoint the body of Jesus were also understandably afraid at the appearance of the angelic guard. The angel immediately comforted the women with the words that they themselves had heard from Jesus:

> *Matt. 28:5–6*
> *And the angel answered and said to the women, "Do not be afraid; for I know that you are looking for Jesus who has been crucified. He is not here, for He has risen"*

> *Luke 24:5–6*
> *Why do you seek the living One among the dead? He is not here, but He has risen. Remember how He spoke to you while He was still in Galilee,*

The Roman guard reported some version of these events to Caiaphas who now made what would be his final attempt to deny Jesus's Resurrection.

> *Matt. 28:11–14*
> *Now when they were going, behold, some of the watch came into the city, and shewed unto the chief priests all the things that were done.*

> *And when they were assembled with the elders, and had taken counsel, they gave a large [sum of] money unto the soldiers, Saying, Say ye, His disciples came by night, and stole him away while we slept. And if this come to the governor's ears, we will persuade him, and secure you. So they took the money, and did as they were taught: and this saying is commonly reported among the Jews until this day.*

The events surrounding Jesus, the Son of God, which we have just considered were considered prophetically long before the 15th Nisan, A.D. 30. Accepted or not, such prophecies are true and truly amazing. I have selected two prophecies in this consideration of *The Man Who Took Him Down* for comment: Psalm 22 and Isaiah 52:13–53:12. These two passages are considered in the light of their fulfilments between the 14th-17th of Nisan, 30 A.D. Where necessary, I have modified the KJV of Psalm 22 and Isaiah 52–53 to reflect more pointedly the Hebrew of these passages.

Prophetic Delineation in Psalm 22

The best example of prophetic delineation in Scripture is in Genesis 3:14–15

> *And the LORD God said unto the serpent, Because thou hast done this, thou art cursed above all cattle, and above every beast of the field; upon thy belly shalt thou go, and dust shalt thou eat all the days of thy life: And I will put enmity between thee and the woman, and between thy seed and Her Seed; He shall bruise thy head, and thou shalt bruise His heel.*

In Christian Theology, Genesis 3:14–15 is the Protoevangelium, the first statement of the salvation to come *in the fullness of time* through Jesus Christ, the Son of the Virgin, the Seed of the Woman. If you will accept it, the Gospels of Matthew and Luke begin with the birth of the Seed of the Woman and conclude with the crushing of the head of the Serpent and the bruising of the heel of the Savior. Both take place at the Crucifixion of Jesus Christ at which time Joseph of Arimathea enters the narrative of the History of Redemption.

Another example of prophetic delineation is in Psalm 110:1. After Jesus's Resurrection and Session, He reigns at the Right Hand of God the Father until the Consummation when His enemies will all be subdued beneath His feet, the last of which is death itself. Paul meditates on this prophetic delineation in 1 Corinthians 15:25–26.

> *For He must reign, till He hath put all enemies under His feet. The last enemy that shall be destroyed is death.*

One final illustration of prophetic delineation comes from Psalm 2:7–8. The first part of Psalm 2:7 is a statement of the Ontological Sonship of the Christ, Messiah:

> *I will declare the decree: the LORD hath said unto Me, Thou art my Son;*

From the revelations in the New Testament we learn that God became a Man and dwelt among us, and as writes the Apostle John, *we beheld His glory as of the Only Son of God.*

The prophetic delineation in the second part of Psalm 2:7 pertains to the Resurrection of Jesus from the dead: this day have I called Thee forth.[19] As a consequence of His Death and Resurrection, the Lord Christ claims the nations as His inheritance.

> *Ask of me, and I shall give thee the heathen for thine inheritance, and the uttermost parts of the earth for thy possession. (Ps.2:8)*

The Book of Revelation, The Book of Blessing, is the prophetic statement of the New Testament proclaiming the coming of the nations to salvation in Jesus Christ.

In a manner similar to Psalm 2, Psalm 22 contains a prophecy of the Crucifixion of Jesus Christ and the glories to follow

His Resurrection. Ps. 22:1 begins with what we identify as Jesus's Fourth Word from His Cross:

> *My God, my God, why hast thou forsaken me?*

The following statements are offensive to some and rejected by not a few, but are nevertheless truthful. Such rejections and offenses are not surprising, although sad. Jesus was Himself despised and rejected, a man of sorrows and acquainted with grief; and at the same time, the embodiment of truth. The following excerpts from Psalm 22 are chosen to illustrate the relevance of this Psalm to the narratives of the Four Gospels where we have the record of Jesus's Crucifixion and are therefore important for our consideration of *The Man Who Took Him Down.*

As noted, Ps. 22:1 is claimed by Jesus in Matt. 27:46, and in Mark 15:34 with slight modification:

And about the ninth hour Jesus cried with a loud voice, saying, Eli, Eli, lama sabachthani? That is to say, My God, my God, why hast thou forsaken me? (Matt.27:46)

> *Mark 15:34 And at the ninth hour Jesus cried with a loud voice, saying, Eloi, Eloi, lama sabachthani? Which is, being interpreted, My God, my God, why hast thou forsaken me?*

The mockery and taunting of Jesus's enemies appear prophetically in Psalm 22:7–8 and are realized and recorded in their fulfilment in Matthew 27:39–44:

> *All they that see me laugh me to scorn: they shoot out the lip, they shake the head, saying, He trusted on the LORD that he would deliver him: let him deliver him, seeing he delighted in him.*

> *Matt. 27:39–44*
> *And those passing by were hurling abuse at Him, wagging their heads, and saying, You who are going to destroy the temple and rebuild it in three days, save Your-*

> *self! If You are the Son of God, come down from the cross. In the same way the chief priests also, along with the scribes and elders, were mocking Him, and saying, He saved others; He cannot save Himself. He is the King of Israel; let Him now come down from the cross, and we shall believe in Him. He trusts in God; let Him deliver Him now, if He takes pleasure in Him; for He said, I am the Son of God.*

Psalm 22:16–18 prophesies the crucifixion in a manner that is truly startling. There are objections to the translation of the Hebrew Text given in the KJV and challenges to the Hebrew Text itself, but the Text stands secure and the translation is correct:

> *For dogs have surrounded me; A band of evildoers has encompassed me; They pierced my hands and my feet. I can count all my bones. They look, they stare at me; They divide my garments among them, And for my clothing they cast lots.*
>
> *John 20:25*
> *The other disciples therefore said unto him, We have seen the Lord. But he said unto them, Except I shall see in his hands the print of the nails, and put my finger into the print of the nails, and thrust my hand into his side, I will not believe.*

Psalm 22:27–29 prophesies beyond the Cross to the Resurrection, Ascension, Session, to the Coming of the Nations to Christ, and the Consummation:

> *All the ends of the earth will remember and turn to the LORD, And all the families of the nations will worship before Thee. For the kingdom is the LORD's, And He rules over the nations. All the prosperous of the earth will eat and worship, All those who go down to the dust will bow before Him, Even he who cannot keep his soul alive.*

Prophetic Delineation in Isaiah 53

Like Psalm 22, Isaiah 52:13 to 53:12 is a prophecy about the Christ, the Servant of the LORD, in remarkable terms. As with Ps. 22 above, I am only selecting a few items from Isaiah's Prophecy that have an obvious bearing upon the events where Joseph of Arimathea is involved. Though frequently left unread, even by those who know the Hebrew language, this Prophecy from Isaiah included Joseph of Arimathea, the rich man, and the malefactors, the wicked, crucified with Jesus. Isaiah 53 also implies the reconciliation achieved by the death and resurrection of Jesus as the basis for peace with God. Before concluding this essay, let me gather the items from Isaiah 53 that are reflected in the narratives in the Gospels about *The Man Who Took Him Down*.

> *Isaiah 53:1–12*
> *Who has believed what he has heard from us? And to whom has the arm of the LORD been revealed? For he grew up before him like a young plant, and like a root out of dry ground; he had no form or majesty that we should look at him, and no beauty that we should desire him. He was despised and rejected by men, a man of sorrows and acquainted with grief; and as one from whom men hide their faces he was despised, and we esteemed him not. Surely he has borne our griefs and carried our sorrows; yet we esteemed him stricken, smitten by God, and afflicted. But he was pierced for our transgressions; he was crushed for our iniquities; upon him was the chastisement that brought us peace, and with his wounds we are healed. All we like sheep have gone astray; we have turned—every one— to his own way; and the LORD has laid on him the iniquity of us all. He was oppressed, and he was afflicted, yet he opened not his mouth; like a lamb that is led to the slaughter, and like a sheep that before its shearers is silent, so he opened not his mouth. By oppression and judgment he was taken away; and as for his generation, who considered that he was cut off out of the land of the living, stricken for the transgression of my*

> *people? And they made his grave with the wicked and with a rich man in his death, although he had done no violence, and there was no deceit in his mouth. Yet it was the will of the LORD to crush him; he has put him to grief; when his soul makes an offering for guilt, he shall see his offspring; he shall prolong his days; the will of the LORD shall prosper in his hand. Out of the anguish of his soul he shall see and be satisfied; by his knowledge shall the righteous one, my servant, make many to be accounted righteous, and he shall bear their iniquities. Therefore I will divide him a portion with the many, and he shall divide the spoil with the strong, because he poured out his soul to death and was numbered with the transgressors; yet he bore the sin of many, and makes intercession for the transgressors.*

I conclude this essay on *The Man Who Took Him Down* with this tribute to my friend of more than 50 years, John H. White, whom I know as "Jack." Not to say too much or to draw inordinate parallels, but the situation in this essay is one old man writing a tribute to another old man based upon the records of two old men who honored Jesus Christ with their gifts, their talents, and their reputations. To Him the four of them, and countless others, have entrusted their souls.

We look to Jesus Christ for salvation. When we are saved by His grace, we bring our differing gifts and talents and times to His service. Jack, you have served well with the gifts, talents and in the time allotted to you. May you also, dear Reader, look to the Lord Jesus for salvation; and may you use your gifts, talents and time in the interest of the Kingdom of God and the Lord Jesus Christ.

Joseph of Arimathea and Nicodemus gave Jesus a burial befitting a King, and so He was, and is. He was at birth *King of the Jews* and He died under the indictment: *Jesus of Nazareth King of the Jews.* Fitting indeed was the new tomb, the linen cloth and the great quantity of myrrh and aloes purchased at great cost to honor Jesus at His death and burial, even though it lasted but a few hours.

Both Joseph and Nicodemus were concerned to be included within the Kingdom of God as was one of the malefactors crucified with Jesus. Both of these old men referred to in the Synoptics and John now understood that the Kingdom of God involved the lifting up of the Son of Man as Moses lifted up the serpent in the wilderness.[20] Just as those who looked to the bronze serpent placed upon a pole for deliverance from death at the command of Moses, so we at the command of the Gospel look to Jesus once lifted upon the Cross now exalted above the heavens for deliverance from death eternal.

John's Gospel does not conclude with John 20:1–8 but the narrative involving Joseph of Arimathea does. Following the announcement by Mary Magdalene that the tomb of Jesus was empty, Peter and John ran to the burial place. John outran Peter and he gives this description of his arrival at the tomb.

> *John 20:1–8*
> *The first day of the week cometh Mary Magdalene early, when it was yet dark, unto the sepulchre, and seeth the stone taken away from the sepulchre. Then she runneth, and cometh to Simon Peter, and to the other disciple, whom Jesus loved, and saith unto them, They have taken away the Lord out of the sepulchre, and we know not where they have laid him. Peter therefore went forth, and that other disciple, and came to the sepulchre. So they ran both together: and the other disciple did outrun Peter, and came first to the sepulchre. And he stooping down, and looking in, saw the linen clothes lying; yet went he not in. Then cometh Simon Peter following him, and went into the sepulchre, and seeth the linen clothes lie, And the napkin, that was about his head, not lying with the linen clothes, but wrapped together in a place by itself. Then went in also that other disciple, which came first to the sepulchre, and he saw, and believed. For as yet they knew not the Scripture, that he must rise again from the dead.*

Upon the stone where the body of Jesus was placed lay the costly linen wrappings, and apart from them lay the wrappings that covered His face and head. The scene inside the tomb was not one of chaos but of the miraculous. Peter and John pondered and recorded the testimonies of these wrappings and their implications: *He is not here. He has risen.* From that time onward, we have in these words, *He is not here. He has risen.* The essence of the Gospel of the Lord Jesus Christ, *the Word that became flesh and tabernacled among us.*

Joseph of Arimathea and Nicodemus are not mentioned by name in John 20:1–10. However, the fragrance in the tomb and the linen cloths which once enshrouded the body of Jesus were witnesses to the ministries of these two old men on behalf of their Savior. Wherever the Gospel of the Lord Jesus Christ is preached, what they did in tribute to Him is spoken of as a memorial to them, Nicodemus, and Joseph of Arimathea—*The Man Who Took Him Down.*

Notes

[1]JH. Friedlieb, *Archäologie der Leidensgeschichte unsers Herrn Jesu Christi: nach den Grundsätzen der Evangelien-Harmonie historisch-kritisch bearbeitet,* [*Archeology of the Passion of our Lord* Jesus] p. 142 "There was a twofold manner of crucifixion. Either the condemned were lifted up to the cross, already erected, or they were fastened to it while it was still on the ground; the former manner seems to have been the more usual."

See also: J. P. Lange, *The Life of the Lord Jesus Christ*, translated by Marcus Dods (London: T&T Clark, 1872) Vol. III, p. 292 [Lipsius shows that both modes were used. Of Pionius, the martyr^ he quotes, that he divested himself of his garments, stretched himself on the cross, and gave the soldiers liberty to fix the nails, and then *eum igitur ligno fixum erexerunt.* [the wooden piece between the legs? EAR] But he shows that it was much more common first to erect the cross, and then to set the condemned on the small projecting bar and proceed with the fixing to the cross. It seems doubtful whether ladders were used for this purpose. Bynseus agrees with Salmasius in thinking that the ordinary height of the feet of the crucified above the ground was no more than three or four feet, although in some cases it was undoubtedly much greater. The hyssop stalk on which the sponge was presented to our Lord on the cross was only a foot and a half long; and the stroke of the spear was probably a level thrust, and not from below upwards.]

[2]The best discussions of the difficulties in reconciling the time elements between the Synoptic Gospels and John are in Leon Morris, *The Gospel According to John* (Grand Rapids: Eerdmans, 1971), p. 158 n. 90; pp. 774–786; 799–801. There were several different methods of time keeping among the Jews and the Romans, and between the Jews and the Romans. Among the Romans and Jews there was Roman Popular and Jewish Popular time-keeping which counted the day from sunrise to sunrise. Roman Legal Time counted days from midnight to midnight. Jewish Approximate Time was not precise. In John 1:39, "about the 10th hour" in Roman Legal Time is *about 10 a.m.* In Jewish Approximate Time the 10th hour falls somewhere between the 9th and 12th hour, i.e. 3–6 p.m. (Compare: John 1:39; 4:6, 52–53; 11:9; 19:14; Matt 27:45; Mark 15:25; Luke 23:44; Acts 2:5; 2:1; 10:3,9)

[3]*Matt. 27:57 When the even was come, there came a rich man of Arimathaea, named Joseph, who also himself was Jesus' disciple:*

John 19:38 And after this Joseph of Arimathaea, being a disciple of Jesus, but secretly for fear of the Jews, besought Pilate that he might take away the body of Jesus: and Pilate gave him leave. He came therefore, and took the body of Jesus. Luke 23:49–52 *And all his acquaintance, and the women that followed him from Galilee, stood afar off, beholding these things. And, behold, there was a man named Joseph, a counsellor; and he was a good man, and a just: (The same had not consented to the counsel and deed of them;) he was of Arimathaea, a city of the Jews: who also himself waited for the kingdom of God. This man went unto Pilate, and begged the body of Jesus.*

[4]*John 18:36–37 Jesus answered, My kingdom is not of this world: if my kingdom were of this world, then would my servants fight, that I should not be delivered to the Jews: but now is my kingdom not from hence. Pilate therefore said unto him, Art thou a king then? Jesus answered, Thou sayest that I am a king.*

[5]Matt. 27:55–61; Mark 15:35–47; Luke 23:49–56; John 19:28–42

[6]Repeatedly during the Last Week of Jesus' Public Ministry, references are made to the Hebrew Scriptures. When references are made *to Moses and the Prophets and the Psalms* (Luke 24:44–45 is one example of many) the entirety of the Hebrew Scriptures is meant. Here is the reason for this footnote. In John 19:35 John swears his oath to the truthfulness of what he saw and wrote. In John 19:36, John writes *Not one of His bones will be broken* and *They will look on Him whom they pierced.* Why, however, with all of the important details in this narrative does John include that Nicodemus brought *a mixture of myrrh and aloes ...*? You have in these three items *Not one of His bones will be broken...they will look on Him whom they pierced...myrrh and aloes, Moses and the Prophets and the Psalms.* The whole of the Hebrew Scriptures bears witness to Jesus, Messiah, the Son of God.

[7]Edward A. Robson, *Kai-Configurations in the Greek N.T.* Unpublished Ph.D. Dissertation, Syracuse University, 1980.

[8]John 19:22 ἀπεκρίθη ὁ Πιλᾶτος· ὃ γέγραφα, γέγραφα. -Pilate used the perfect tense in the twice repeated verb, γέγραφα. Of course, all that Pilate had in mind was that he was not changing his mind and would not remove the accusations as he had written it. Ever thereafter, however, Pilate's words on the placard bear an ironic witness to the profound truth that Jesus is the King of the Jews, and the Ruler of all of the Kings of earth for all time.

[9]*John 19:35* καὶ ὁ ἑωρακὼς μεμαρτύρηκεν, καὶ ἀληθινὴ αὐτοῦ ἐστιν ἡ μαρτυρία, καὶ ἐκεῖνος οἶδεν ὅτι ἀληθῆ λέγει, ἵνα καὶ ὑμεῖς πιστεύ[σ]ητε. = *and the one having seen [perf. Participle] bears testimony that continues from that point onward [perfect tense] and his witness is true and that one knows by revelation that he is speaking the truth so that you believe.*

[10]*John 19:31 The Jews therefore, because it was the preparation, that the bodies should not remain upon the cross on the sabbath day, (for that sabbath day was a high day.) besought Pilate that their legs might be broken, and that they might be taken away.*

[11]*Mark 15:39 And when the centurion, which stood over against Him, saw that He so cried out, and gave up the ghost, he said, Truly this man was the Son of God.*

[12]William Hendriksen, *John* (Grand Rapids: Baker, 1954), Vol.II, p.

436 "At times the Sanhedrists could be very scrupulous in observing the details of the ceremonial law. Was it not true that the land would be defiled if a body was hanging all night upon a tree? See Deut. 21:23. Such defilement would be even worse if bodies remained on the cross on the sabbath. It was getting later in the afternoon (the afternoon of the Preparation, that is, of Friday; see on 19:14, 42); it was going toward sun-set, that is, toward sabbath. Moreover, this particular sabbath was "very great," for it was the sabbath of the Pass-over-feast, a feast of seven days."

[13]Luke 23:42 *And he said unto Jesus, Lord, remember me when thou comest into thy kingdom. And Jesus said unto him, Verily I say unto thee, today shalt thou be with me in paradise. [*striking that like Nicodemus and Joseph, this young man was also concerned about the Kingdom of God.]

[14]ὡς λίτρας ἑκατόν = Roman pound, a weight of 12 ounces in a Roman measure, about 325 grams. The KJV simply translates, *an hundred pound weight.* The ESV gives the equivalent of the Roman measure in avoirdupois = 75 lbs.

[15]σινδών = linen cloth of a high quality. Four of the six references in the NT to linen are in Mark's Gospel: Mark 14:51,52; 15:46; 4 out of the 6 references are to the linen cloth purchased by Joseph of Arimathea: Matt. 27:59; Luke 23:53; Mark 15:46.

[16]*Matt. 27:63–66 Sir, we remember that that Deceiver said, while He was yet alive,* After three days I will rise again. *Command therefore that the sepulchre be made sure until the third day, lest his disciples come by night, and steal him away, and say unto the people,* He is risen from the dead*: so the last error shall be worse than the first. Pilate said unto them, Ye have a watch: go your way, make it as sure as ye can. So they went, and made the sepulchre sure, sealing the stone, and setting a watch.*

[17]*Matt. 28:12 And when they had assembled with the elders and taken counsel, they gave a sufficient sum of money to the soldiers*

[18]πείσομεν from πείθω meaning to convince someone to believe something; seduce; mislead. Used only three times in Matthew: Matt. 27:20; 27:43; 28:14.

[19]Acts 13:33; Heb. 1:5; 5:5

[20]*John 3:14 And as Moses lifted up the serpent in the wilderness, even so must the Son of Man be lifted up; Numbers 21:9 And Moses made a bronze serpent and set it on the standard; and it came about, that if a serpent bit any man, when he looked to the bronze serpent, he lived.*

CHAPTER FIVE

The Mystery of Predestination

Byron G. Curtis

"The gifts and the call of God are irrevocable."
Romans 11:28–29 (NET Bible)

"...in order that God's purpose in election might stand: not by works, but by him who calls."
Romans 9:11–12 (NIV)

A Personal Word

Summer, 1972. That was the time I first heard the word *predestine* used positively. Not that I'd heard it much. I was seventeen, a recent convert to Christianity, and attending an event at Geneva College for new students and their parents. On that day the College's "Dean of Religious Services" offered a prayer for us all. In that prayer I was shocked to hear words about the God who *predestined* a people for glory. Predestine? The mere word can chill or thrill the soul. In 1972, "chill" described my soul's response. Back home, I told similarly chilled friends, "They'll never get me to believe *that*!" Little did I know.

As classes began that September, I volunteered to sing in another oddity for me: a chorus that sang only the Psalms, recruited by that same Dean of Religious Services, Dr. John H. White. I would later learn to call him "Jack"—and learn to call him "friend."

In 1972, I measured Calvinism as ice cold, with predestination its absolute Kelvin-scale zero. That icy estimate would shatter. The ice held firm over months of intense discussion of the Scriptures with classmates. Then, one cold night, like an *Arktika* ice-breaker through the Bering Straits and into a calm Pacific, Paul's Epistle to the Romans broke through. Here's the ice-breaking sentence:

> As far as the gospel is concerned, they [the Jews] are enemies for your sake; but as far as election is concerned, they are beloved on account of the patriarchs, for the gifts and the call of God are irrevocable. (Romans 11:28–29)

Paul's ice-breaker declares that in the special case of ethnic Israel, Jewish unbelief does not nullify Israel's election.[1] Ethnic Israel's special case, Paul says, operates by the same rule that applies to election everywhere else, including the election of individuals. That rule is summed up in one omnipotent word: *irrevocable*. Election is permanent. A divine decree *decrees*. How could it be otherwise?

I had believed that people decide to become Christians by the power of their own free will. *Free will*: that term, I thought, marked off the sacred sector of God's universe where He'd decreed never to decree. There He'd sovereignly renounced His sovereignty. *Huh?* So, I reasoned, if by the power of free will people decide to become Christians, they could just as readily *undecide* to be Christians. True converts could be lost. *I* could be lost. That fear dogged my days and haunted my nights.

But "*irrevocable*"? If, under divine election, the gift and calling of conversion cannot be revoked, then a true convert could *never* be lost. What if *God* calls people to faith in Christ—effectively and permanently? The shock of Paul's "irrevocable" shattered my Arctic ice. It opened the way for me to an abiding peace, an assurance of salvation—and to the vocation of a theologian. With deep gratitude for the part he played in my spiritual, intellectual, and professional formation, in 1972, and in the many years since, I dedicate this essay to my good friend, Jack White, who shocked me with the God who predestines a people for glory.

Turtles on Fenceposts

There's a proverb among Calvinist preachers: "*If you see a turtle on a fence post, you know he didn't get there by himself.*"[2] Christians are like turtles on fence posts. We didn't get here by ourselves; we got here by God's power. He is ever wooing, wounding, working in us to accomplish God's glorious plan. As Paul writes, "*It is because of Him that you are in Jesus Christ*" (1 Corinthians 1:30).

There should be no doubt among biblically minded Christians that God is a God who predestines. If I had been paying better attention, I would have learned it from the Bible, rather than from Jack White. No less than six times the New Testament uses the Greek verb *pro-orizo*. In English versions of the Bible, that verb is variously translated as "decide beforehand," "foreordain," "determine," or "predestine" (Acts 4:28; Romans 8:29–30 twice; 1 Corinthians 2:7; Ephesians 1:5; and Ephesians 1:11). The verb in each of these six occasions has God as its subject and is grammatically positive. In two of these passages, it is explicit that God pre-determines not merely a few things, or even many things, but "all things." The focus of five of the six is the future for Christians: "*destined for glory before time began*" (1 Corinthians 2:7). The other is the plot to kill Jesus: *foreordained* (Acts 4:28). Together, these six teach that God decides things beforehand: God foreordains. God destines. God predestines. God works His plan. The plan never fails. And the plan is glorious. So, the question for Bible-believing Christians is not, "Should I believe that God is a God who predestines?" Rather the question is, "What kind of predestination should I believe in?"[3]

Three Testy Terms

A few definitions are in order: three key terms Christians have used to parse the Bible's teachings on this potentially chilling theme. These terms often enough elicit debate—or provoke fights—among Christians. Sometimes Christians turn testy over them. Sometimes they're used as tests of theological wisdom. Nonetheless, it seems that the warmth of the Bible requires of our English-language minds these terms, or something exactly like them.

1. *Providence*: God's acts of governing His universe.
2. *Foreordination*: God's act of determining events before hand.
3. *Predestination*: God's act of election, graciously choosing sinners for everlasting life.

These three definitions sing a warm triadic harmony: *Providence* is the general term for what God does when He rules the world.[4] *Foreordination* is what God does in the wise predetermination of these acts of providence. *Predestination* is what God does in the kind of foreordination that, for a vast company of otherwise hell-bound sinners like you and me, results in our everlasting blessedness in Christ, the Redeemer.[5] All three terms are devotedly Trinitarian. They are the deeds of the holy Trinity—Father, Son, and Holy Spirit—the one eternal God in three divine persons, blessed forever.[6]

All Christians believe in providence, foreordination, and predestination. Christians of all stripes believe that the Triune God rules in goodness, and that his good plan cannot be defeated. Christians believe this despite the massive evils of the world, for God has demonstrated His beauty, truth, and goodness not only in starry skies and verdant earth, but in the incarnate life of the Son of God, Jesus Christ, crucified resurrected, reigning on high. Because of this astonishing past, Christians trust the *future* victory of Jesus Christ over sin and death. Christians believe that the Church (carefully defined) shall certainly be saved. Christians even believe that the world itself (likewise carefully defined) shall certainly be saved. The true *destination*, a destination *planned* for the world in the wise, merciful, and secret counsels of the Triune God, shall be achieved.

These events, although future, are certain. But (1) how big is this providence? (2) How much of life does God foreordain? And (3) what kind of predestination should Christian believe in? In this essay, I pursue those three questions.

How Big is Providence?

Two Minutial Texts, Two Maximal Texts, and Two Conclusions

Matthew 10:29. We begin with certain texts that I'll call "minutial" texts—that is, texts that speak of small things, of the miniscule. In Matthew 10:29, Jesus asks His disciples, *"Are not two sparrows sold for a penny? Yet not one of them will fall to the ground apart from the will of your Father"* (NIV 1984). The KJV puts the second clause this way: "one of them shall not fall on the ground *without your Father*"; the NASB puts the final phrase, "*apart from your Father*" (emphases mine). These renditions well convey the meaning of Matthew's Greek.[7] They also prove far superior to the 1960 paraphrase by J. B. Phillips, which says that no sparrow falls "without your Father's *knowledge*"; and the 1971 *Living Bible* which says, "without your Father *knowing it*" (emphases mine). [8]

Surely the Father *does* know, but Matthew's Greek asserts nothing about knowing. The text instead denies that our falling sparrow falls "without" or "apart from" the Father: not a single one. The 1984 NIV smoothed out the Greek's un-English syntax to say, "apart from the will of your Father." The revision of the NIV (2011) does it perhaps even better: *"Are not two sparrows sold for a penny? Yet not one of them will fall to the ground outside your Father's care."* Thus we learn that the Father's tender care embraces even the slightest events in mortal history—even the death of a sparrow. Far better than divine cognition, that divine care comes as comfort to the soon-to-be persecuted disciples in

Matthew 10, now sent out "to the lost sheep of the house of Israel" (10:6). On that journey they shall face all sorts of perils, but these disciples take that trek not merely with the Father's awareness of their plight, but within the Father's fatherly care. When the great gospel-and-jazz vocalist Ethel Waters sang "His Eye is on the Sparrow," she didn't think the Father merely *knew*: "His eye is on all of us sparrows."[9] Jesus concludes His exhortation with these words of comfort: *"Do not fear: you are worth many sparrows"* (Matt 10:31).

Proverbs 16:33, our second text, speaks in a similarly minutial mode. *"The lot is cast into the lap, but its every decision is from the LORD."*[10] The Bible's proverbs usually come in single sentences of two poetical clauses, serving up some canny observation or moral admonition about daily life. This proverb asserts that even casting lots—drawing straws? throwing dice?—finds its outcome from the will of God.

Some interpreters see Proverbs 16:33's "lot" (Hebrew = *goral*) as the eerie *Urim* and *Thummim* of Israel's high priests, cast to evoke a divine answer to some crucial question in Israel's national life. The high priest bore the *Urim* and *Thummim* ("lights" and "perfections"?; see Exodus 28:30 and Numbers 27:21) in his ephod for such mysterious inquiries.[11] For some debaters, that move limits the range of Proverbs 16:33 to exclusively sacred functions. Hence (they say) not all chancy actions are claimed by the proverb as divinely determined. Joshua and Eleazar the high priest's allotting the lands of Israel, tribe-by-tribe, *yes*. The eleven apostles' choice-by-lot of Matthias over Justus to replace Judas, *yes*.[12] Some prodigal son's unlucky snake-eyed gamble, *no*.

But the Book of Proverbs pays little attention to the priestly practices of ancient Israel. The wisdom literature of the Old Testament is rooted in the Israelites' daily world, the world of families and friends, farmers and fields, busyness and businesses. Hence, Proverbs 16:33 is not likely to evoke the lot of Israel's priests. Elsewhere, Proverbs tells of the common use of casting lots in settling un-neighborly disputes between neighbors: *"The lot puts an end to quarrels and decides between powerful contenders*" (Prov 18:18). In Psalm 22:18, the lot's a gambler's toss. The point of our proverb? God exerts his providential control over even trivial actions—even a toss of dice. In his excellent discussion of Proverbs 16:33, Bruce Waltke rightly insists, "there are no exceptions."[13]

Three classic sources of Christian teaching agree. Thomas Aquinas (1225–1274) and John Calvin (1509–1564). Thomas writes,

> It is clear that even acts of human willing and choosing must be subject to divine providence... since [God] is the cause of our act of choice and volition, our choices and will-acts are subject to divine providence.
> –Thomas Aquinas, *Summa Contra Gentiles*, 3.90.1–2

Calvin concurs with that totality.

> Providence means not that by which God idly observes from heaven what takes place on earth, but that by which, as keeper of the keys, he governs all events.
> –John Calvin, *Institutes of the Christian Religion*, 1.16.4

The *Westminster Larger Catechism* (1648) asks and answers the same issue well:

> Q. 18. What are God's works of providence?
> A. God's works of providence are His most holy, wise, and powerful preserving, and governing all his creatures; ordering them, and all their actions, to His own glory.

Other theologians and other miniscule texts could be chosen, but let these, and falling sparrows and tumbling lots suffice. We conclude: God's good and holy will is intimately involved in the slightest, the most trivial aspects of life in this universe. That's very good news.

Two Maximal Texts: Our two miniscule texts agree with two maximal texts. These maximals speak of "all things" under God's good providence. That "all" translates Greek's *panta*; "all." The form *ta panta* means "the all," or, far better, "everything." These two maximal texts are Romans 8:28 and Ephesians 1:10–11.

Romans 8:28. The King James Version (KJV) famously declares, "We know that all things work together for good to them that love God, to them who are the called according to His purpose."[14] That KJV declaration is quoted far and wide, enshrined on living room walls and magnets on the fridge. What wondrous comfort to know that even the bad serves the good, and the worst, the best.

Some have taken that comfort in a wrong direction. The KJV's "*All things work together for good*" is less theologically explicit than most recent English versions of Romans 8:28. For example, the NIV reads, "We know that *in all things God works* for the good of those who love him, who have been called according to His purpose" (emphasis mine). "*All things working together for good*" is, of course, a circumlocution, a roundabout way of saying that God is working them. But that well-trafficked roundabout allows some interpreters to chauffeur God's limousine some distance away from the hub where "all things work together." An exhaust of deism wafts through. Is there an alternative warranted by Paul's Greek? Perhaps so. C.E.B. Cranfield finds no less than eight syntactical options for this verse [15] Let's explore three of the more interesting alternatives. Some see the subject of verse 28 as supplied by verses 26–27: "the Spirit." The *Revised English Bible* (REB) casts it accordingly as the conclusion of a long sentence:

> 26 We do not even know how we ought to pray, but through our inarticulate groans the Spirit himself is pleading for us, 27 and God who searches our inmost being knows what the Spirit means, because He pleads for God's people as God himself wills; 28 and in everything, as we know, He [the Spirit] cooperates for good with those who love God and are called according to His purpose. (Romans 8:26–28 REB 1992)

This option allures us, not least because the ministry of the Holy Spirit is Romans 8's great theme. The REB also rises to a finely crafted elegance. And we find a true and lovely idea about the Holy Spirit, who woos us, indwells us, prays within our prayers, leads us to love God rightly, and works within our will, in accordance with His sanctifying work among those whom the Father calls. Philippians 2:13 says much the same about the God who "works in you to will and to act in order to fulfill his good purpose." But Paul's habits of rhetoric raise an important objection against it. Persistently in Paul, the verb "we know" (*oidamen*) marks rhetorical shifts—new emphases, new sentences, and especially new paragraphs.[16] That verb heads verse 28. Hence, it is hard to consider verse 28 as anything other than a new sentence, and likely a new paragraph. The REB stands virtually alone in making verse 28 part of the preceding sentence. That paragraph break, then, readily aligns verse 28 not with the subject of verses 26–27, the Holy Spirit, but rather with the subject in verse 29: God the Father.[17] The alluring Holy Spirit option for 8:28 remains unlikely.

Far from our limousine's roundabout is another rendering preferred by a few commentators. These interpreters (1) follow a textual variant in the Greek found in few NT manuscripts such as the papyrus designated P46, the oldest manuscript of collected Pauline letters. This expertly copied codex preserves most of the Pauline Epistles, plus Hebrews, and is usually dated to about 200 AD. The reading in P46 includes a subject noun, "*ho theos*," "the Deity," after the verb *sunergei*, "work together."[18] These interpreters also suggest (2) that the verb *sunergei* applies not to "all things," but to "those who love God." The result of following these two options? "*We know that in all things God works for good with those who love Him*" (GNT, 1992, emphasis mine). The resulting doctrine? God cooperates *with those who love God, and they with Him*, to bring good in all sorts of things, even bad things.[19]

The strength of this view is that the Greek verb "work together" (*sunergeo*) often takes a direct object: the verb's subject works together with someone or something else. For example, in an all-too-florid late appendix to Mark's Gospel, the variant called the "Long Ending," we read this: "Then the disciples went out and preached everywhere, and the Lord *worked with them* (*sunergountos*, participle; 16:20). And in James 2:22 we read that Abraham's faith "was working together (*sunergei*) *with his works*." That syntax seems to support their preferred rendering of verse 28, "in all things God works for good *with those who love Him*."

The doctrinal claim about divine-human cooperation is, on some quite lowly level, true. But to claim it as the apostle's meaning in Romans 8:28 is hardly satisfying. In Romans 8, Paul is working up to a grand climax on the absolute safety of all who are in Jesus Christ:

> Neither death nor life, neither angels nor demons, neither the present nor the future, nor any powers, neither height nor depth, *nor anything else in all creation*, will be able to separate us from the love of God that is in Christ Jesus our Lord. (Romans 8:38–39 NIV, emphasis mine)

Death and life, angels and demons, present and future, powers, heights, and depths? — That's a whole universe. It is well warranted, then, to take the "all things" in verse 28 as not merely "all the sorts of things in which we and God cooperate for good," but rather, as anticipating verse 38, "all things" in the absolute sense: all events in all of Creation.

That conclusion is strengthened by this observation: in Paul's syntax the phrase, "in all things" is "fronted," placed first. That's an odd emphatic order. The fronting gives further weight to those things that are denoted by the "all things," making it even less likely that "all things" means only "some things," the things with which Christians have to do. It is not that we and God cooperate for good in the many things that we encounter, true though that may be. All things *without exception* are directed to the good of those who love God.

That "good" is no Pollyanna wish-dream. In Romans 8 the "all things" include everything that would otherwise drive not only us but also the angels to hot noontime sweats and cold midnight anguish:

> Who shall separate us from the love of Christ? Shall trouble or hardship or persecution or famine or nakedness or danger or sword? As it is written: "For your sake we face death all day long; we are considered as sheep to be slaughtered." (Romans 8:35–36 NIV)

Even amid deadly perils the Christian can join in the Apostle's bold reply: "No, in all these things (*tois pasin*) we are more than conquerors through him who loved us" (Romans 8:38 NIV).[20] Romans 8:28, then, is not about God working with us for good in all sorts of things. That claim is not nearly bold enough.

Before we rest the case and rest in Paul's final claim, there's one more important alternative for Romans 8:28's syntax. As we have seen, Paul's Greek can track with the KJV, with the "all things" understood as the subject of verb "work together": "*We know that all things work together for good.*"[21] But form-for-form equivalence of Paul's Greek can also yield this awkward but understandable result: "*And we know that to the ones who love God, [God] works all things for good to the ones who are, according to [His] purpose, called.*"[22] The seemingly natural objection that the KJV mistakes the plural "all things" (*panta*) as the subject of the singular verb "works together" (*sunergei*) fails, because the neuter plural *panta* "all" ordinarily takes a singular verb. American English similarly mixes our "all." "All are"? Or "All is"? That singular syntax works well in our Hellenistic author's less-than-classical Greek.

However, the verb "works together" (*sunergei*) may better fit an implied subject, "God." That subject is perhaps introduced at the end of the preceding clause by the accusative form *ton theon*, "the Deity," "God." In the phrase about "those who love God" (*tois agaposin ton theon*), the *ton theon* may do double duty, serving as the direct object ending one clause, and implying the unexpressed nominative subject of the next verb. *"To those who love God* (ton theon), *[God] works all things for good."*[23]

As we saw above, a few manuscripts such as the impressive P^{46} actually include "*ho theos,*" "the Deity," "God," after the verb *sunergei*, "work together." This longer reading is widely thought to be an anxious scribe's attempt to clarify a misunderstood text. Paul may rather have neatly streamlined his Greek with a double-duty noun, ton *theon,* "God," leading his readers to infer its referent as the next subject. In either case, the following sentence (vv. 29–30) may strengthen the interpretation that God is the subject who "works [all things] together": all the main verbs in Romans 8:29–30 likewise imply a missing *ho theos*, "God," as their subject:

> For those whom He foreknew He also predestined to be conformed to the image of His Son, ...And those whom He predestined, He also called; those He called, He also justified; those He justified, He also glorified. (Romans 8:29–30)

The resulting alternative, *"God works all things for good,"* with "God" as the stated or implied subject, lies behind most of the recent English versions. Translators, it seems, now prove reluctant to follow the KJV's "all things work together for good." Better, perhaps, the rendering that makes God's engagement with all things unmistakably explicit: *"God works all things for good."*[24] Even without the seemingly repetitive *ho theos* ("God") in P^{46} and its textual kin, this syntax works well enough.

In our survey of translation options, we see that two alternatives survive scrutiny:

> *"We know that all things work together for good..."*
> *"We know that God works all things for good..."*

Whichever way we choose to translate the line, Romans 8:28 proves to be a maximal text. If we go with the plausible but roundabout *"all things work together for good,"* we need not take that limousine far from that roundabout's hub. We need simply to assert that if indeed "all things work together for the good of those who love God," they do so not because of their own inherent machinery, but because *God Himself* works them so. We might cite Bruce Waltke's wise comment on Proverbs 16:33 again here: "there are no exceptions." [25] If, on the other hand, we go with the explicit *"God works all things for good for those who love Him,"* we arrive at the same blessed destination.

That destination is the Christian's trust that every created entity, every creaturely event—whether neutral, benevolent, or malevolent—somehow serves God's good purpose for those who love him. *God Himself works them so.* "There are no exceptions."

Thus, the Christian is sure to arrive at the planned destination: glorious conformity to Christ, "the firstborn among many brothers and sisters" (Romans 8:28b NIV). Christ becomes thus not only eldest, but model, prototype, "pioneer and perfecter" of our faith (Hebrew 12:2). Christ's unbreakable bond of love with His Bride grows ever stronger every moment of all the everlasting ages yet to come. In him at last we find the death of death, and the life of life.

Ephesians 1:10–11. Our second maximal text bears an even greater glory. Romans 8 has taken us far; Ephesians 1 takes us farther. In Romans 8, Paul taught us that the focus of God's predestinating plan is to bring guilty sinners, graciously elected in Christ, at last to a blessed destination. Can Ephesians 1 top *that*?

It does. Ephesians, after all, is the eagle-eyed epistle, soaring far above earth and winging toward the ethereal. If Romans is the New Testament's most detailed account of redemption in Christ, Ephesians is its most heavenly. But this heavenly account is no earthless idealism. Rather, in Ephesians Christ binds earth to heaven and heaven to earth. The Christ "who descended" in incarnation, death, and burial "is the very one who ascended higher than all the heavens, in order to fill the whole universe" (Ephesians 4:10). Thus Ephesians sets forth "unity in the inaugurated new creation," a unity achieved by this very Christ in an astonishment of grace founded in the divine wisdom before and beyond all ages.[26]

Breaking into the middle of the New Testament's longest sentence, here's how Paul puts it in our second maximal text:

> ...[God] made known to us the mystery of his will according to His good pleasure, which He purposed in Christ, [10] to be put into effect when the times reach their fulfillment—to bring unity to all things [*ta panta*] in heaven and on earth under Christ. [11] In him we were also chosen, having been predestined according to the plan of Him who works out everything [*ta panta*] in conformity with the purpose of His will, [12] in order that we, who were the first to put our hope in Christ, might be for the praise of His glory. (Ephesians 1:8b–12 NIV)

Not only does God work "all things" (*ta panta*) "for the good" (Romans 8:29), but he also predestines us to be His holy children in accordance with the gracious plan that works everything (*ta panta;* Ephesians 1:11) for His purpose, fitting everything into everything else and pressing it toward His chosen goal. And what is this goal? That "all things (*ta panta*) in heaven and on earth" shall be brought together "under one head, even Christ" (Ephesians 1:10).

This union of earth and heaven in Christ is already present in principle in the very Incarnation of Christ. This is what the "Father of Orthodoxy," Athanasius the Great (c296–373 AD), insisted upon against the Christ-denying Arians so long ago. In one of the greatest treatises on that subject, *On the Incarnation of the Word*, he exhorted the "true lovers of Christ":

> The first fact that you must grasp is this: *the renewal of creation has been wrought by the Self-same Word Who made it in the beginning.*"[27]

The Incarnation of God-in-Man contains within itself the reconciliation of earth and heaven, of creation and Creator. It presses the corruptible into the incorruptible; sin into sanctity; endless death into everlasting life.

Yet the implications of this Incarnation must be worked out in time, in eschatology. Because of the Incarnate Christ, all heaven and earth shall stand renewed, refreshed, reconciled. In his own God-Man personhood, Jesus Christ effects the marriage of heaven and earth. The destination of predestination is nothing short of this: the resurrection of the dying cosmos under Christ's living lordship.

Those who promote the Rapturist anti-vision of "The Late Great Planet Earth" miss the future great point. Creation is not abandoned.[28] Earth is not consigned to some cosmic trash can. The new Heavens and New Earth are the renewal of the old, borne out of the old into incorruptibility.[29] The whole creation groans as if in childbirth—not in despair over a stillborn child, but in hope of its own life in glory (Romans 8:21–22).

Responding to Ephesians 1, Irenaeus, the second century Bishop of Lyons and the ancient Church's most astute reader of Paul, expanded Paul's point:

> God recapitulated in Himself the ancient formation of man, that He might kill sin, deprive death of its power, and vivify man. (*Against Heresies*, Book III.18.7)

And again,

> [God] took up man into Himself, the invisible becoming visible, the incomprehensible being made comprehensible, the impassible becoming capable of suffering, and the Word being made man, thus summing up all things in Himself:...and, taking to Himself the pre-eminence, as well as constituting Himself Head of the Church, He might draw all things to Himself at the proper time. (*Against Heresies*, Book III.16.6) [30]

For Irenaeus, the Incarnation "recapitulates" the creation in such a way that the human race and the Creation itself, though fallen in Adam and therefore subject to corruption and death, is reframed, reclaimed by this Christ, the "second Adam," the "last Adam," so that Creation is liberated from corruption, and the race redeemed from sin and death, summed up under Christ in the eschaton. It brings the marriage of heaven to those who were hellish; and a glory better than gold to the humblest dust of the earth. Astonishing.

Earlier in this essay I raised three questions: (1) How big is this providence? (2) How much of life does God foreordain? And, (3) What kind of predestination should Christian believe in? Two answers are now in order. (1) Providence is as big as the mighty universe and as small as the merest mite. (2) Second, foreordination is total. Nothing is omitted from the purposes of God. But, lest we send them astray, these answers must be given their proper origin and their intended goal. They arise from the Triune counsel in eternity. They reach their goal in the consummation of the universe in Jesus Christ. Thus every iota of all creation serves the purpose of God the Father: the glory of Jesus Christ in the fullness of the Holy Spirit. This Triune origin and Triune goal of the one eternal decree help us answer our third question, "*What kind of predestination should we believe in?*"

The Westminster Confession of Faith (WCF) on God's Eternal Decree

To answer that question, "*What kind of predestination?*" we now we turn to the text of the document that my mis-adventurous freshman year at Geneva College at last led me to study. *The Westminster Confession of Faith* (WCF, 1646) is the principal doctrinal standard for many a Reformed Church. Its chapter 3 addresses our third question with wonderful clarity, gaining the assent of multitudes of Christians worldwide. Our discussion shall attempt to show how astutely the Westminster Confession's author expressed the biblical doctrine of predestination in such a way as to do what Paul did with it: to exalt the utter graciousness of grace in the gospel of Christ.

First, we note the title of the chapter: "*Of God's Eternal Decree.*" Decree: the word is singular. The mind of God is so immensely vast that the whole plan of God for the whole of time and space, for the whole fabric of human history, is subsumed in one single enormous thought. God does not need to make many decrees, to test out plans to see how well they work, and then propose more plans. One single decree is all it takes. It takes no time, and there's never enough time for it. This decree is in eternity. It is the one Decree-About-Everything.

Here we must distinguish among timed, timeful, and timeless terms. We'll avoid what Augustine pondered: "What then is time? If no one asks me, I know: if I wish to explain it to one who asks, I know not."[31] Suffice it to say that what is *timed* ends within its time. What is *everlasting* endlessly endures within time. And what is *eternal* exists without time. Thus "everlasting" is timeful; but eternity is timeless. Finite, creaturely existence is necessarily timed. But by God's good gift, human life, once begun, continues forever. The soul, though perishable in its creatureliness, is not permitted to die. Like the ray in geometry, it starts at one point and goes on forever. It gains heaven or suffers hell. The New Testament routinely calls the blessed side of that future *zoe aionios*, "the life of the age [to come]." English translations often make this "eternal life," as in John 3:16, or sometimes "everlasting life." The second of these is the better, for an "age," as in "the age to come," is timeful. Some Bible versions may declare that "*time* [chronos] *shall be no longer*" (Revelation 10:6, Douay-Rheims; similarly, KJV) but this is mistranslation. The old American Standard Version (ASV) got it right in 1901: "*There shall be delay* [chronos] *no longer.*" In Revelation 10, the time of final salvation draws near: no calling "Time!" No delay of the God's holy game. Despite the persistence of the "timeless" error in gospel hymns, nearly every English version since 1901 since has followed suit: "No more *delay*!"[32]

The resurrected Christian's immortal forever is thus timeful. We are timeful. God's experience cannot be. In technical precision, Christians receive *everlasting* life; but God alone possesses timeless *eternity*.[33]

Yet even here the word "time*less*" can mislead. It is not that God's experience is *less* than our timeful life. God is time's Maker and therefore time's Master. His eternity is the Timefulness beyond time.[34] Hence, "timeless" implies no disability in God.[35] God's infinite personhood reaches into time—and thus the words by which Moses blessed Israel prove true: "The eternal God is your refuge, and underneath are the everlasting arms" (Deuteronomy 33:27).

Which brings us at last to chapter 3 of the *Westminster Confession*. Our time-bound minds must consider many aspects of the one great Decree; and so the theologians speak of the "decrees" of God, and of their logical (not temporal) order. But fully and properly considered, "there is but one, and that one, ever."[36] God needs no time. Hence, the chapter title: "Of God's Eternal Decree." Now to the text that title introduces:

> I. God, from all eternity, did, by the most wise and holy counsel of his own will, freely, and unchangeably ordain whatsoever comes to pass: yet so, as thereby neither is God the author of sin, nor is violence offered to the will of the creatures; nor is the liberty or contingency of second causes taken away, but rather established.

Here we see that the *Westminster Confession*, like the Bible, teaches total foreordination: "*whatsoever comes to pass.*" Yet it does so with certain conditions attached. These conditions help us see our answer to the question, "*What kind?*"

> . . . yet so, as thereby neither is God the author of sin, nor is violence offered to the will of the creatures; nor is the liberty or contingency of second causes taken away, but rather established.

These conditions are threefold:

(a) God orders His universe in such a way that, despite the totality of the decree, God remains morally pure; He is not the author of sin. There is no Sithian "dark side" to God; no need for Yoda's famous warning: "*Young Skywalker, beware the dark side of the Force.*" There is no such admonition in Christianity. There is no need for it, for "there is no unrighteousness in

Him!" (Psalm 92:15). "God is light; in Him there is no darkness at all" (1 John 1:5). This, of course, is mystery. But if we never encounter mystery in religion, then we have downsized God. The French polymath Blaise Pascal (1623–1662) said it well in his *Pensées*, # 585:

> Any religion which does not affirm that God is hidden is not true; and any religion which does not give the reason of it is not instructive. Our religion does all this: *Vere tu es Deus absconditus.*[37]

(b) God ordains the acts of his creatures in such a way that no violence is offered to the will of the creature. Thus, we choose according to our nature, according to our strongest motive at the time of choosing. Our choices arise not arbitrarily, but from our own character, free and uncoerced.[38] This, too, is mystery. But every alternative proves morally repugnant: either God does not rule the world; or humans have no will. The first alternative insults God; the second insults the image of God. Wise and foolish Christians alike assert the contrary as simultaneous truths when they pray, "God is great. God is good. And we thank him for this food." God is great: he truly rules. God is good: his creation basks in the outflow of his love.

(c) God ordains the events of the universe in such a way that his ordaining them does not abolish "second causes," but rather establishes them. In classic Christian theology God is the "first cause" of all things. He created everything. "In Him we live and move and have our being" (Acts 17:28). As the first cause of all things, God establishes all other causative powers. These powers are the "second causes." They include the various physical forces, such as inertia, entropy, and gravity They also include the choices of free creatures: angels and human beings. God includes the use of second causes in His all-embracing decree. Unless we exercise our wills to do something, *it will not be done*. Zero-sum games of fifty/fifty, or sixty/forty, or ninety-nine/one are rejected. Our choosing and God's choosing co-exist in concursus, a mystery of consent beyond our understanding.

II. Although God knows whatsoever may or can come to pass upon all supposed conditions, yet hath he not decreed anything because he foresaw it as future, or as that which would come to pass upon such conditions.

In Romans 8:29–30, "foreknowledge" is foreknowledge of the elect themselves, not merely of their decisions or actions. Paul asks, "Did God reject His people whom He foreknew?" (Romans 11:2). In biblical foreknowledge, God enters into a personal, covenantal relationship with people before they even existed. "Those he foreknew he also predestined" (Romans 8:29). Thus "foreknown" is *foreloved.*

III. By the decree of God, for the manifestation of his glory, some men and angels are predestinated unto everlasting life; and others foreordained to everlasting death.

Why God did not choose all is a mystery. That God chose some is also a mystery—the mystery of mercy. For God could have chosen none—that would be justice. And that would not have been a mystery.

John Wesley thought that God was obliged to offer salvation to all.[39] Today's liberal Protestants think that God is obliged to save all. Neither claim understands grace well enough. Grace is not merely "undeserved favor." We sinners deserve its opposite. Had He resolved to save none, God's goodness would remain forever untarnished. Those who rebel against this thought should reflect: God sends no saving mission to Satan and His minions. So it could have been for the guilty human race.

IV. These angels and men, thus predestinated, and foreordained, are particularly and unchangeably designed, and their number so certain and definite, that it cannot be either increased or diminished.

Romans 8:29–30, the "Unbreakable Chain of Salvation," is famous on the point. It requires that the number of the elect remain definite and constant. Those whom God foreknew in love are the same as those who attain to final glory, *"for the gifts and call of God are irrevocable"*:

> For those God foreknew He also predestined to be conformed to the image of His Son, that He might be the firstborn among many brothers and sisters. [30] And those He predestined, He also called; those He called, He also justified; those He justified, He also glorified. (Romans 8:29–30 NIV)

Those who marginalize Paul on such questions may not feel quite the same about the words of Jesus. Yet his words require the same conclusion:

> This is the will of Him who sent me, that I shall lose none of all those He has given me, but raise them up at the last day. [40] For my Father's will is that everyone who looks to the Son and believes in Him shall have eternal life, and I will raise them up at the last day." (John 6:39–40 NIV)

Paul paraphrased: All whom the Father foreknew and predestinated shall certainly be called by the gospel, justified by faith, and glorified in the resurrection. Jesus, paraphrased: Of all that the Father has given me, I shall lose none, but raise them up to perfection at the last day. Thus, in both Jesus and Paul, election makes glorification absolutely certain. To be a Christian is to be everlastingly safe.

> V. Those of mankind that are predestinated unto life, God, before the foundation of the world was laid, according to His eternal and immutable purpose, and the secret counsel and good pleasure of His will, hath chosen, in Christ, unto everlasting glory, out of his mere free grace and love, without any foresight of faith, or good works, or perseverance in either of them, or any other thing in the creature, as conditions, or causes moving Him thereunto; and all to the praise of His glorious grace.

"Predestinated unto life"—that is the authors' conscious choice for the wording of the WCF here. Predestination is for the elect; foreordination is for those whom God passed by. God *actively* destines some, chosen in mercy, to the glorious destiny of the children of God. Those who are not so predestined, are *passively* left to their own nature, sinful nature, and thus to the hellish outcome of their self-determined revolt.

The decree of election must stand as a real and determinative decree of God. The Arminian interpretation of the decree does away with the gravity of election. It makes divine election dependent upon our foreseen, persevering faith, dependent upon our response to the gospel, dependent upon some surviving seed of virtue in us that leads us, unlike others, to choose Christ. But this stance takes away the power of election altogether. In Arminianism we are said to become elect because we determine it ourselves through our act of believing. God foresees our act of faith, and accordingly elects us to everlasting life.

But the Bible will not support this interpretation of predestination. In Acts 13:48, when the Gentiles hear the good news preached by Paul and Barnabas, "they were glad, and honored the word of the Lord; and all who were appointed for everlasting life believed." Here saving faith is the result of the divine appointment—election—and occasioned by the preaching of the gospel—and freely chosen by astonished pagans! In Romans 9:11, Jacob was chosen and Esau passed by "before the twins were born or had done anything good or bad—in order that God's purpose in election might stand—not by works, but by him who calls."

Thus, the Arminian view that election is based on foreseen persevering faith is clearly overruled.[40] God's purpose stands. That purpose is for all things to serve the glory of God the Father through Jesus Christ our Lord in the power of the Holy Spirit. As Paul writes to the Corinthians, "It is because of him that you are in Jesus Christ." Hence, "Let him who boasts boast in the Lord" (1 Corinthians 1:30–31).

VI. As God hath appointed the elect unto glory, so hath He, by the eternal and most free purpose of His will, foreordained all the means thereunto. Wherefore, they who are elected, being fallen in Adam, are redeemed by Christ, are effectually called unto faith in Christ by his Spirit working in due season, are justified, adopted, sanctified, and kept by his power, through faith, unto salvation. Neither are any other redeemed by Christ, effectually called, justified, adopted, sanctified, and saved, but the elect only.

The decree of election is not a bare and naked decree, working its will apart from the intimate engagement of human beings. God decrees the end, the destiny of salvation; He also decrees the means to that end, the gospel of salvation. Without the gospel, that destiny fails. Only if Jesus dies can people be saved; only if the gospel is preached can they be saved; only if the Holy Spirit effectually calls them can they be saved; only if people believe the gospel can they be saved. Without the means, the end fails. God decrees both the end and the means. Augustine (354–430) puts it this way:

> If a certain order of causes does exist in the mind of God, it does not follow that nothing is left to the free choice of our will. For our wills themselves are included in the order of causes which is certain to God and contained within His foreknowledge."[41]

The devout New Testament scholar H. C. G. Moule (1841–1920), who taught at both Oxford and Cambridge and served as Bishop of Durham, gives Augustine's answer a personal and pastoral turn, and thus helps us answer the question, "*What kind of predestination?*"

> If we could not it was because we would not. If you cannot it is because, somehow and somewhere, you will not; will not put yourselves without reserve in the way of the sight. "Oh, taste and see that the Lord is

> good"; oh, love the eternal Love. But those who thus simply and genuinely love God are also, on the other side, "purpose-wise, His called ones"; "called," in the sense which we have found above to be consistently traceable in the Epistles; not merely invited, but brought in; not evangelised only, but converted. In each case of the happy company, the man, the woman, came to Christ, came to love God with the freest possible coming of the will, the heart. Yet each, having come, had the Lord to thank for the coming. The human personality had traced its orbit of will and deed, as truly as when it willed to sin and to rebel. But lo, in ways past our finding out, its free track lay along a previous track of the purpose of the Eternal; its free "I will" was the precise and fore-ordered correspondence to His "Thou shalt." It was the act of man; it was the grace of God.[42]

> VII. The rest of mankind God was pleased, according to the unsearchable counsel of His own will, whereby He extendeth or withholdeth mercy, as He pleaseth, for the glory of His sovereign power over His creatures, to pass by; and to ordain them to dishonor and wrath for their sin, to the praise of His glorious justice.

As *the Westminster Confession* teaches, God elects some despite their sin, to mercy and heaven. God passes by others because of their sin, and thereby leaves them to condemnation. Thus God's decree of election and His "passing by" are not equal decrees in the mind of God. Election is *active*: in it God makes use of means, the means of grace, the death of Jesus, the preaching of the gospel, the effectual call of the Holy Spirit. He makes vigorous use of means in order to secure the full salvation of the elect. His "passing by" is indeed *passive*. In it God makes no use of means. God does not tempt people to sin; He does not draw people to evil. "God is light, and in Him there is no darkness at all" (1 John 1:5). There is no unrighteousness in Him!" (Psalm

92:15). God, as it were, leaves evil to itself, to its own naturally destructive consequences. Augustine says as much in his little manual on the Christian life, *The Enchiridion* [Handbook] *on Faith, Hope and Love*:

> He who is saved has no basis for glorying in any merit of his own; nor does the man who is damned have a basis for complaining of anything except what he has fully merited.[43]

Thus, heavenly saints have no one to thank but God; and hell-bound sinners have no one to blame but themselves. We are the power of our own damnation; God alone is the power of our deliverance.

Four More Testy Terms

With this discussion so far, perhaps we are better prepared to understand four more of the testy terms Christians have used to discuss the Bible's teachings on this difficult issue. Again, it seems that the Bible requires of our English-language minds either these terms, or something exactly like them.

1. *Preterition*: God's passing over or passing by the non-elect, leaving them in the condemned mass of fallen humanity.
2. *Reprobation*: God's decree to punish those guilty ones who are passed by for their sins.

For those with the eyes to see, the *Westminster Confession's* chapter 3 is "infralapsarian." This term has reference to a controversy within Reformed Christianity between the *infralapsarians* and the *supralapsarians*. This controversy has to do with the mind of God in his unique eternity, and the order of his decrees (note the plural) about creation, election, sin and the fall of the human race. The key question was this: what is the *logical* order of decrees in the mind of the eternal God? To put it more specifically, the issue is "whether the decrees to create and to permit the fall were means to the decree of redemption." [44]

3. *Supralapsarianism* (the term means "above or prior to the fall")[45] holds that God in logical priority first decreed . . .
   a. "to glorify Himself through the salvation of some and the perdition of other rational creatures"; He then decreed…
   b. "to create those who were thus elected and reprobated"; He then decreed…
   c. "to permit them to fall"; lastly, He decreed…
   d. "to justify the elect and to condemn the non-elect."[46]

It's easy to forget that these decrees are actually happening at one and the same "instant" in the one immense Decree-About-Everything in the eternal, Triune mind of God. We are speaking of logical order, not chronological order. Again, there's never enough time for such a decree. Time has nothing to do with it. It's in eternity.

Supralapsarianism accordingly presents itself as the way of properly recognizing the absolute sovereignty of God. In "*Supra*," God is the absolute sovereign, since He creates and disposes of His creatures according to His own sovereign choice, without regard to the condition of the creature.

4. *Infralapsarianism* (the term means "below or subsequent to the fall"[47]) holds to a different order of decrees. In "*Infra*," the order of God's eternal wisdom resembles the order of events as they work out in time. This semblance happens because history obeys the eternal decree. Again, there's never enough time for such a decree. Time has nothing to do with it. The decree is in eternity. In "*Infra*," God first decreed . . .
   a. to create the human race "in holiness and blessedness." He then decreed…
   b. to permit the human race to fall "by the self-determination of His own will."
      He then decreed…
   c. "to save a certain number" out of this guilty mass of fallen humanity.

He then decreed…

d. "to leave the remainder in their self-determination in sin," and to subject them to the punishment that their sin deserves.

In its emphasis on God's choosing some despite their sin, while passing over others because of their sin, the *Westminster Confession* is implicitly *infralapsarian*. In Infralapsarianism, God reprobates because of foreseen sin. This is not the case with supralapsarianism. In supralapsarianism, God elects and reprobates without regard to foreseen sin. God's decree of election and reprobation comes *before* (supra-) His decree to permit the fall. This stance leaves supralapsarianism open to the charge that God is arbitrary, that He reprobates those whom He does not yet consider wicked.

Infralapsarianism is more sensitive to the issue of the justice of God. God is not an arbitrary ruler; God passes by and reprobates those whom He already considers as sinfully wicked. As Rowland Ward writes, "God did not create men in order to damn them." Rather, "He created men who, having fallen…receive the just reward for their sin, unless they are embraced in His gracious election."[48]

For this reason, most Reformed theologians through the centuries have been Infralapsarians. *The Canons of Dordt* (1618) and *The Westminster Confession* (1646) are both implicitly Infralapsarian.

VIII. The doctrine of this high mystery of predestination is to be handled with special prudence and care, that men, attending the will of God revealed in His Word, and yielding obedience thereunto, may, from the certainty of their effectual vocation, be assured of their eternal election. So shall this doctrine afford matter of praise, reverence, and admiration of God; and of humility, diligence, and abundant consolation to all that sincerely obey the gospel.

The *Westminster Confession*'s final paragraph in Chapter 3 gives effective pastoral counsel for our wise use of this difficult doctrine. Predestination is a "high mystery," requiring "special prudence and care. Predestination is to be preached, for there is no teaching in the Word of God, the Holy Scriptures, that is not profitable for the people of God (2 Timothy 3:16–17). But predestination is to be preached with appropriate wisdom.

Its neglect is tragic for so many Christians. Believing that their salvation was gained by the natural power of their own free will, they likewise believe that their salvation can just as willfully be lost.

Not long after I heard Jack White in that summer of 1972 thanking God for His predestinating grace, I consulted my pastor back home about it. Citing John 10:29, he looked me in the eye and assured me with soul-chilling confidence words to this effect: "Jesus said, 'No one can snatch them out of my Father's hand.' *But you can snatch yourself away*." Thus I stood assured that I had no ground to stand assured.

If so, there is no safety in Christ. Yet the New Testament massively assures Christians of their everlasting safety. *"My Father is greater than all; no one can snatch them out of my Father's hand"* (John 10:29). Grounded in the Triune counsel of eternity, our election can never be annulled. *"The gifts and calling of God are irrevocable." "God's purpose election stands"* (Romans 11:29; 9:11).

Misunderstandings abound; it is up to the Church to correct them. Rightly used, the doctrine gives great comfort to the people of God—for whoever truly believes the gospel is certainly one of God's elect. As the preacher's proverb has it, *"If you see a turtle on a fence post, you know he didn't get there by himself."* We make our calling and election sure—to us—by doing nothing other than believing the Good News. We make it still more sure —to us and to others—by bearing the fruit of a converted life (2 Peter 1:5–11). By recognizing this doctrine, we exalt the graciousness of grace, the irrevocable grace that converts us forever. "*It is because of him that you are in Jesus Christ*" (1 Corinthians 1:30). This mystery of predestination humbles us; it also exalts us beyond the stars.

Notes

[1]According to Romans 9–11, Israel's ethnic election differs in one important way from the election of individuals. Elect individuals will be converted, and never lost. Yet unconverted individuals from elect ethnic Israel can be lost; for "*For not all who are descended from Israel are Israel*" (Romans 9:6). Even so, Paul assures us, the end result of national Israel's election will be massive Jewish salvation through faith in Jesus Christ (Romans 11:11–16). By Romans 11's grand finale, we discover that salvation for Jews and Gentiles alike shall prove vastly generous in number and in mercy (11:32).

[2]I first heard this saying thirty-some years ago in a Sunday evening sermon by Dr. Steve Brown at the General Assembly of the Presbyterian Church in America (PCA), meeting at Calvin College, Grand Rapids, Michigan, June, 1987. Steve Brown attributes it to Allan Emery. See Brown's article, "It's Him...the Holy Spirit." *Key Life*, August 29, 2018. https://www.keylife.org/articles/its-him...the-holy-spirit, accessed July 26, 2019. A similar saying is also attributed to Alex Haley, author of *Roots*.

[3]I first heard *that* question in a lecture by Dr. R.C. Sproul at the Ligonier Valley Study Center, about 1975.

[4]Classic Christian theology assesses God's acts as twofold: works of creation and works of providence. Thomists and Calvinists alike use the distinction as an organizing idea in theology. For example, Thomas Aquinas's famous *Summa Contra Gentiles* (c1259–1265 AD), "The Doctrinal Summary against the Unbelievers," is composed of four topical sections in logical order: God, Creation, Providence, and Salvation. The last of these addresses a special type of providence, the providence of redemptive grace. See the edition translated by Anton C. Pegis, *et alia* (Notre Dame, IN: University of Notre Dame Press, 1975).

[5]Christian theologians sometimes use the terms *predestination* and *foreordination* interchangeably. However, in the *Westminster Confession of Faith* and other standards of Reformed orthodoxy, predestination is exclusively a matter of mercy.

[6]See the valuable discussion of the subject in Paul Helm, *The Providence of God* (Contours of Christian Theology; Downers Grove, IL: InterVarsity Press, 1994).

[7]Matthew 10:29's Greek reads in transliteration, *kaì hen ex auton ou peseitai epi ten gen aneu tou patros humon.* In near absolute word-for-word equivalence, barbarous though it be, that's *"And one out of them does not fall upon the ground without your Father."*

[8]*The New Testament in Modern English.* Translated by J. B. Phillips. London: Bles, 1960. *The Living Bible.* Translated by Kenneth N. Taylor. Carol Stream, IL: Tyndale House, 1971.

[9]Civilla D. Martin, lyrics, and Charles Gabriel, music, "His Eye is On the Sparrow" (1905). Ethel Waters (1896–1977) made it her theme song, and used its title for her autobiography. For the final quotation, see Ron Hale, "The Sparrow that Soared," *The Christian Index* (May 2, 2016). https://christianindex.org/ethel-waters-sparrow-soared/. Accessed September 9, 2019.

[10]The Hebrew reads, *baheyq yutal et-haggoral, umeYHWH kôl-mishpatô.* In extreme formal equivalence, this becomes, *"Into the lap it is thrown—the lot—but from Yahweh [is] all its judgment."*

[11]For brief discussion of the complexities of the *Urim* and *Thummim,* see C. Van Dam, "*Urim,*" in volume 1 of *The New International Dictionary of Old Testament Theology and Exegesis,* ed. W. A. VanGemeren (Grand Rapids: Zondervan:1985), 325–27. For exhaustive discussion, including the demonstration that the *Urim* and *Thummim* did not function exclusively as revelation-by-lottery, but required further "light" from God, often oracular in nature, see C. Van Dam, *The Urim and Thummim: A Means of Revelation in Ancient Israel* (Winona Lake, IN: Eisenbrauns, 1997).

[12]Tribal lands chosen by lot: Joshua 14:1; 19:51. Matthias chosen by lot: Act 1:26.

[13]B. K. Waltke, *The Book of Proverbs, Chapters 16–31*; New International Commentary on the Old Testament (Grand Rapids: Eerdmans, 2005), 38.

[14]Romans 8:28 transliterated reads, *Oidamen de hoti tois agaposin ton theon panta sunergei eis agathon, tois kata prothesin kletois ousin.*

[15]See the superb discussion in Cranfield's *Critical and Exegetical Commentary of the Epistle to the Romans*, International Critical Commentary (Edinburgh: T & T Clark: 1975), I: 425–31. Less daunting is his aptly named *Romans: A Shorter Commentary* (Eerdmans, 1985), 202–205.

[16]Paul's letters use *oidamen* "we know" eleven times, nearly all of them to mark rhetorical divisions, such as (in English) new paragraphs. Romans 2:2; 3:19; 7:14; 8:22, 26, 28; 1 Corinthians 8:1, 4; 2 Corinthians 5:1, 16; and 1 Timothy 1:8. The NIV takes ten of them as paragraph markers; the KJV and ESV, seven; the NRSV, nine.

[17]For this argument I am aided by Thomas Schreiner's *Romans*, Baker Exegetical Commentary on the New Testament (Grand Rapids: Baker Academic) 1998, 448–49. So also Douglas Moo, *Romans*, 528,

[18]P^{46} = Papyrus 46, one of the eleven "Chester Beatty Papyri." Eighty-six leaves of this codex survive. Daniel Wallace calls P^{46} "priceless." For photos, text, and translation, see http://www.csntm.org/manuscript/View/GA_P46. That same verb + noun combination, *sunergei ho theos, "God works all things,"* is likewise attested in the great fourth and fifth century codices Vaticanus and Alexandrinus; and several other Greek, Coptic, and Ethiopic sources, a minority reading. For Daniel Wallace's comment on P^{46}, see his on-line blog, "Some Notes on the Earliest Manuscript of Paul's Letters": https://danielbwallace.com/2013/06/08/some-notes-on-the-earliest-manuscript-of-pauls-letters/. Accessed August 13, 2019.

[19]This rendering is defended by Barclay M. Newman and Eugene A. Nida, *A Translators Handbook on Paul's Letter to the Romans* (London: United Bible Societies, 1973), 165–67. The *Good News Translation* (GNT), quoted above, is Newman's work.

[20]Romans 8:38's "all these things" translates *tois pasin*. The form *pasin* is the neuter plural dative of *pas*, "all." The word therefore resumes the theme of the *panta*, "all things," likewise from *pas*, "all," in verse 28. The form *panta* is likewise neuter plural and either nominative or accusative, depending on how we assess the syntax. The *pasin* and *panta* of Romans 8:28 and 8:38 thus assert the same totality in God's providence.

[21]This is the understanding defended by Cranfield (1975; 1986), and by Douglas Moo, *The Epistle to the Romans*, New International Commentary on the New Testament (Grand Rapids: Eerdmans, 1996), 527–31.

[22]Again, Romans 8:28's Greek: *Oidamen de hoti tois agaposin ton theon panta sunergei eis agathon, tois kata prothesin kletois ousin.*

[23]If Paul had restated his subject, we'd read a rather awkward repetition: *tois agaposin ton theon, ho theos panta sunergei*. Or *tois agaposin ton theon, panta sunergei ho theos*. Either is excessive.

[24]Here the "all things" (*panta*) may be taken as an accusative of respect: "in regard to all things." See the discussion, *pro* and *con*, in Douglas Moo, *Romans* (1996), 527–28.

[25]B. K. Waltke, *The Book of Proverbs, Chapters 16–31*, 38

[26]So S. M. Baugh in his superb commentary, *Ephesians* (Evangelical Exegetical Commentary; Bellingham WA: Lexham Press, 2016), 35.

[27]*On the Incarnation of the Word* 1.1. https://www.ccel.org/ccel/athanasius/incarnation. Accessed September 7, 2019. Emphasis original to the translator. This ancient book earned a famous introduction by C. S. Lewis, which can be found here: workhttps://www.uccfleadership-network.org/resource/introduction-to-athanasius-on-the-incarnation. Accessed September 7, 2019.

[28]Hal Lindsey, with C. C. Carlson, *The Late, Great Planet Earth* (Grand Rapids: Zondervan, 1970).

[29]Revelation 21:1's "New Heavens and New Earth" (*ouranon kainon kai gen kainen*) are not described by Greek's *neos,* "new in kind," but by *kainos*, suggesting "new in quality." New creation thus comes not *ex nihilo*, "out of nothing," but as creation *renewed*. For an excellent exposition of biblical eschatology, see Anthony Hoekema, *The Bible and the Future* (Grand Rapids: Eerdmans, 1979); or more recently, Richard Middleton, *A New Heaven and a New Earth: Reclaiming Biblical Eschatology* (Grand Rapids: Eerdmans, 2014); also Herman Bavinck, *Holy Spirit, Church, and New Creation*; volume 4 in *Reformed Dogmatics* (ed. John Bolt; trans. John Vriend; Grand Rapids: Baker Academic, 2008; transl. from Dutch of the 4th edition, 1928).

[30]Irenaeus, *Against Heresies* (transl. by Alexander Roberts and William Rambaut; from *Ante-Nicene Fathers*, Vol. 1; ed. Alexander Roberts, James Donaldson, and A. Cleveland Coxe; Buffalo, NY: Christian Literature Publishing Co., 1885). Revised and edited for New Advent

by Kevin Knight. <http://www.newadvent.org/fathers/0103318.htm>. Accessed September 9, 2019.

[31] *Confessions*, Book 11.

[32] Alas, James Milton Black's hymn of 1889 is marred by the error: "When the trumpet of the Lord shall sound, and *time shall be no more*, / and the morning breaks eternal bright and fair; / when the saved of earth shall gather over on the other shore, / and the roll is called up yonder, I'll be there."

[33] Thus "eternity" is one of the incommunicable attributes of God. See Herman Bavinck, *God and Creation*; volume 2 of *Reformed Dogmatics* (four volumes; Grand Rapids: Baker Academic, 2008; translation of the Dutch original's fourth edition, 1928), 192–97.

[34] My case-sensitive claim that God in eternity is the "Time beyond time" is parallel to the thought from Jonathan Edwards that God is the Space beyond space. See Edwards, "Of Being" and "Of Mind." *Scientific and Philosophical Writings,* Volume 6, *The Works of Jonathan Edwards* (New Haven: Yale University Press), 1980.

[35] Contrary to so-called "Open Theists," who suppose that the timeless, spaceless God of classic Christian theology is as unable to relate to us in our world of time and change as Aristotle's "Unmoved Mover." See the failed project, now largely abandoned, in *The Openness of God: A Biblical Challenge to the Traditional Understanding of God*, by Clark Pinnock, Richard Rice, John Sanders, *et alia* (Downers Grove, IL: InterVarsity Press) 1994. For persuasive criticisms of Open Theism, see *Beyond the Bounds: Open Theism and the Undermining of Biblical Christianity*, edited by John Piper, Justin Taylor, and Paul Kjoss Helseth (Wheaton, IL: Crossway, 2003).

[36] From "Easter," by George Herbert, from his immortal collection, *The Temple* (1633).

[37] "Truly you are a God who hides Himself" (Isaiah 45:15, Vulgate). Blaise Pascal, *Pensées,* translated by W.F. Trotter (Grand Rapids: Christian Classics Ethereal Library), 2002: 94. http://www.ntslibrary.com/PDF%20Books/Blaise%20Pascal%20Pensees.pdf

[38] As is taught in the Westminster Confession, Chapter 9, "Of Free-Will." The greatest defense of this definition of free will is found in

Jonathan Edwards, *Freedom of the Will* (1754). For the definition itself, see the Yale edition, edited by Paul Ramsay, volume 1 in *The Works of Jonathan Edwards* (Yale University Press: New Haven, 1957).

[39]See the discussion in John Gerstner, *Jonathan Edwards, Evangelist* (Orlando: Northampton Press, 2018), 93. Original title: *Steps to Salvation in the Evangelistic Message of Jonathan Edwards* (Philadelphia: Westminster Press, 1959).

[40]For an attempt to thwart this classic criticism of Arminianism, see Roger Olsen, *Arminian Theology: Myths and Realities* (Downers Grove, IL: 2006).

[41]Augustine, *The City of God*, 5.9.

[42]H.C.G. Moule, *The Epistle to the Romans* (Expositor's Bible Commentary; ed. W. Robertson Nicoll; Seventh Series, 1893–94. London: Hodder and Stoughton, 1894). https://biblehub.com/commentaries/expositors/romans/8.htm. Accessed August 5, 2019.

[42]Augustine, *Enchiridion: On Faith, Hope and Love,* Book 25.99. Transl. Albert Outler. 1955. http://www.tertullian.org/fathers/augustine_enchiridion_02_trans.htm#C25

[43]Louis Berkhof, *Systematic Theology* (Grand Rapids: Eerdmans, 1941), 119.

[44]Richard Muller, *Dictionary of Latin and Greek Theological Terms* (Grand Rapids: Baker, 1985), 292.

[45]Berkhof, 119–120.

[46]Muller, *Dictionary of Latin and Greek Theological Terms*, 155.

[47]Rowland Ward, *The Westminster Confession of Faith: A Study Guide. New Expanded Edition* (Wantirna, Australia: New Melbourne Press, 2004), 63–72.

Recommended Reading

Herman Bavinck, *Reformed Dogmatics*. 4 volumes. Ed. John Bold; transl. John Vriend. Grand Rapids: Baker Academic, 2003–2008.

Louis Berkhof, *Systematic Theology*. 4th edition. Grand Rapids; Eerdmans, 1941. Chapter 9, "Predestination," pages 109–125.

Michael Horton, *The Christian Faith: A Systematic Theology for Pilgrims on the Way*. Grand Rapids: Zondervan, 2011. Chapter 9, "The Decree: Trinity and Predestination," pages 309–323.

Richard Mouw, *He Shines in All that's Fair: Culture and Common Grace*. The 2000 Stob Lectures. Grand Rapids: Eerdmans, 2001. Chapter 4, "Infra- "versus "Supra-," pages 53–74.

Rowland S. Ward, *The Westminster Confession of Faith: A Study Guide. New Expanded Edition*. Wantirna, Australia: New Melbourne Press, 2004. Chapter 3, "God's Eternal Plan," pages 63–72.

The Westminster Confession of Faith (London, 1646; many editions available in print and on-line). Chapter 3, "Of God's Eternal Decree."

CHAPTER SIX

What Was the Old Testament Referent in John 7:38? Observations on the Freed-Carson Proposal

C. Scott Shidemantle

Introduction

In John 7:37–38, Jesus is presented as speaking these words on the last and greatest day of the Feast of Tabernacles:

> On the last and greatest day of the Feast, Jesus stood and said in a loud voice, "If anyone is thirsty, let him come to me and drink. Whoever believes in me, as the Scripture has said, streams of living water will flow from within him" (John 7:37–38 NIV).

To what Old Testament Scripture does John 7:38 refer? During the past 50 years, numerous evangelical and non-evangelical scholars alike have revisited this question without much consensus resulting from their efforts.[1]

The reason for the lack of scholarly consensus is due to the complexity of issues surrounding John 7:37–39. Not only is there a punctuation issue in the Greek text that results in ambiguity regarding from whom the living water will flow (Jesus or the believer), but no matter which punctuation is accepted, no specific Old Testament passage using the phrase *ek tês koilias autou* can be found.[2] Also, there is a lack of consensus concerning the meaning of the singular *graphê* in the phrase "as the Scripture [*graphê*] said." Some scholars argue that because *graphê* is in the singular form, one specific Old Testament passage must be in view.[3] Others argue that *graphê*, even though it is singular, can still refer to the Scriptures as a whole such that the phrase "as the Scripture said" introduces a summary of the teaching of the Scriptures as a whole regarding the abundance of the Spirit under the New Covenant.[4] Because of this lack of consensus, some researchers have proposed going outside of the canonical Old Testament in order to find a source for the Scripture referenced in John 7:38.[5]

The purpose of this essay is not to settle the issue. To attempt to do so would be somewhat presumptuous given the complexity of the issues and the volume of scholarly writings by researchers with more experience working with this text than this current writer. Rather, the purpose of this essay is to present and then make a few observations regarding a proposal that was initially articulated by E. D. Freed in his book titled *Old Testament Quotations in the Gospel of John* and subsequently developed by D. A. Carson in his commentary *The Gospel According to John*.[6] Hereafter, this proposal, which will be explained more fully below, will be referred to in this essay as the Freed-Carson proposal. Interestingly enough, the Freed-Carson proposal has not generated much scholarly discussion. It is the hope of this writer that the Freed-Carson proposal will take its place in the conversation.

A Brief Survey of Proposals

A variety of proposals have been made by those who have studied this issue. Most of these proposals have two things in common: first, they attempt to demonstrate verbal parallels between John 7:38 and a certain Old Testament passage, and second, they attempt to demonstrate contextual parallels between John 7:38 and a certain Old Testament passage.

Maarten Menken has proposed Psalm 78:16,20 (Ps 77:16,20 LXX) as the source of the quotation.[7]

> He brought streams out of a rocky crag and made water flow down like rivers... When he struck the rock, water gushed out, and streams flowed abundantly (Ps 78:16,20 NIV).
>
> Kai eksêgagen udôr ek petras kai katêgagen ôs potamous udata... epei epatakse petran kai erruêsan udata kai cheimarroi kateklusthêsan (Ps 77:16,20 LXX).

Based on the assumptions that *graphê* indicates that one passage is in view and that John seems to interact with the Septuagint (LXX) when citing from the Old Testament, Menken goes to the LXX to find that one passage. He determines that Psalm 77:16,20 has the strongest verbal parallels with John 7:37–39. The verbal parallels are fourfold. Both passages contain forms of these three words: *potamoi*, *reô*, and *udôr*. Also, the phrase *ek tês koilias autou* in John 7:38 finds a parallel idea in the phrase *ek petra* in Ps 77:20.

Zane Hodges, following A. T. Hanson and a variety of other scholars, has argued that Ezekiel 47:1–11 was the source passage for John 7:38.[8] It is argued that Ezekiel 47:1–11 (in the LXX) and John 7:38 have two key verbal parallels: first, the water is "living" (*zôntos*) and second, both passages concern a "river"(*potamos*). Hodges also argued that there are clear connections between the Temple scene in Isaiah 47:1–11 with water flowing from the Temple, and the water libation ceremony, which is the context for Jesus's words in John 7:37–39.

Aileen Guilding has argued that Zechariah 14:8 is the background passage. When Guilding deals with the source of the quotation of John 7:38, she approaches the question by reconstructing the lectionary readings that would have been present (so she argues) in Jewish synagogues during the first century A.D. Guilding argues that early Johannine Christians adopted this Jewish lectionary and transformed it in light of their new Christian faith. One of the passages that would have been read during the Feast of Tabernacles, according to Guilding, was Zechariah 14:8, which happens to have verbal parallels with John 7:38. The verbal parallels are: first, in both passages the water is "living" (*zôntos*), and second, the Hebrew phrase "out from Jerusalem" (*miyirusalem*) in Zechariah 14:8 parallels the phrase *ek tês koilias* in John 7:38.

Joel Marcus, among others, has argued that Isaiah 12:3 may be the Old Testament passage being referred to in John 7:38:[9]

> With joy you will draw water from the wells of salvation (Isa 12:3 NIV).
>
> *Kai antlêsete udôr met' eufrosunês ek tôn pagon tou sôteriou* (Isa 12:3 LXX).
>
> *Yushavte-mayim veseson mimaana hayeshuah* (Isa 12:3 MT).

Marcus points to several Talmudic passages that closely associate Isaiah 12:3 with the Feast of Tabernacles and the water libation ceremony, which is the context in John 7 for Jesus' speech.[10] Marcus goes on to argue that the original *Sitz im Leben* of Isaiah 12:3 itself might have been a water libation ceremony which, according to the rabbinical literature, took place on the mornings of the Sukkot.[11]

A variety of other proposals have been put forth on this issue, but time and space does not permit a more detailed survey. Among these proposals are Isaiah 28:16, Isaiah 58:11, Proverbs 18:4, a combination of Exodus 17:1–7 and Numbers 20:11, and Psalm 40. Suffice it to say, the plethora of proposals is an illustration of the lack of consensus regarding this issue.

Overview of the Freed-Carson Proposal

Freed, when treating John 7:38 in his book *Old Testament Quotations in the Gospel of John*, actually concluded that the singular *graphê* in John 7:38 referred to the Scripture as a whole and not one particular passage. Therefore, at the end of his treatment of John 7:38 he concluded that a cluster of Old Testament passages was probably behind John 7:38 and not one singular passage. However, after making this argument, he seemingly backtracked when he stated that if indeed one Old Testament passage was behind John 7:38, it was probably Nehemiah 9:20. Freed made this statement based on his observation that in the Old Testament the manna miracle and the water from the rock miracle were often linked together. It was his contention that John 6 and 7 form a linked literary unit, driven by the frequent Old Testament linkage of manna and water from the rock, such that in John 6 Jesus is presented as the true bread/manna from heaven and in John 7 Jesus is presented as the water from the rock. Based on this literary relationship, he observed that only Nehemiah 9:20 brings together the three elements of manna, water, and the Spirit:

> You gave your good **Spirit** to instruct them. You did not withhold your **manna** from their mouths, and you gave them **water** for their thirst (Neh 9:20 NIV).

As Freed stated, "John could have had the trio of this passage in mind during the creative, artistic composition of his gospel."[12] Unfortunately, Freed did not develop his thoughts regarding this possible connection. He merely stated this possibility in one short paragraph.

Freed's suggestion lay dormant for almost 30 years in the published scholarly discourse until Carson in his commentary on John took it up in more detail. Carson agrees with Freed that Nehemiah 9:20 is the only Old Testament passage where Spirit, manna, and water all come together. But, Carson adds, it is also the only Old Testament passage where these three elements come together within the context of the Feast of Tabernacles, which is the context of John 7.[13]

As Carson argues, Nehemiah 9:13–15 begins by discussing the act of God giving the law to Israel on Mount Sinai and ends by discussing the act of God giving Israel the physical provisions of manna and water from the rock. In Hebrew, these three verses are syntactically connected showing further how the provision of God's law and God's provision of food and water in the twin miracles are linked. By Nehemiah 9:20 the link has shifted. Rather than the gift of the law being linked with the twin miracles, it is God's gift of the Spirit that is linked with the twin miracles. A comparison between Nehemiah 9:13–15 and Nehemiah 9:20 demonstrates this shift in linkage:

> You came down on Mount Sinai; you spoke to them from heaven. You gave them regulations and laws that are just and right, and decrees and commands that are good.
>
> You made known to them your holy Sabbath and gave them commands, decrees and laws through your servant Moses. In their hunger you gave them bread from heaven and in their thirst you brought them water from the rock (Neh 9:13–15 NIV).
>
> You gave your good Spirit to instruct them. You did not withhold your manna from their mouths, and you gave them water for their thirst (Neh 9:20 NIV).

Carson notes that in Nehemiah 9:20 the provision of the Spirit was bound up with the instruction of the people of Israel in the law.[14] So, in Carson's view, the giving of the law and the giving of the Spirit in Nehemiah 9:13–20 is symbolized by the provision of manna/water.[15] This is the link that John 7:37–39 makes. As Carson argues,

> If this is correct, Jesus in John 7:37–39, prompted perhaps by the Feast of Tabernacles, thinks of that Feast in Nehemiah 9, and that chapter's use of the accounts of the provision of water from the rock, and the connection Nehemiah draws between water/manna and law/Spirit. But he [Jesus] takes one further step,...he insists he alone can provide the real drink, the satisfying Spirit...John himself explicitly confirms the connection between water and Spirit (v. 39).[16]

Observations Regarding the Freed-Carson Proposal

What do we make of the proposal that Freed initially developed and that Carson amplified? Let us move forward by making three observations regarding the Freed-Carson proposal.

First, a major strength of the Freed-Carson proposal is of course the recognition that both Nehemiah 9:20 and John 7:37–39 share a Feast of Tabernacles background. In Nehemiah 8–10 Ezra has gathered the returned exiles together and he reads the Book of Moses. While reading it, they discover the requirements for the Feast of Tabernacles and that they should be observing it. Afterward, there was a great gathering in which the history of God's dealing with his people was recounted, followed by a covenant agreement ceremony. In John 7:37–39 it is clear that the "Feast" during which Jesus stood up and spoke was the Feast of Tabernacles based on John 7:2, "But when the Jewish Feast of Tabernacles was near..."

Second, both Nehemiah 9:20 and John 7:37–39 offer reflections on the water from the rock miracle. Nehemiah 9 explicitly mentions the miracle of water twice: verses 9:15 and 9:20. While the water from the rock miracle is not explicitly mentioned in John 7, the words of Jesus in John 7:37–39 have long been associated with the water libation ceremony that was performed each day during the Feast of Tabernacles in the Second Temple period. Its existence during the Second Temple period is not seriously debated, even though some have debated how it originated.[17] The ceremony would begin with a ritual procession from the temple courtyards to the pool of Siloam where the priest would fill a flask with the water.[18] Then, the ritual procession would proceed to the altar area where he would fill a bowl. The water would drain off through a pipe onto the altar. All of this would occur with a throng of pilgrims looking on.[19] This ceremony would be repeated each of the seven days of the feast. It has been argued that the water libation ceremony was originally introduced sometime during the Second Temple Period as a reenactment of the water from the rock miracle in order to serve as a reminder of God's provision of water during the 40 years of wandering.[20] This should not be surprising because the Feast of Tabernacles as a whole was originally intended to remind Israel about their lives during the forty years of wandering (Leviticus 23:43).

Third, both Nehemiah 9 and the broader context of John 7 seem to do similar things with the manna and water from the rock imageries in relationship to the law and the Spirit. As has been mentioned earlier, Carson argued that an exegesis of Nehemiah 9 shows the connection that the writer of Nehemiah made between manna/water and law/Spirit. In favor of Carson's argument we may turn to John Pryor's observation that in both the canonical scriptures and in the rabbinic literature, the imagery of eating and drinking the law most likely finds its origins in the imagery of eating manna and drinking the water from the rock.[21] Could it be possible that this imagery of eating the law and drinking the law is behind the syntactical connection between manna/water from the rock and the law in Nehemiah 9:13–15? In light of this background, it is striking that in Nehemiah 9:20 it is the gift of the good Spirit that instructs the Israelites, not the law as one would expect.

John 6–7 has interesting parallels at this point. In John 6:25–71 the eating of manna is connected not with the eating of the law, as one might expect, but rather with the eating of Jesus. As John 6:51 (NIV) states:

> I am the living bread that comes down from heaven. If anyone eats of this bread, he will live forever. This bread is my flesh, which I will give for the life of the world.

The subsequent misunderstanding and murmuring that occurs in John 6:60 highlights the significance of Jesus's teaching at this point (misunderstanding is a technique frequently used by the writer of John's Gospel to highlight a spiritual truth that is inconceivable to all except the elect). According to this language in John 6, Jesus and the Spirit that he offers are doing something new in redemptive history that the law could not accomplish. Specific reference to the Spirit in connection with the eating of Jesus as the bread of life is found in John 6:61–62 (NIV):

> Aware that his disciples were grumbling about this, Jesus said to them, "Does this offend you? What if you see the Son of Man ascend to where he was before! The Spirit gives life; the flesh counts for nothing. The words I have spoken to you are spirit and they are life."

Peder Borgens identifies further comparisons that are made in John 6 between the Spirit and the law. Rabbinic thought understood that the law gave life, most likely drawing from such familiar passages as Psalm 1. The language of John 6:61 replaces the law with the Spirit; it is the Spirit who gives life.[22]

In John 6 there are other contrasts between the provisions under the old covenant and the provisions under the new covenant. One of the key comparisons is between the bread that Moses gave (manna) and the bread that Jesus gives (Himself). In fact, the words of Jesus in John 6:32 point out that the manna that Moses gave came not from Moses but from God Himself. Jesus offers a greater manna to eat: Himself.

Turning our attention to John 7:39, it is clear from the editorial comment ("By this He meant the Spirit, whom those who believed in Him were later to receive..." John 7:39 NIV) that the living water that Jesus spoke about is the Holy Spirit. It is also clear that no matter what punctuation one takes for John 7:37–39, Jesus is claiming that He is the ultimate source of the living water (the Holy Spirit). The spiritually thirsty person is urged to come and drink from the water that Jesus offers.

Borgen argues that given the Old Testament and rabbinic evidence that Jews were urged to eat and drink the law, Jesus is using the imagery of manna (in John 6) and the water from the rock (in John 7) to clarify that He and the Spirit that He offers have become the objects of the believer's affection under the new covenant. Rather than urging His disciples to eat and drink of the law, they are urged to eat Him (John 6) and drink of the water He gives (John 7). Therefore, a comparison and contrast between new covenant and old covenant permeates John 6 and 7. Jesus, and the Spirit that He offers, becomes the focus under the new covenant. The law is seen as having a particular redemptive-historical function under the old covenant that is now brought to completion in Christ under the new covenant. Hints of this coming shift in the redemptive-historical function of the law emerges in Nehemiah 9:20; where we would expect the law to do the instruction (Neh 9:13–15), it is the Spirit.

Contrasting Freed-Carson with Other Proposals

At this point we can contrast the Freed-Carson proposal with the four proposals surveyed earlier in this paper. Menken's argument that Psalm 77:16,20 (LXX) is the correct background has strong verbal parallels with John 7:37–39. However, it does not contain the explicit Spirit language, which appears to be so important to John that he includes a narrative comment regarding the third person of the Trinity in John 7:39.

Guilding, while attempting to be sensitive to the Feast of Tabernacles background of John 7:37–39 when she suggests a Zechariah 14:8 background, fails to provide a passage with explicit Spirit language. That the water is "living" in Zechariah 14:8 certainly comes closer to Spirit language, however, than does the language of Psalm 77:16,20 (LXX).

Hodges's suggestion of Ezekiel 47:1–11 certainly has some of the same language as John 7:37–39 has (*zôntos* and *potamos*) as well as the same Temple setting. However, John 7:37–39 also occurs in the Temple. And, John 7:37–39 and Nehemiah 9 both occur during the Feast of Tabernacles.

Marcus's suggestion also attempts to be sensitive to the Feast of Tabernacles background of John 7 by pointing out the Talmudic references that connect Isaiah 12:3 to the water libation ceremony. His assertion, however, that the writer who penned Isaiah 12:3 may have actually written it with the water libation ceremony in mind is problematic since most scholars agree that the ceremony was not instituted and practiced until late in the second temple period.[23] Therefore, Marcus's argument assumes a very late date for the writing of Isaiah, an assertion that is contrary to the mainstream of evangelical scholarship.[24] More to the point, while it could be argued that there might have been a trajectory of rabbinical thought that connected Isaiah 12:3 to the water libation ceremony in the second temple period, as evidenced in the Talmudic tradition, Isaiah 12:3 does not contain other key contextual themes found in John 6 and 7. Most notable is the reality that Isaiah 12:3 does not contain Spirit or law language, which is central to the context of John 6 and 7.

Weaknesses of the Freed-Carson Proposal

Let us now transition into mentioning some of the weaknesses of the Freed-Carson proposal. Carson's main point is this: Nehemiah 9:20 is the only passage in the Old Testament where Spirit, manna, and water from the rock language all appear in the context of the Feast of Tabernacles. He then argues that this is also the case in John 6 and 7. However, this is not entirely accurate. John 6, while it has Spirit and manna language, does not share a Feast of Tabernacles context with John 7. Rather, its context is actually the Passover (John 6:4).

A second weakness of the Freed-Carson proposal is that it assumes that *graphê* points to one specific Old Testament passage. It is entirely possible that John (Jesus) had in mind a matrix of Old Testament Spirit/water passages in John 7:37–39.[25]

For Further Research

The fact that John 7:37–39 is such a contested passage, and that the Freed-Carson proposal has not received much attention, ought to bring new life to the discussion. This writer has identified a couple of areas that might push an analysis of the Freed-Carson proposal further.

First, what would a more detailed analysis of Nehemiah 9 reveal in terms of the shift in emphasis between the law in Nehemiah 9:13–15 and the Spirit in Nehemiah 9:20? In 1988, Loren Bliese published an article in which he argued for a chiastic structure in Nehemiah 9, with the Spirit language in Nehemiah 9:20 being at the apex.[26] It would be interesting to take a critical look at Bliese's work to determine, a) if there is indeed warrant for a chiastic structure in Nehemiah 9, and b) if there is a chiastic structure how might it inform the law/Spirit replacement idea that Carson identifies.

Second, since the manna language of John 6 does not actually appear in the context of the Feast of Tabernacles, does that seriously weaken the proposal put forth by Freed and Carson? Perhaps an initial response to this weakness could be the following: If Borgen's and Pryor's analyses are correct, that the symbolic imagery of eating and drinking the law finds its background in the manna and water from the rock miracle, *and* if the Spirit language in John 6 and 7 is part of a broader law/Spirit replacement theme in John's Gospel, *and* if Nehemiah 9:20 is the only place in the Old Testament where the Spirit/law contrast motif emerges explicitly connected with a reference to the manna/water from the rock miracles, *then* does it really matter that only John 7 (and not John 6) is connected with the Feast of Tabernacles because sufficient parallels with Nehemiah 9:20 already exist?

Summary

The purpose of this essay was certainly not to settle the complicated issue at hand. Rather, the purpose of this essay was to raise awareness of a proposed solution to the Old Testament referent of John 7:37–39. Based on an initial examination of the Freed-Carson Proposal, enough possible parallels exist to consider it alongside some of the other prominent proposals. Much more work needs to be done to probe this proposal.

Notes

[1]To name just a few: M. E. Boismard, "De son ventre couleront des fleuves d'eau," *RB* 65 (1958): 523–546; "Les citations targumiques dans le quatrième évangile," *RB* 66 (1959): 374–378; E. D. Freed, *Old Testament Quotations in the Gospel of John* (NovTSup 11; Leiden: E. J. Brill, 1965), 21–22; Dale C. Allison, "The Living Water," *St. Vladimir's Theological Quarterly* 30 (1986): 143–157; Bruce Grigsby, "If Any Man Thirsts... The Rabbinic Background of John 7,37–39," *Bib* 67 (1986): 101–108; Glenn Balfour, "The Jewishness of John's Use of the Scriptures in John 6:31 and 7:37–38 *TynBul* 46 (1995): 357–380; Maarten J. J. Menken, "The Origin of the Old Testament Quotation in John 7:38," *NovT* 38 (1996): 160–175; Henry M. Knapp, "The Messianic Water Which Gives Life to the World," *Horizons in Biblical Theology* 19 (1997): 109–121; Joel Marcus, "Rivers of Living Water from Jesus' Belly (John 7:38)," *JBL* 117 (1998): 328–330; Michael A. Daise, "'If Anyone Thirsts, Let That One Come to Me and Drink'": the Literary Texture of John 7:37b-38a," *JBL* 122 (2003): 687–699.

[2]The two major punctuation options are:

Punctuation Option One (the so-called believer centered reading):

Ean tis dipsai erxesthô me kai pinetô. Ho pisteuon eis eme kathôs eipen hê graphê potamoi ek tês koilias autou reusousin udatos zôntos.

If anyone thirsts let him come to me and drink. The one who believes in me, just as the Scripture said, rivers of living water will flow from the midst of him.

Punctuation Option Two (the so-called Christocentric reading):

Ean tis dipsai erxesthô me kai pinetô ho pisteuon eis eme. Kathôs eipen hê graphê potamoi ek tês koilias autou reusousin udatos zôntos.

If anyone thirsts let him come to me and let the one who believes in me drink. Just as the Scripture said, rivers of living water will flow from the midst of him.

[3]This view of *graphê* is assumed by Marcus (et. al.). Joel Marcus, "Rivers of Living Water from Jesus' Belly (John 7:38)," *JBL* 117 (1998): 328–330.

[4]This view of *graphê* is assumed by Knapp (et. al.). Henry M. Knapp, "The Messianic Water Which Gives Life to the World," *Horizons in Biblical Theology* 19 (1997): 109–121.

[5]Rendell Harris is an example of one who argued that John 7:38 is a quote from an extrabiblical first century Christian Testimonies text. Rendel Harris, "Rivers of Living Water," *The Expositor* 20 (1920): 192–202.

[6]E. D. Freed, *Old Testament Quotations in the Gospel of John* (NovT-Sup 11; Leiden: E. J. Brill, 1965), 21–22; D. A. Carson, *The Gospel According to John* (Grand Rapids: Eerdmans, 1991), 326–328.

[7]Maarten J. J. Menken, "The OT Quotation in John 7:38," *NovT* 38 (1996): 160–175.

[8]Zane Hodges, "Rivers of Living Water—Jn 7:37–39," *BSac* 136 (1979): 239–248. See also A. T. Hanson, *Jesus Christ in the Old Testament* (London: S. P. C. K., 1965), 111f.

[9]Joel Marcus, "Rivers of Living Water from Jesus' Belly (John 7:38)," *JBL* 117 (1998), 328.

[10]b. *Suk.* 48b; 50b; y. *Suk.* 51.

[11]Marcus, "Rivers of Living Water from Jesus' Belly (John 7:38)," *JBL* 117 (1998), 328.

[12]E. D. Freed, *Old Testament Quotations in the Gospel of John* (Leiden: E. J. Brill, 1965), 37.

[13]D. A. Carson, *The Gospel According to John* (Grand Rapids, MI: Eerdmans, 1991), 326 n.2.

[14]Ibid., 327.

[15]This type of symbolic link is not unusual in the Old Testament. In Deut 8:3, for example, the giving of manna to Israel during their wilderness wanderings is tied to God's teaching his people that, "Man does not live on bread alone but on every word that comes from the mouth of the Lord" (Deut 8:3 NIV).

[16]D. A. Carson, *The Gospel According to John* (Grand Rapids, MI: Eerdmans, 1991), 328.

[17]Some have argued that the ceremony finds its roots in a "magic tradition" by which the god was appeased and called upon to send rain. Jacob Milgrom, "The Water Libation in the Festival of Booths," *BibRev* 12 (1996): 55–56.

[18]m. *Suk.* 4.9.

[19]For a fuller discussion of the water libation ceremony, including the scholarly discussion surrounding it, see Jeffrey L. Rubenstein, *The History of Sukkot in the Second Temple and Rabbinic Periods* (Atlanta, GA: Scholars, 1995), 117.

[20]Bruce H. Grigsby, "'If Any Man Thirsts...': The Rabbinic Background of John 7:37–39," *Bib* 7 (1986): 107.

[21]For a brief survey see John Pryor, *John: Evangelist of the Covenant People* (Downers Grove, IL: InterVarsity, 1992), 31.

[22]Peder Borgen, *Bread from Heaven* (Leiden: E. J. Brill, 1965), 148–149.

[23]In fact, Marcus cites a footnote in Rubenstein's book *The History of Sukkot in the Second Temple and Rabbinic Period* as evidence for his point. Interestingly enough, Rubenstein himself in this footnote actually is quite critical of those who argue that there is biblical evidence for the existence of a water libation ceremony. Instead Rubenstein argues that the water libation ceremony was either a late second temple period development or was created out of hand by the rabbinic tradition. Jeffrey Rubenstein, *The History of Sukkot in the Second Temple and Rabbinic Periods*, p. 148 n. 168.

[24]What is interesting here is that Isaiah 12 is typically in First Isaiah, for those who hold to either a two-part or a three-part book. Such a late date for First Isaiah falls well outside of even the most liberal of Old Testament biblical scholarship.

[25]As argued by Knapp. See Henry M. Knapp, "The Messianic Water Which Gives Life to the World," *Horizons in Biblical Theology* 19 (1997): 109–121.

[26]Loren F. Bliese, "Chiastic Structures, Peaks and Cohesions in Nehemiah 9:6–37," *BT* 39 (1988): 209.

CHAPTER SEVEN

Faithfulness Within Modern Pluralism

Calvin L. Troup

As political and economic freedom diminishes, sexual freedom tends compensatingly to increase. And the dictator...will do well to encourage that freedom.
—Aldous Huxley, "Preface," *Brave New World*, 1932

How did Aldous Huxley know? Huxley observes in 1932 that "the sexual promiscuity of *Brave New World*" is not a projection into a distant future; he suggests that in some American cities the divorce rate already equaled the marriage rate.[1] What he envisions is not merely a sexual revolution that authorizes promiscuity, but that the dark underbelly of this kind of sexual freedom would involve a political tyranny to rival the overt statism of *1984*.[2] And we recognize that the dictatorial government in *Brave New World* distracts its subjects from their servitude through a constant supply of pleasures: from solely recreational, promiscuous sex; to round-the-clock access to entertainment; to endless opportunities for consumption of food, opiates, world travel, etc. The simple transaction turns on promises of sexual pleasure and economic security in exchange for freedom of human thought, personal decision-making, and independent civic association.[3] In *Brave New* World, the list of prohibited civic relationships begins with marriage, family, and the church.[4]

A technologically instituted sexual revolution is a central premise in Huxley's *Brave New World*. The sexual revolution dawned as a societal reality in the 1960s, propelled by an array of contraceptive and reproductive technology and policy. However, the philosophical, political, and scientific predicates of the sexual revolution that informed Huxley's work (including the serious embrace of eugenics by American intellectual elites prior to the second world war) did not anticipate either the timing or the consequences of the sexual revolution.[5] But Huxley did see well beyond the first days of the sexual revolution when he posited absolute unity in the authoritarian state's work to support the façade of, and to suppress all opposition to, sexual autonomy.

Anthony Giddens, renowned sociologist and historian, documents and explains the establishment of sexual autonomy via the technologies and policies of the sexual revolution in his 1992 book, *The Transformation of Intimacy: Sexuality, Eroticism, and Love in Modern Societies*. Reproductive technologies—from contraception and fertility procedures, to legalized abortion and gender transition surgery and therapies—have effectively separated sexual relations from procreation. Sex has been reduced to recreation alone, and sexual relationships have been liberated from religious, community, and legal controls. In the process, Giddens identifies an entirely new expectation concerning sexuality and intimacy: autonomy in sexual preference and practice is now associated personal identity—a personal social construct rather than a given condition of personal human identity. He calls it *plastic sexuality*.[6]

Giddens's account explains much about the deadly serious commitment to autonomous gender identity that dominates political, legal, and regulatory discourse today.[7] Giddens himself is an optimistic advocate of the transformation, viewing it as progress in human society and personal democracy. The socio-sexual revolution Giddens suggests might someday emerge has advanced rapidly.[8] We now live in a society that will not endure serious public challenges to sexual autonomy.

A regime of sexual autonomy places Christians and Christian institutions committed to biblical truth, ethics, and morality in a serious public dilemma concerning human identity, sexual relations, marriage, and family. As early as 1966, Philip Reiff noted, "Historically, the rejection of sexual individualism (which divorces pleasure and procreation) was the consensual matrix of Christian culture."[9] More recently, Reiff corroborated Giddens's expectation that the advance of modern psycho-social ideology would produce essentially devotional commitments to personal autonomy manifested through changes in sexual identity.[10] Today, Christian schools across North America face government pressure designed to secure affirmation of sexual orientation and gender identity (SOGI) and institute SOGI as a protected legal class under civil rights statutes and regulations. Such rules already exist in Canada, in many U.S. municipalities, and in several states.

Whether by statute or regulation, measures that mandate affirmation of sexual autonomy violate the institutional mission of orthodox Christian schools grounded on the gospel of Jesus Christ and historic creeds and confessions that recognize the Bible as God's inspired, inerrant, and infallible Word. And many SOGI initiatives target religious organizations, prohibiting religious exemptions and characterizing Christian sexual virtues as immoral and unjust. They aim to enforce a government mandate without regard for religious liberty.[11] Although the sexual revolution began in earnest in the late 1960s, the shift in expectation from tolerance of sexual liberation to conformity under a regime of sexual autonomy seems sudden, intense, and relentless.

SOGI laws create a worldly litmus test to establish conformity on sexual autonomy, not limited to any particular sexual orientation or behavior. Rather, SOGI laws function as a pledge of allegiance to sexual autonomy. By force of law, all must affirm absolute sexual self-determination—that every individual should be able to do what is right in their own eyes, applying all available resources and technologies to craft oneself in the image they desire. The right to choose one's own identity on one's own terms—according to "my truth"—is inviolable.

Under such conditions, where can Christian schools stand? The range of responses we will consider fall under the umbrella of Christian pluralism. Christian pluralism begins by recognizing that the government has authority from God distinct from other human spheres such as the church and the family. And the governmental sphere in which the responsibility for public order and civic life includes a broad spectrum of groups working from different presuppositional grounds, particularly in the modern era. The biblical starting points that distinguish the sphere of government from church and family spheres commend our commitment as Christians to temporal pluralism in civic and public life. George M. Marsden has cogently argued for Christian intellectual engagement—institutionally and personally—with an appropriately pluralistic mindset.[12] The tension between our Christian identity and cultural engagement presents constant challenges in a pluralistic society. As David S. Dockery suggests, Christian higher education must enact Christ's dictum—to be in the world but not of the world—living *between* the gospel and the culture: "One of the challenges for Christian higher education is to maintain a distinctive Christian presence that stands without reservation on the uniqueness of the gospel in contexts where the gospel is not well received."[13] The emergence of SOGI and political action to establish a regime of sexual autonomy in law intensifies the pressure on Christian pluralism in ways that threaten confessional fidelity. In the remainder of this essay, I will first describe a form of Christian pluralism that informs one stance some Christian organizations have taken. Second, I will discuss deficiencies, particularly in light of a regime of sexual autonomy. Finally, I will propose an alternative form of Christian pluralism.

An alliance of Christian organizations prepared a proposal to advocate for SOGI as warranting protected-class civil rights status in exchange for religious exemptions in civil rights laws.[14] According to the proposal, to deny employment, housing, or accommodations on the basis of SOGI would constitute illegal discrimination, as a revision to federal law that prohibits discrimination on the basis of race, sex, disability, etc. The proposal attempts to advance public justice and religious liberty simultaneously, believing that political conditions preclude expansion of religious liberty if not accompanied by SOGI discrimination regulations. The proposal includes exemptions for churches and other religious institutions as a religious liberty concession, given the considerable value and support for the public services, ministries, and education provided. Apparently, many people support some religious liberty exceptions if SOGI rights are secured. Non-exempted Christians and organizations would be legally obligated to conform; the proposal would hold nonconformity to the SOGI laws, even for the sake of religious conscience, as a violation of public justice and, by extension, a sin against God.

How does an association of Christian organizations arrive at a public position that would censure Christian opposition to sexual autonomy as a case of public injustice—a violation of civil rights? The SOGI initiative with limited religious exemptions is informed by a form of pluralism that renders public justice the priority in the sphere of government and focal point of pluralistic political action. Public justice pluralism seeks common cause in government on justice issues with other societal groups. This approach to pluralism begins with the principle that every person is made *imago Dei,* in the image of God, accompanied by the doctrine of common grace—that God extends His gracious blessing to all of humanity, despite their rebellion against Him. Sometimes referred to as "confident pluralism," the approach suggests that although Christians involved in the public sphere should be working from biblical principles and precepts, they must translate biblical truth into non-religious categories of public justice, since non-Christian citizens and groups do not accept and will not respond to biblical authority in the public sphere. Looking for common cause in political life, public justice pluralism does not expect conformity to biblical standards of moral conduct, but looks for points of intersection through which to develop a critical mass of public support.[15] In sum, this form of Christian pluralism focuses on temporal public justice within current conditions. Through Christian engagement and collaboration, public justice pluralism works for societal transformation by demonstrating the gospel's cultural relevance.

In the case of sexual autonomy and SOGI legislation, the commitments of public justice pluralism result in substantial deficiencies for Christian institutions seeking to maintain confessional fidelity in practice.

First, a public justice orientation to pluralism positions us to call sexual autonomy, an evil, "good." A Christian cannot advocate anything associated with sexual autonomy without *believing* that such a policy establishes a public good, based on identifying sexual autonomy as a positive manifestation of *imago Dei*. Public justice pluralism argues precisely this case, elevating SOGI to a civil right and proscribing religious objections as unjust, save for limited exceptions. But the Scriptures faithfully and overwhelmingly teach that sexual autonomy *violates* the created order. In common sense terms, Christians need to uphold civil rights that protect all people according to the created order—*imago Dei*—and according to biblical teaching (e.g., maintaining a common civic law for the sojourner and alien as well as the native-born citizen). Such rights are referenced in Scripture directly.[16] Because each person is *imago Dei*, no law that advances sexual autonomy and a regime of sexual autonomy establishes public justice; the grounds, the worldview, and the practices of sexual autonomy advanced by SOGI laws and regulations irreproachably contradict and violate *imago Dei*.

Second, a public justice orientation to pluralism positions us to call biblical sexual ethics, a good, "evil." By affirming sexual autonomy as a civil right, public justice pluralism necessarily treats public censure of sexual autonomy by Christians as moralizing, misplaced pietism that compromises the gospel. Public support for civil rights that advance sexual autonomy is equated with an expression of love for neighbor, in the hope of creating conditions through which people might be more open to the gospel. Conversely, opposition to sexual autonomy as a civil right is critiqued as a lack of grace. According to the public justice proposal, to resist sexual autonomy publicly perpetuates injustice, violates the second Great Commandment, and compromises the message of the gospel.

Third, a public justice orientation to pluralism relinquishes a place for God's word in the public sphere by self-censorship. Asserting that a pluralized, secularized public sphere will not listen to the Scripture disregards its public power and acts as though God's word is limited by the receptivity of the human hearer. Ironically, such a mindset creates a functional dualism that limits consideration of God's word to a purely religious, private sphere that should remain separate from public life. The Bible is appropriate within the walls of a church building and in private homes, but not in the public square. That is, scripture is deemed publicly impotent as a ground for public deliberation—public justice must proceed from shared assumptions without reference to the Bible because non-Christians reject its authority.

The basic deficiencies described above are not hypothetical. They have been repeated since my days as a college student in the early 1980s; and they have been articulated in thought and manifested in policy through the first quarter of the 21st century. My purpose here is to consider the problem in this case, without making light of thoughtful and committed Christian colleagues who espouse public justice pluralism which retains merit in other contexts. In fact, we share substantial presuppositions. We all believe deeply that every human being is made in the image of God, that the image of God has been profoundly corrupted by sin in each person and in the human race. We believe that the gospel of Jesus Christ is the only remedy for sin; and that despite our sinful corruption, God deals with all mankind in our temporal lives according to His grace—no living person experiences the full effects of His just wrath in this life. We also believe that God has ordained government with the power of the sword; government authority is under Christ's rule directly, not derived from the family or the church.

However, advocating SOGI laws and regulations cannot be reconciled with basic teaching that spans the spectrum of biblical revelation concerning justice. What cannot be commended as a good anywhere in Scripture cannot become a common good for Christians or anyone else in public. To call SOGI rules good turns faith, hope, and love on their heads. To argue for SOGI as public justice suggests an erroneous equivalency of SOGI with *imago Dei*-based civil rights; offers a mistaken sense of neighbor love; and conforms to public worldliness. The gospel publicly calls every group, every nationality, every man and woman out of false identities and false autonomy; and the gospel publicly calls everyone into their God-given identity under the grace and truth of Jesus Christ.

But what alternative do we have, particularly if we confirm that Christians must work within a pluralistic public sphere? Thankfully, Augustine provides an alternative approach to pluralism for Christians that answers our paradoxical dilemma in a biblically robust fashion.

As I have written elsewhere, Augustine explains in *City of God* that the present age is essentially pluralistic.[17] Guided by the parable of the Wheat and the Tares, he reminds us that we inhabit an earthly city of churches, communities, and societies constituted as a mixed multitude that include members of the City of God and the City of Man.[18] The two cities exist intermingled until the last great day when God will sort them out. Augustine's argument for commonwealth and against empire in the earthly city establishes civic pluralism in commonwealths as desirable and attainable, at least in a proximate sense, on biblical grounds.[19] He advocates a robust cultural pluralism that reflects the commitment of the kingdom of God to a citizenship from every tribe and language and people and nation. By contrast, empires impose tyranny and prejudices by force of power; they divide and conquer.[20]

What then are the boundaries of Christian pluralism? The nature of a pluralistic society demands tolerance—true tolerance, in which we are called to abide a range of beliefs, customs, practices, and laws in a civic commonwealth, even many that may conflict in some way with our own convictions and commitments for the sake of maintaining a community. The tolerance required for healthy pluralism must be mutual and reciprocal. Yet, members of a pluralistic society, including Christians, still must ask, "Where do we draw the lines?"

At the most basic level, we find ourselves to be in the world, but not of the world—a paradoxical dilemma. Christ has not taken us out of a world of evil and an evil age. We remain in it for the sake of gospel salt and light to live and act redemptively. And we have clear indicators that civil society *is* a sphere distinct from the church. As the apostle Paul says, "I wrote to you in my letter not to associate with sexually immoral people—not at all meaning the sexually immoral of this world, or the greedy and swindlers, or idolaters, since then you would need to go out of the world.[21] Is the apostle suggesting that Christian pluralism demands tolerance of all sexual immorality as a matter of public policy?

The question of sexual immorality tests the limits of tolerance for Christian pluralism. And the answer is not simplistic. Augustine helps us. Remembering that he lived in the decadence of the late Roman empire, and that his bondage to sin included a long battle with sexual immorality, he urges us to push our tolerance for civic customs and laws to the limits of divine law. What we can abide as long as society either supports or at least permits the public practice of faithfulness is expansive. But, he says, when civic laws and customs call us to publicly contradict divine law, no accommodation is possible and we must follow God's word. What is Augustine's test case in the *Confessions*?

> Therefore, vicious deeds that are contrary to nature, are everywhere and always detested and punished, such as

> were those of the men of Sodom. Even if all nations should do these deeds, they would all be held in equal guilt under the divine law, for it has not made men in such fashion that they should use one another in this way. For in truth, society itself, which must obtain between God and us, is violated, when the nature of which he is the author is polluted by a perverted lust.[22]

Laws and regulations, some in place and others proposed, demand that we affirm SOGI as good and right, and to denounce publicly as evil and immoral any person or institution who would challenge the sexual autonomy these laws instantiate. The script of scorn alleging judgmentalism concerning sexual autonomy is an old one: "This fellow came to sojourn, and he has become the judge! Now we will deal worse with you than with them." Today as in the past, we are expected to affirm sexual autonomy in principle and SOGI as a civil right or be excoriated as bigots.

We need not determine a boundary; SOGI laws impose a definitive public line on us. If we do not respect the line, we might well be cast out. As Stanley Fish notes, such cases test the limits of civic tolerance; a civic order defines the boundaries of tolerance by locating its own intolerances.[23] Our society is in flux and our culture is grappling with the definitions of what it will prohibit.[24] In little more than a generation, the United States has moved from public limits on sexual practice and promiscuity to public prohibition of any restraint on sexual practice or identity. Sexual autonomy is on the move. The lines have been drawn. The only question is, *where* will we stand in reference to the regime of sexual autonomy and, finally, *will* we stand?

As Augustine asserts, to stand on the side of sexual autonomy and affirm SOGI laws as a positive statement of public justice violates divine law *for all societies*. God visits similar judgment on Sodom and Benjamin, on Gentiles and Jews, on Canaanites and on Nicolaitans. God's judgment against the nation of Israel and on the church in the New Testament often turns on specific laws revealed uniquely to God's people in Scripture. God's judgment against other nations concerns divine mandates for civic order and civil government that apply to all societies. The line for civil law on sexual autonomy in Scripture is thick and well-defined; public; international; unequivocal; and...redeemable. But not by accommodation or capitulation.

The worldliness associated with sexual autonomy deals with a violation of the essence of *imago Dei*; the issue is morally charged, but not remotely moralistic—the question goes to the heart of the whole human race, without regard for local practice, custom, or taboo. The violation is societal—engaged in the public sphere by government authority, not only in the sphere of church or family authority. Sexual autonomy violates God's created order and cultural mandate for society; the generations of society are ordained to proceed through families constituted and reconstituted through the marriages of men to women. With a move to mandate affirmation of sexual autonomy, government oversteps the bounds of its God-given authority.

We do not expect worldly leaders to acknowledge divine law. No matter; the boundaries of divine law call for civic law and custom and supersede them simultaneously. Christian pluralism must follow the same order. On one hand, we cannot and do not expect sexual fidelity in the earthly city; on the other hand, we cannot and will not affirm sexual autonomy in any society. Neither love of God nor love of neighbor can affirm SOGI as a civil rights status—particularly any rule that would force us to profess sexual autonomy as a public good or as a good manifestation of *imago Dei*.

The question remains, what options are available? Augustine anticipates such dilemmas. And he counsels Christians to proceed with humility if they must object to such policy initiatives or disobey such public laws, regulations, or customs. There is no place for pride or arrogance. We may express our distress; we must profess the truth of God's gracious public rule; and we need to affirm the goodness of His created order under which all are called and commanded to live faithfully. But Augustine goes further. He instructs us to acknowledge that our objections and non-compliance create difficulties for our local governmental leaders.[25] Yet we must stand publicly.

And standing on our good confession is sufficient. That is, we must remain immovable on such points, seeking true pluralistic tolerance even if the public affirmation *of our stance* is unlikely in a particular moment.[26]

Why, for the sake of the gospel, would we maintain such a stand? The question is fair since we have called into question the strategy of seeking gospel relevance through cultural accommodation and political pragmatism. In Scripture, the gospel proceeds in public. When Caiaphas the high priest questions Jesus about His teaching, Jesus says, "I have spoken openly to the world. I have always taught in synagogues and in the temple, where all Jews come together. I have said nothing in secret."[27] Similarly, toward the end of his apostolic ministry, Paul reminds people that he taught and argued openly in public.[28]

Jesus Christ institutes the public preaching, teaching, and gospel mission of the first disciples with the Great Commission, which begins with worship. The disciples encounter the risen Christ and worship Him. As they worship Him, Jesus Christ proclaims, "All authority in heaven and on earth has been given to me." With His full authority already established He states the Great Commission: "Go therefore and make disciples of all nations." That is, we are authorized to engage in gospel discipleship under Christ's public authority, enacted through public baptism into the name of the Father, and of the Son, and of the Holy Spirit. The commission ends with instruction, teaching them "to observe all that I have commanded you."[29] An order Jesus taught in summary through the two Great Commandments and enacted in the giving of the Great Commission: worship—that is, love God; then teach—go and make disciples of all nations—that is, love your neighbor. Accordingly, gospel work follows the order of the Great Commandments.

The temptation is strong to invert the Great Commandments. Public justice pluralism falls into this error by predicating public proclamation of the gospel on perceptions of cultural relevance and cultural conditions. Instead of starting with worship of Christ and faithful observation of all He has commanded, this course of action begins with the world's sense of justice and adapts to cultural norms as a manifestation of neighbor love. Thus inverted, the second Great Commandment dismisses the first, at least in public matters; the capitulation presents itself as pragmatic but is principal and deeply spiritual. As Os Guinness has noted, the inversion of the order on SOGI subverts the gospel:

> Let there be no misunderstanding: the greatest crisis now facing the church in the West today is the crisis of authority caused by the church's capitulation to the pressures of the sexual revolution, and in particular to the bullying agenda of the Lesbian-Gay-Bisexual-Transgender-Queer Coalition. This is no time for Christian apologists to miss their moment and to duck the unpopular issues out of a mistaken concern for the narrow priorities of 'preaching the gospel' to those outside the church.[30]

The objection, that the Apostle Paul taught us to "become all things to all people that some might be saved," fails in the context of his words to his young protégé, Timothy, through whom he indicates that the clarity of gospel teaching was a path toward persecution.[31] The necessary clarity of the gospel message against worldliness was not a path of peace with the world on its own terms through cultural relevance. We are taught to avoid gratuitous offenses,[32] but the offense of the cross to the world is no small offense.[33]

We must retain both Great Commandments in their given order, which presents a poignant theological and practical challenge. The world pushes us to forsake one or the other. To keep both well places us in a position of extreme tension. Dutch Theologian Herman Bavinck explains the difficulty in an essay on the modernist theology of Albrecht Ritschl:

> ...Whereas salvation in Christ was formerly considered primarily a means to separate man from sin and the world, to prepare him for heavenly blessedness and

> to cause him to enjoy undisturbed fellowship with God there, Ritschl posits the very opposite relationship: the purpose of salvation is precisely to enable a person, once he is freed from the oppressive feeling of sin and lives in the awareness of being a child of God, to exercise his earthly vocation and fulfill his moral purpose in this world. The antithesis, therefore, is fairly sharp: on the one side, a Christian life that considers the highest goal, now and hereafter, to be the contemplation of God and fellowship with him, and for that reason (always being more or less hostile to the riches of an earthly life) is in danger of falling into monasticism and asceticism, pietism and mysticism; but on the side of Ritschl, a Christian life that considers its highest goal to be the kingdom of God, that is, the moral obligation of mankind, and for that reason (always being more or less adverse to the withdrawal into solitude and quiet communion with God), is in danger of degenerating into a cold Pelagianism and an unfeeling moralism. Personally, I do not yet see any way of combining the two points of view, but I do know that there is much that is excellent in both, and that both contain undeniable truth.[34]

The purpose of this essay is to advance a Christian pluralism that embraces fully Bavinck's sense of the tension, owning that the tension resides in the midst of the two Great Commandments.[35] The Great Commandments call for unequivocal love of God with genuine piety yet without pietism; they command unconditional love of neighbor and God's creation with no hint of worldliness. As G.K. Chesterton suggests in *Orthodoxy*, faith in Christ calls us to retain such apparent antitheses, without moderation.[36] We must keep both Great Commandments fiercely—genuine piety allied with full cultural engagement—as our spiritual imperative for life between the ages. The gospel of the Kingdom is redemption: profoundly personal and extending to all of Creation once and for all.

We dare not disengage from our neighbors in a pluralistic world, but we must disengage fully from worldliness. And Scripture associates worldliness—in personal and corporate conduct—directly with the impulse and inclination to sexual autonomy. We remember that the first letter to the church in Corinth teaches that faithfulness means sexual holiness in practice; but permits association with worldly people. Immoral sexual practice must not be tolerated in the church; but must be tolerated to be in the world at all. The call to live in the world but not be of the world burdens us, even if our burdens are light.

We can tolerate the public line between ourselves and the world, but we cannot be forced to cross a line that denies legitimacy to public tolerance and insists on public affirmation. Even if we are pilloried as unloving, bigoted, or hateful because of our stand, we must remain steadfast while we continue working toward reformation and relief from escalating human vulnerabilities caused by the sexual revolution. The inevitable human consequences are well-documented, are escalating, and have a profound impact on the weakest members of our communities. No one is exempt from the withering practical effects visited on society by a regime of sexual autonomy. But the pressures are enormous to capitulate. Christian institutions might lose public reputations, public accreditation, and public funding—such losses would be momentous and devastating.

When we know the place to stand and on whom we stand, how do we finally stand? We need to remember, in the most practical terms, that the battles we face are spiritual, not political; the battles are the Lord's, not ours. Even as battles rage in our midst, the lines do not fall along the conventional spectrum of electoral politics, the news media, or social media—such lines are misleading. Because we do not wrestle against flesh-and-blood, we can practice humility and hospitality in good faith. We can continue to engage our neighbors—fellow sojourners, siblings, and even enemies—with love and affection. We maintain the careful commitments to accept our neighbors as *imago Dei*, without denying *imago Dei* in false affirmation of sexual autonomy.[37] We are called to stand; and to engage within our communities as good friends, family members, and neighbors. We cannot force our neighbors to reciprocate, but we can unswervingly live within the gospel of love. Finally, we need to remember the faithfulness of those who have taken such stands in the past, who did not capitulate, accommodate, or lose heart even when compelled. As Francis Schaeffer warned during a battle for the inerrancy and infallibility of Scripture a generation ago, to capitulate on a seemingly small point of doctrine when under attack by the world and the devil even when I "profess with the loudest voice and clearest exposition every portion of the truth of God," means that "I am not confessing Christ, however boldly I may be professing Christ."[38]

At the most basic level, Christian institutions in every age feel pressure from the world to dissociate themselves from the person, the work, and the name of Jesus Christ in public. The temptation persists to suppress our identification with Jesus Christ as we work in a pluralistic world. The present popularity of the maxim, "Preach the gospel at all times; use words if necessary," reflects the pressure we face. Wrongly attributed to St. Francis of Assisi, a prolific and influential preacher in his own day, the maxim's use subordinates the public proclamation of the gospel—as though preaching and teaching Christ would diminish His public impact.[39]

Like Luther and many others before us, we must count the cost *and stand* for the Lord Jesus Christ, for His faithful word, and for His gracious rule over every ruler, authority, principality, and power in perfect accord with His revealed will in the Scripture. We need to be prepared to stand and confess the grace and truth of Jesus Christ, not against any person, but in opposition to a regime of sexual autonomy in league to advance tyranny in the name of justice. To take this stand means being willing to give ourselves up *and to give our institutions up*, not before the battle, but to remind ourselves to whom the real battle belongs. As a wise man once said, he is no fool who gives that which he cannot keep to gain that which he cannot lose.

Notes

[1]Aldous Huxley, *Brave New World and Brave New World Revisited* (New York: Harper Perennial, 1932), 12–13.

[2]Ibid., 264.

[3]Ibid., 11–13.

[4]Ibid., 44–45; 207–209.

[5]*Op cit*, 12.

[6]Anthony Giddens, *The Transformation of Intimacy: Sexuality, Love & Eroticism in Modern Societies* (Stanford, CA: Stanford University Press, 1992), 2; 28–34.

[7]Ibid., 184–199.

[8]*Op cit*, 181.

[9]Philip Reiff, *The Triumph of the Therapeutic: Uses of Faith after Freud* (Wilmington, DE: ISI Books, 2006), 13. Reiff's book was first published in 1966 by Harper & Row.

[10]Philip Reiff, *Life among the Deathworks: Illustrations of Aesthetics of Authority* (Charlottesville, VA: University of Virginia Press, 2006), 8–11.

[11]Equity Act of 2019, H.R. 5, 116th Cong. (2019).

[12]George M. Marsden, *The Soul or the American University: From Protestant Establishment to Established Nonbelief.* (New York: Oxford University Press, 1994), 439; *The Outrageous Idea of Christian Scholarship* (Oxford: Oxford University Press, 1997), 1–12; 99–100.

[13]David S. Dockery, *Renewing Minds: Serving Church and Society through Christian Higher Education* (Nashville, TN: B&H Academic, 2008), 143–144.

[14]Shapri D. LoMaglio, "Fairness for All," *CCCU Magazine*, Spring 2017, https://www.cccu.org/magazine/fairness-for-all/.

[15]John D. Inazu, *Confident Pluralism: Surviving and Thriving through Deep Difference* (Chicago: University of Chicago Press, 2016).

[16]Proverbs 29:7, 31:9 (English Standard Version).

[17]Calvin L. Troup, "Augustine the African: Critic of Roman Colonialist Discourse," *Rhetoric Society Quarterly 25*, (1995), 91–106. See also, "Humility & Hospitality," Forum 4:15: Conversations about Faith and Communication, Spring Arbor University, Spring Arbor, MI, presented June 15, 2017.

[18]Augustine, *The City of God against the Pagans*, ed. and trans. By R. W. Dyson, (Cambridge, UK: Cambridge University Press, 1998), X1.2, XV.22.

[19]Augustine, *City of God*, XIX.15–7, 21–24.

[20]Ibid., XV.5.

[21]1 Corinthians 5:9–10.

[22]Augustine, *Confessions* III.viii.15, p. 87.

[23]Stanley Fish, "Mission Impossible: Settling the Just Bounds between Church and State," *Columbia Law Review*, 97, no. 8, (1997), 2272, 2279.

[24]Philip Reiff, *Deathworks*, 1.

[25]Augustine, *City of God*, XIX.17.

[26]Augustine, *City of God.*

[27]John 18:20.

[28]Acts 18:28; 20:20.

[29]Matthew 28:17–20.

[30]Os Guinness, *Fool's Talk: Recovering the Lost Art of Christian Persuasion* (Downers Grove, IL: InterVarsity Press, 2015), 212.

[31]See II Timothy 3.

[32]I Corinthians 10:32–33.

[33]Galatians 5:11.

[34]John Bolt, editor's introduction to *Reformed Dogmatics, v. 4: Holy*

Spirit, Church and New Creation, by Herman Bavinck, trans. by John Vrend and ed. by John Bolt (Grand Rapids, MI: Baker Academic, 2008), 19.

[35]Note that Bavinck echoes the teaching of Colossians 2–3, avoiding both worldly asceticism and worldly permissiveness.

[36]Gilbert K. Chesterton, *Orthodoxy* (Garden City, NY: Image Books, 1952), 91–97.

[37]See for example, *The Gospel & Sexual Orientation: A Testimony of the Reformed Presbyterian Church of North America*, ed. Michael LeFebvre (Pittsburgh, PA: Crown & Covenant, 2012) and *Gender as Calling: The Gospel and Gender Identity*, ed. Michael LeFebvre (Pittsburgh, PA: Crown & Covenant, 2017).

[38]Francis A. Schaeffer, *No Final Conflict: The Bible Without Error in All that It Affirms* (Downers Grove, IL: InterVarsity Press, 1975), 13.

[39]Guinness, *Fool's Talk*, 175; Glenn T. Stanton, "Misquoting Francis of Assisi," *Factchecker* (blog), *TGC: The Gospel Coalition*, July 10< 2012. https://www.thefospelcoalition.org/article/factchecker:misquoting-francis-of-assisi/.

References

Augustine. *The City of God Against the Pagans*. Edited and Translated by R. W. Dyson. Cambridge, UK: Cambridge University Press, 1998.

Bolt, John. Introduction to *Reformed Dogmatics, v.4: Holy Spirit, Church, and New Creation,* by Herman Bavinck. Translated by John Vrend and edited by John Bolt. Grand Rapids, MI: Baker Academic, 2008.

Chesterton, Gilbert K. *Orthodoxy.* Garden City, NY: Image Books, 1952.

Dockery, David S. *Renewing Minds: Serving Church and Society through Christian Higher Education.* Nashville, TN: B&H Academic, 2008.

Fish, Stanley. "Mission Impossible: Settling the Just Bounds between Church and State." *Columbia Law Review* 97, no.8, (1997): 2255–2333.

Giddens, Anthony. *The Transformation of Intimacy: Sexuality, Love & Eroticism in Modern Societies.* Stanford, CA: Stanford University Press, 1992.

Guinness, Os. *Fool's Talk: Recovering the Lost Art of Christian Persuasion.* Downers Grove, IL: InterVarsity Press, 2015.

Huxley, Aldous. *Brave New World and Brave New World Revisited.* New York: Harper Perennial, 1932.

Inazu, John D. *Confident Pluralism: Surviving and Thriving through Deep Difference.* Chicago: University of Chicago Press, 2016.

LeFebvre, Michael, ed. *Gender as Calling: The Gospel and Gender Identity.* Michael LeFebvre Pittsburgh, PA: Crown & Covenant, 2017.

LeFebvre, Michael, ed. *The Gospel & Sexual Orientation: A Testimony of the Reformed Presbyterian Church of North America.* Pittsburgh, PA: Crown & Covenant, 2012.LoMaglio, Shapri D. "Fairness for All," CCCU Magazine, Spring 2017, https://www.cccu.org/magazine/fairness-for-all/.

Marsden, George M. *The Soul of the American University: From Protestant Establishment to Established Nonbelief.* New York: Oxford University Press, 1994.

The Outrageous Idea of Christian Scholarship. Oxford: Oxford University Press, 1997.

Reiff, Philip. *My Life among the Deathworks: Illustrations of the Aesthetics of Authority.* Charlottesville,VA: University of Virginia Press, 2006.

_____. *The Triumph of the Therapeutic: Uses of Faith after Freud.* Wilmington, DE: ISI Books, 2006.

Schaeffer, Francis A. *No Final Conflict: The Bible Without Error in All that It Affirms.* Downers Grove, IL: InterVarsity Press, 1975.

Stanton, Glenn T. "Misquoting Francis of Assisi." *Factchecker* (blog). *TGC: The Gospel Coalition*, July 10, 2012. https://www.thegospelcoalition.org/article/factchecker-misquoting-francis-of-assisi/.

Troup, Calvin L. "Augustine the African: Critic of Roman Colonialist Discourse." *Rhetoric Society Quarterly* 25, (1995): 91–106.

CHAPTER EIGHT

Calvin's Development of the Marks of the Church in *The Institutes*, and His Legacy of Confessional Influence

Barry York

With the shadows of medieval history and the Church of Rome looming large, the European Reformers needed to clarify what constituted a true church. For the leaders who had first sought reform within the Roman Catholic Church, but then were forced to bring it from without, what were their views? How did their definition of the church differ from the Catholic Church? How did their understanding of the church impact their life and ministry? As the Reformation progressed, how was the visible church defined in the development of the Protestant confessions? These questions are perhaps best answered in seeing the development of John Calvin's doctrine of the church and his influence as captured in the Reformation confessions.

Yet before exploring Calvin, it is important to examine first the teaching of the Roman Catholic Church on the constitution of the church as a backdrop. By reviewing the Council of Trent's counterstatements to the Protestant Reformation (particularly as seen in the catechism that came forth from Trent), Rome's official teachings regarding the church can be understood and their view of the church's identity established.[1] Calvin's work and legacy regarding the constitution of the church is then more readily recognized.

The Roman Catholic Church's Views on the Marks

In the medieval period, a developing belief solidified in Rome over what constituted the true church and what were its necessary characteristics. By the 13th century, "The Fourth Lateran Council declared that: 'There is one universal Church of unassailable "attributes."'"[2] These attributes were four in number, as the Roman Catholic Church relied on the Nicene Creed statement which declares, "We believe in one holy catholic and apostolic Church." In the early decades of the Reformation, Rome struggled for a period with limiting itself to these four qualities.

> In the 16th century the fertile imagination of the Roman apologists distinguished a varied number of "notae ecclesiae"; seven, then ten, then fifteen, and one apologist (Bozio, in 1591) even went so far as to enumerate a hundred! But very soon, and fortunately, the "notae" were reduced to the four qualities whereby the Symbol of Nicaea defined the Church: unity, sanctity, catholicity and apostolicity.[3]

Rome's use of these four attributes can be seen most clearly in the catechism that came from the Council of Trent, called by Pope John III in 1545 (and continued until 1563 under the supervision of five popes in total[4]) to counter the growing Protestant Reformation. In "Article IX: I believe in the Holy Catholic Church; the Communion of Saints," under the section "The Marks of the Church," each of the four attributes above are treated individually and with the claim that all within the church should know these marks. "The distinctive marks of the Church are also to be made known to the faithful, that thus they may be enabled to estimate the extent of the blessing conferred by God on those who have had the happiness to be born and educated within her pale."[5] With the Council's emphasis on the pope's rule of the church and the claim that the Church of Rome was the ultimate church, these marks as defined by Rome became one of their focal points to create a definition of what truly constitutes the visible church.

To understand how Rome treated the marks, consider the first mark of unity. The Council of Trent stated:

> The first mark of the true Church is described in the Nicene Creed, and consists in unity: My dove is one, my beautiful one is one. So vast a multitude, scattered far and wide, is called one for the reasons mentioned by St. Paul in his Epistle to the Ephesians: One Lord, one faith, one baptism. The Church has but one ruler and one governor, the invisible one, Christ, whom the eternal Father hath made head over all the Church, which is his body; the visible one, the Pope, who, as legitimate successor of Peter, the Prince of the Apostles, fills the Apostolic chair.[6]

In prescribing the pope as the visible ruler over the visible church, the Council was seeking to ensure that other movements, particularly the Reformed and Lutheran camps, were viewed as schismatic, having broken off from the mother church. The Council of Trent believed that it was "the unanimous teaching of the Fathers that this visible head is necessary to establish and preserve unity in the Church," and cited numerous church fathers to support its claim.[7]

Holding forth this first attribute, Trent's teachings then set forth the next marks of holiness, catholicity, and apostolicity as issuing from the oneness of papal authority. In concluding that the Holy Spirit had conferred legitimacy on the Catholic Church through these marks, the catechism states further that "just as this one Church cannot err in faith or morals, since it is guided by the Holy Ghost; so, on the contrary, all other societies arrogating to themselves the name of church, must necessarily, because guided by the spirit of the devil, be sunk in the most pernicious errors, both doctrinal and moral."[8] Thus, clearly Rome viewed Protestant congregations as illegitimate based on their definition of the marks.

The Protestant Response to Rome's Marks

Though the Reformers differed from Rome on how the preceding four qualities were manifested in the church, they did not deny that they were legitimate attributes of the church. "It is striking in this connection that the four words themselves were never disputed, since the Reformers did not opt for other 'attributes.'"[9] Second, they disagreed with Rome's view that these attributes were suitable for defining what constitutes a true church compared to a false one. As Berkouwer further points out:

> Ultimately, such a static ecclesiology no longer allows room for discussion about the ecclesiastical reality; and to the extent that one is willing to embark on such a discussion, it can have relation only to the Church's periphery, which is separated from her unassailable 'essence.' In contrast, in the Reformation it was precisely the *notae* that took on decisive significance, with the result that it was impossible to use the 'attributes' apologetically as an unthreatened and unassailable, aprioristic reality. The Reformers could not refer simply to the factual reality of the Church: *una, catholica, apostolica, and sancta*. The question of the *notae* reached an apex in various tensions in Church history in connection with the question of the true Church, the *ecclesia vera*.[10]

Third, as the above quote indicates, part of the unsuitability of the Nicene qualities was a confusion over the need to identify a true, visible church rather than speaking more generally regarding the invisible church. Finally, this dilemma in identifying a proper visible church led the Reformers to make a distinction between the essential marks, or the *notae,* and the more general attributes of the church. As James Bannerman states, "First, there is an important distinction between what is necessary to the being of a Church, and what is necessary to its wellbeing."[11] Defining the church and how to care for her properly was at the heart of the concern of the Reformation leaders, as can be seen particularly in John Calvin.

John Calvin's Development of the Marks

In the fourth book of *Institutes of the Christian Religion*, aptly entitled "The External Means or Aims by Which God Invites Us into the Society of Christ," Calvin makes the careful distinction of what constitutes a church. In this section of *The Institutes*, Calvin discussed the topics of "the church, its government, orders, and power; then the sacraments; and lastly, the civil order."[12] His commitment to the visible church echoes past theologians such as Cyprian of Carthage and Augustine.

> So powerful is participation in the church it keeps us in the society of God... But as it is now our purpose to discourse of the visible Church, let us learn, from her single title of Mother, how useful, nay, how necessary the knowledge of her is, since there is no other means of entering into life unless she conceive us in the womb and give us birth, unless she nourish us at her breasts, and, in short, keep us under her charge and government, until, divested of mortal flesh, we become like the angels (Matt. 22:30).[13]

Central to the church nurturing the people of God, in Calvin's development, is the preaching of the Word of God. After quoting from Ephesians 4, which cites pastors as Christ's gift to the church, Calvin states, "We see that God, who might perfect his people in a moment, chooses not to bring them to manhood in any other way than by the education of the Church. We see the mode of doing it expressed; the preaching of celestial doctrine is committed to pastors."[14] After tracing this central mark of teaching through the Old Testament into the New Testament, from priests and prophets to apostles and preachers, he defends God's use of human agents in the propagation of his Word.

> Those who think that the authority of the doctrine is impaired by the insignificance of the men who are called to teach, betray their ingratitude; for among the many noble endowments with which God has adorned the human race, one of the most remarkable is, that he

> deigns to consecrate the mouths and tongues of men to his service, making his own voice to be heard in them. Wherefore, let us not on our part decline obediently to embrace the doctrine of salvation, delivered by his command and mouth; because, although the power of God is not confined to external means, he has, however, confined us to his ordinary method of teaching.[15]

Calvin testifies both to the Lord's use of ministers and God's claim that all spiritual work belongs to him. He did not view preaching exclusively as proclamation from the pulpit. "Christ did not ordain pastors on the principle that they only teach the Church in a general way on the public platform, but that they care for the individual sheep, bring back the wandering and scattered to the fold, bind up the broken and crippled, heal the sick, support the frail and weak."[16]

As Calvin continues, he distinguishes between the invisible and visible church, and then denotes how the latter is made evident.

> Often, too, by the name of Church is designated the whole body of mankind scattered throughout the world, who profess to worship one God and Christ, who by baptism are initiated into the faith; by partaking of the Lord's Supper profess unity in true doctrine and charity, agree in holding the word of the Lord, and observe the ministry which Christ has appointed for the preaching of it.[17]

Calvin acknowledges how vital it is for the Lord to have made clear for his people what the church is in order to recognize it. "Accordingly, inasmuch as it was of importance to us to recognize it, the Lord has distinguished it by certain marks, and as it were symbols."[18] He then repeatedly points to the Word and sacraments as the marks of the church.

> And, since assurance of faith was not necessary, he substituted for it a certain charitable judgment where-

> by we recognize as members of the church those who, by confession of faith, by example of life, and by partaking in the sacraments, profess the same God and Christ with us. He has, moreover, set off by plainer marks the knowledge of his very body to us, knowing how necessary it is to our salvation...Wherever we see the Word of God purely preached and heard, and the sacraments administered according to Christ's institution, there, it is not to be doubted, a church of God exists [cf. Eph. 2:20].[19]

As such, Calvin warned against the attempts to remove these two marks. "For there is nothing that Satan plots more than to remove and do away with one or both of these. Sometimes he tries by effacing and destroying these marks to remove the true and genuine distinction of the church."[20]

In pointing out the word and sacraments only as the two distinguishing traits, Calvin appears to depart somewhat from Martin Bucer, his mentor during his Geneva exile in Strasbourg from 1538–41, who included the third mark of discipline.

> At Geneva, Calvin himself did not include discipline as a mark of the Church, but the tension between the objectivity of grace and the subjective response to that grace raised questions as to the validity of the definition. Significantly, the later Reformed confessions were to follow Bucer's lead and to include discipline *sub regno Christi* as a third mark."[21]

However, a closer reading of *The Institutes* and other of Calvin's writings gives needed clarification to this assessment. Calvin saw the preaching of the truths of God's Word as the chief and ultimate mark. As such, he often made statements in discussing the marks that could seem to invalidate the other ones. "Let it therefore be a fixed point, that a holy unity exits amongst us, when, consenting in pure doctrine, we are united in Christ alone."[22] He warned against trusting in outer signs or symbols of God's kingdom with this belief in view.

> Therefore, although they put forward Temple, priesthood, and the rest of the outward shows, this empty glitter which blinds the eyes of the simple ought not to move us a whit to grant that the church exists where God's Word is not found. For this is the abiding mark with which our Lord has sealed his own: 'Everyone who is of the truth hears my voice' [John 18:37].[23]

For another example, in the "Articles of the Faculty of Paris," Calvin stated, "We all confess that there has been a universal Church ever since the beginning of the world, and that it must continue until the end. The question is, what are the outward signs by which we can discern it? In our conviction it is the Word of God which is the mark of the Church."[24] Thus, based on a limited sample of statements such as these, a similar charge could be made to the one of Calvin not including discipline, namely, that Calvin did not view the sacraments as a mark, which is clearly untrue. Herman Bavinck, commenting on the Reformers' practice of identifying preaching as the chief mark, states that "a true church has only one mark, the Word," yet he goes on to add that the Word is "variously administered and confessed in the church's preaching, sacraments, discipline, and life."[25]

Next, the marks were viewed as ranked and interdependent on one another, with preaching, as indicated above, viewed as chief, followed by the sacraments, yet with both needing the support of discipline to maintain their integrity.[26] One can hear the need for discipline to accompany the preaching and administration of the sacraments in statements such as the following ones from *The Institutes* (emphasis added):

> We have laid down as distinguishing marks of the church the preaching of the Word and the observance of the sacraments. These can never exist *without bringing forth fruit* and prospering by God's blessing...and *no one is permitted to spurn its authority, flout its warnings, resist its counsels, or make light of its chastisements*—much less to desert it and break its unity.[27]

> For in it alone is kept safe and uncorrupted that doctrine in which *piety stands sound* and the use of the sacraments ordained by the Lord *is guarded*...we are neither to renounce the communion of the church nor, remaining in it, to disturb its peace and *duly ordered discipline*.[28]

Third, Calvin makes it clear that a holy lifestyle must accompany faith in the Word of God and practice of the sacraments. "If churches are well ordered, they will not bear the wicked in their bosom. Nor will they indiscriminately admit worthy and unworthy together to that sacred banquet."[29] In his letter to Cardinal Sadoleto, Calvin decried the cardinal's attempt to draw the Genevan Protestants back into Rome's fold. In so doing, he faults Sadoleto's definition of the church, which consists primarily of appeals to unity and catholicity, asking, "[W]hat comes of the Word of the Lord, that clearest of all marks?"[30] Then, as he proceeds, Calvin writes that there are "three things on which the safety of the Church is founded, viz., doctrine, discipline, and the sacraments..."[31] Clearly Calvin upheld discipline as necessary.

Later in the twelfth chapter in Book 4 of *The Institutes,* Calvin treats more formally the subject of discipline by starting with its necessity. "But because some persons, in their hatred of discipline, recoil from its very name, let them understand this: if no society, indeed, no house which has even a small family, can be kept in proper condition without discipline, it is much more necessary in the church."[32] He then encourages those in the church to be open to receiving correction from others.

> The first foundation of discipline is to provide a place for private admonition; that is, if anyone does not perform his duty willingly, or behaves insolently, or does not live honorably, or has committed any act deserving blame—he should allow himself to be admonished; and when the situation demands it, every man should endeavor to admonish his brother.[33]

Calvin further treats the common text on this subject, Matthew 18:15–20, by giving direction on how to handle private and public sins and lists the sins that could lead to exclusion from the fellowship.

As he offers three purposes for discipline, Calvin demonstrates the interplay between the marks. He states that the first purpose is for separating the righteous from the wicked, "that they who lead a filthy and infamous life may not be called Christians, to the dishonor of God, as if his holy church [cf. Ephesians 5:25–26] were a conspiracy of wicked and abandoned men."[34] According to him, this separation preserves the order and sanctity of the Lord's Supper. The next rationale he offers for discipline is that it preserves purity in the church. "The second purpose is that the good be not corrupted by the constant company of the wicked, as commonly happens."[35] He then follows this with discipline's restorative purpose. "The third purpose is that those overcome by shame for their baseness begin to repent."[36]

Given Calvin's reputation as being severe, his pastoral heart should be noted particularly with respect to the subject of discipline. He advises great patience in applying formal discipline, saying that official acts should not take place "until the sinner becomes obstinate."[37] Even then, the discipline is to be done in a spirit of gentleness, and speaks of the cruelty of ancient church practices where undue lengthy judgments would have created despair. He instead stresses that love should be seen in disciplinary measures: "This gentleness is required in the whole body of the church, that it should deal mildly with the lapsed and should not punish with extreme rigor, but rather, according to Paul's injunction, confirm its love toward them [2 Cor. 2:8]."[38] Even those who are to be excommunicated "are not cast into everlasting ruin and damnation" as was practiced by Rome, but are warned with a hope that "in hearing that their life and morals are condemned, they are assured of their everlasting condemnation unless they repent."[39]

Calvin believed the marks were placed into the hands of ordained leadership to administer. Back in the third chapter of

Book 4, "The Doctors and Ministers of the Church, Their Election and Office," Calvin lays out the biblical case for the church's governance. Using Ephesians 4:4–16, he goes through the five offices listed there, showing the first three (apostles, prophets, and evangelists) were of the apostolic age and are no longer functioning. He explains that in the New Testament titles such as pastor, teacher, elder, and overseer are used interchangeably. He discusses how the calling to this office involves both the internal call, as a man senses the Spirit's stirring him to this responsibility, and the external calling, which comes from the church as it observes certain men having the sound doctrine and holy lives requisite for this position.

Thus, ministers who have this calling are to be set apart by the church, such as was done in Acts 13. Calvin supports the concept of the elders being elected by the church, based on Acts 14:23 where Paul and Barnabas "appointed elders in every church."[40] He completes this section by discussing ordination and how it is accomplished by the laying on of hands. Clearly ordination in the Protestant churches granted the leadership authority to oversee the marks and was distinct from the Catholic view of apostolic succession and papal-granted authority.

The Confessional Legacy Calvin Regarding the Marks

The varied confessions from the nations where the Reformation was birthed and spread attest to the impact that Calvin had on the church's identity. Certainly not all the confessions relied solely upon him. Yet a good number of the confessions were greatly influenced by Calvin and testify to the necessity of the marks.[41]

The *Geneva Confession* of 1536, written for the Swiss church by John Calvin and William Farel, declares, "The proper mark by which to rightly discern the church of Jesus Christ is that his holy gospel be purely and faithfully preached, proclaimed, heard, and kept, and his sacraments be properly administered, even if there be some imperfections and faults, as there always will be among men."[42] This document testifies to the place of ministers in the ministry of the Word and sacraments, and to keeping due order in the church with the positive side of discipline. "To these we accord no other power or authority but to conduct, rule, and govern the people of God committed to them by the same Word, in which they have the power to command, defend, promise, and warn, and without which they neither can nor ought to attempt anything."[43]

The *French Confession* (1559), in which Calvin played a central role, stresses the importance of preaching in no uncertain terms: "We detest all visionaries who would like, so far as lies in their power, to destroy this ministry and preaching of the Word and sacraments."[44] The Gallic confession goes on to say that "... [W]e believe it is important to discern with care and prudence which is the true church, for this title has been much abused. We say, then, according to the Word of God, that it is the company of the faithful who agree to follow His Word and the pure religion which it teaches..."[45] However, in citing the first two of the marks directly, the confession does not leave out the third, for it insists that the church are those "who agree to follow the Word and... who advance in it all their lives, growing and becoming more confirmed in the fear of God according as they feel the want of growing and pressing onward."[46]

The *Scottish Confession of Faith* (1560) was drawn up by John Knox, who spent several years with Calvin at Geneva prior to writing it. In "Article 18: Of the Notes, by Which the True Church Is Discerned from the False; and Who Shall Be Judge of the Doctrine," an emerging clarity is seen in adding the third mark of discipline to the description of what constitutes a true church.

> The notes, therefore, of the true Church of God, we believe, confess, and avow to be, first, the true preaching of the word of God, in the which God hath revealed himself unto us, as the writings of the Prophets and Apostles do declare: secondly, the right administration of the Sacraments of Christ Jesus, which must be annexed unto the word and promise of God, to seal and

> confirm the same in our hearts: lastly, Ecclesiastical discipline, uprightly ministered, as God's word prescribeth, whereby vice is repressed, and virtue nourished.[47]

However, perhaps Calvin's influence in viewing the first two marks as prominent is seen in the sentence that follows. "Wheresoever, then, these former notes are seen and of any time continue, (be the number never so few, about two or three), there, without all doubt, is the true Church of Christ; who, according to his promise, is in the midst of them..."[48]

The following year saw Guido de Brés of the Netherlands, influenced greatly by Calvin's teachings and the *Gallic Confession*, publish the *Belgic Confession* (1561). With great clarity the three marks are emphasized in Article XXIX "Of the Marks of the True Church, and Wherein She Differs from the False Church." "The marks by which the true Church is known are these: If the pure doctrine of the gospel is preached therein, if she maintains the pure administration of the sacraments as instituted by Christ; if church discipline is exercised in punishing of sin; in short, if all things are managed according to the pure word of God."[49] This section also indicates how individual Christians are to be discerned, giving special notice that the mark by which they are known in addition to faith is that "they avoid sin, follow after righteousness, love the true God and their neighbor, neither turn aside to the right or left, and crucify the flesh with the works thereof."[50] Increasingly, the confessions emphasize that accompanying the preaching of the Word and the administration of the sacraments is the behavior of the members of the church to live a holy, disciplined life.

The influence of Calvin, flowing down in history through these preceding confessions, is seen in what is called the "crown jewel" of the Reformed confessions. *The Westminster Confession of Faith* (1643) testifies to the marks of the church as well. Beginning by defining the visible church, the importance of the gospel and its truths (a clear reference to the first mark) are highlighted.

> The visible church, which is also catholic or universal under the gospel (not confined to one nation as before under the law) consists of all those, throughout the world, that profess the true religion...and particular churches, which are members thereof, are more or less pure, according as the doctrine of the gospel is taught and embraced, ordinances administered, and public worship performed more or less purely in them.[51]

In the following paragraph, the confession expands to the need for ordained ministers and the other marks with these words (explanations inserted).

> "Unto this catholic visible church Christ hath given the ministry (preachers of the Word), oracles (the holy Scriptures), and ordinances of God (the sacraments and the accompanying commitment to them reflected in discipline), for the gathering and perfecting of the saints, in this life, to the end of the world: and doth, by his own presence and Spirit, according to his promise, make them effectual thereunto."[52]

These confessions, recorded over a century of time, continue to direct the greater Reformed community throughout the world down into our modern era. Thus, paying close attention to Calvin's teaching and influence regarding the true constitution of the visible church should remain a high priority to those holding to these confessions.

Notes

[1]Though the Council of Trent met in the middle of the 16th century and was seen as a response to the Reformation, its teachings espoused the long-held beliefs of the church. Thus, there is little danger of anachronism in looking at Trent's declarations before examining the Reformers.

[2]G.C. Berkouwer, *Studies in Dogmatics: The Church* (Grand Rapids: Eerdmans, 1976), 14.

[3]Charles Westphal, "The Marks of the Church: A Protestant Viewpoint," *Anglican Theological Review* 42 (1960), 91.

[4]The five popes were Paul III, Julius III, Marcellus II, Paul IV, and Pius IV.

[5]J. Donovan, *The Catechism of the Council of Trent* (Chorley, Lancashire, UK: Christian Books Today Ltd., 2009), 74.

[6]Ibid.

[7]Ibid.

[8]Ibid., 79.

[9]G. C, Berkouwer, *Studies in Dogmatics: The Church* (Grand Rapids: Eerdmans, 1976), 14.

[10]Ibid.

[11]James Bannerman, *The Church of Christ* Vol. I (Vestavia Hills, AL: Solid Ground Christian Books, 2009), 55.

[12]John Calvin, *Institutes of the Christian Religion*, ed. John T. McNeill, trans. Ford Lewis Battles. (Philadelphia; London: Westminster John Knox Press, 1960), 4.1.1.

[13]Ibid., 4.1.1.

[14]Ibid., 4.1.3.

[15]Ibid., 4.1.5.

[16]John Calvin, *Acts 14–28: Torrance Edition* (Grand Rapids: Wm. B. Eerdmans Publishing, 1996), 175.

[17]Ibid., 4.1.7.

[18]Ibid., 4.1.8.

[19]Ibid., 4.1.9.

[20]Ibid., 4.1.11.

[21]Westphal, "The Marks," 91.

[22]John Calvin, *The Necessity of Reforming the Church*, (Dallas, TX: Protestant Heritage Press, 1995), 129.

[23]Calvin, *Instit.*,4.2.6.

[24]Westphal, "The Marks", 91.

[25]Herman Bavinck, *Reformed Dogmatics.* Vol. 4 (Grand Rapids: Baker Academic, 2008), 312.

[26]Even today a pastor may be deemed a "minister of the Word and sacraments." This title does not necessarily imply that he does not practice discipline or view it as a mark of his ministry.

[27]Calvin, *Institutes*, 4.1.10.

[28]Ibid., 4.1.12.

[29]Ibid., 4.1.15.

[30]John Calvin, *John Calvin, Tracts and Letters,* Vol. 1, Trans. Henry Beveridge (Edinburgh: The Banner of Truth Trust, 2009), 35.

[31]Calvin, *Tracts and Letters*, 38. Note here Calvin goes on in this sentence to speak of ceremonies as a fourth "mark," but his meaning is that the Church of Rome has added this in a way contrary to God's Word.

[32]Ibid., 4.12.1.

[33]Ibid., 4.12.2.

[34]Ibid., 4.12.5.

[35]Ibid.

[36]Ibid.

[37]Ibid., 4.12.6.

[38]Ibid., 4.12.7.

[39]Ibid., 4.12.8.

[40]The Greek word for "appointed" is ceirotonew, a word used to describe the action of the Greek polis in "electing by a show of hands."

[41]I am indebted to the insights of Robert Reymond for much of the following, per his volume, *A New Systematic Theology*, Second Ed. (Grand Rapids: Thomas Nelson, 2010), 855–859.

[42]Arthur Cochrane, ed. *Reformed Confessions of the Sixteenth Century*, 2nd ed. (Louisville, KY: Westminster John Knox Press, 2003), 125.

[43]Ibid.

[44]Robert Letham, "The Necessity of Preaching in the Modern World," *Ordained Servant: A Journal for Church Officers* 22 (2013), 43.

[45]Schaff, *Creeds,* 3:375.

[46]Ibid.

[47]John Knox, *The History of the Reformation of Religion in Scotland: With Which Are Included Knox's Confession and The Book of Discipline*, ed. by Cuthbert Lennox (London: Andrew Melrose, 1905), 354.

[48]Ibid.

[49]Schaff, *Creeds,* 3:419–20.

[50]Ibid., 3:420.

[51]WCF 25.2.

[52]WCF 25.3

CHAPTER NINE

Networking, Justification, and One Man's Salvation

Bruce R. Backensto

It was during October, 1966, while I was sitting in a morning worship service in the College Hill Reformed Presbyterian Church in Beaver Falls, Pennsylvania, with its then-pastor Rev. John H. "Jack" White preaching, that I was taken back when he said our deeds of righteousness are as filthy rags in God's sight. I remember thinking, "That cannot be true! God welcomes us into heaven based on our good deeds." I had grown up believing my good works (which had to outweigh my bad works) would insure my entrance into heaven. I truly *wanted* to keep God's commandments; at least enough of them to outweigh the ones I did not keep. It is amazing that I believed good works insured my salvation considering I was a communicant member of the Presbyterian Church at Woodbury, New Jersey (PCUSA).

After hearing those words in that sermon, I hurried out of the building and went to my room, opened my leather-bound *Thompson Chain Reference Bible* to the concordance and soon found—much to my surprise—White had paraphrased Isaiah 64:6: "But we are all as an unclean thing, and **all our righteousnesses are as filthy rags**; and we all do fade as a leaf; and our iniquities, like the wind, have taken us away" (KJV) [emphasis added]. The Holy Spirit convicted me of my sin, sinfulness, self-righteousness so that I finally understood the gospel. I realized for the first time in my life that Jesus bore the wrath of His (and now my) Father which I deserved because of my sin. What was of most importance to Paul made sense for me: "For I delivered unto you first of all that which I also received, how that Christ died for our sins according to the scriptures; And that he was buried, and that he rose again the third day according to the scriptures" (1 Corinthians 15:3–4 KJV).

Fast forward to the summer of 1969. I was unofficially interning under White's tutelage when he was the minister of the College Hill Reformed Presbyterian Church. I was a communicant member there and heading to the Reformed Presbyterian Theological Seminary (RPTS) in the fall. The College Hill RPC had a mission outreach in the West Mayfield Chapel. I was given an opportunity to deliver the message one Lord's Day morning. In that message, I cited the Westminster Shorter Catechism 14: Q. *What is sin?* A. *Sin is any want of conformity unto, or transgression of, the law of God.* Having graduated with a BS in Math from Geneva College, I was not a student of the Shorter Catechism, nor of Elizabethan English. It was my understanding the word *want* meant desire; i.e. *sin is any desire to keep the law of God*. Why is that what *want* meant to me at that time in my life? I had only heard *want* used to mean *desire* something. I *wanted* a college degree, therefore I attended and graduated from Geneva College. I had been convicted that basing one's salvation on good works which stemmed from *wanting/desiring* to keep the commandments was wrong. Our deeds of righteousness will not save us!

Because I thought salvation was secured through acts of righteousness, I understood the word *want* in SC 14 to mean *desire*; that is, it clearly was foolishness to believe keeping the law of God earned one's salvation. Surely the Westminster Divines knew that and taught that—*wanting* to keep the commandments to earn salvation—was sin. It was after that service that someone (I think it was a godly elderly woman) kindly spoke to me and informed me of the meaning of *want.* It means *lack*—I *lacked* conformity to the law of God.

Now I had a dilemma. At first, I thought I gained a right standing with God by keeping the law. In other words, it was sin not to *want to* keep the commandments. Now I learned, indeed, it was a sin to *want* conformity to the law of God. How was I to be made right with God?

It was not long in my conversations with White that he told me about justification. I soon learned Shorter Catechism 33: Q. *What is justification?* A. *Justification is God's act of free grace, wherein he pardoneth all our sins, and accepteth us as righteous in his sight, only for the righteousness of Christ imputed to us, and received by faith alone.* There is nothing one does to be justified/ righteous in God's sight. It is all of grace. However, the question arises, at least for me, what role does *faith* play? If I am to believe in order to be justified, isn't *faith*; more specifically, *MY faith* what enables me to have right standing with God?

It was then that I learned about Ephesians 2:8–9. "For by grace you have been saved through faith. And this is not your own doing; it is a gift from God, not as a result of works, so that no one could boast." What a comfort these two verses become in a Christian's life. That I *have been saved through faith* because of God's gift of salvation of me, through *faith*, but not a faith of my own. The faith I exercised when I repented of my, so called, righteous deeds, *is a gift from God* otherwise I could boast of my work of faith which endeared God to me so that He had to forgive me and welcome me into His family. I don't remember if White was the person who encouraged me to learn Ephesians 2:8–9, but I am indebted to the Holy Spirit Who pointed out the difference between the faith every person has at birth, and the faith which embraces Jesus as Lord and Savior.

It happened that Dr. John Gerstner had been invited to visti for four successive Lord's Days to teach the adult class at College Hill Reformed Presbyterian Church where White was the minister. During the month that Gerstner taught in 1966, I asked him, a member of the Presbyterian Church of the United States of

America (PCUSA), for advice concerning whether I should remain a member of the PCUSA or leave the denomination. This was the denomination in which I had become a communicant member at the age of twelve. A part of becoming a communicant member of the Presbyterian Church at Woodbury was to memorize the Westminster Shorter Catechism. I did so, but shortly after being confirmed as a communicant member I forgot most of the 107 questions and answers. It was in the mid-1960s that a new confession was being drafted to bring the denomination's public profession of faith into more relevant language. A new confession was needed. Dr. Gerstner commented that he believed the confession was not orthodox. Among other things, he was concerned with the statement the *New Confession* made regarding the Bible.

Sometime before returning to Woodbury over the Christmas break, I learned my mother had talked with the minister at the church where I was a communicant member. She told him he should speak with me during the time I was home because there was something different about me. The first Sunday I was home the minister invited me to meet with him during that week. I did meet with him in his office. He asked me about why my mother thought I was different. I told him I had become a Christian; that is, I realized I was not going to go to heaven because of my good works. I told him I realized my righteousness is as filthy rags in the Lord's sight. I told him that I finally realized what Jesus meant by His words recorded in Mark 1:15: "The time is fulfilled, and the kingdom of God is at hand; repent and believe in the gospel." The gospel as set forth in passages like Ephesians 2:8–9 and First Corinthians 15:3–8. I had come to realize Jesus died for sinners such as I am. It was through repenting and believing in the finished work of Jesus in my behalf that I was transformed into a Christian. My minister thanked me for sharing my experience with him. Then I asked him what he thought of the *New Confession* the General Assembly's committee was writing for the church. He asked me if I had read it? I had not read it. He handed me a draft of the *New Confession*, asked me to read it and some-time in August we would meet to discuss what questions I might have after I had read it. I agreed and we set a date in August to meet again.

Imagine how I felt as a three-month-old Christian being invited to read what would become known as *The Confession of 1967.* I accepted the challenge and began reading the draft my minister had given to me. I read with a red lead pencil and underlined places where I had questions as to what was being said. In August, when my minister and I met in his office I began pointing out all the places I had questions about the orthodoxy of what I was reading. To my surprise, his reply to my questions was, "That part is back in committee for further work." I finally asked him what he thought about the statements concerning the inspiration and infallibility of the Bible. His answer convinced me I had to leave the PCUSA. He sought to illustrate how what "inspiration of the Bible" meant by comparing it to the light which was coming through the smoked glass window in his office. It would take the reasoning power of humans to understand the intent of the words in the Bible. They are words of human writers. It was their thoughts put to writing concerning God and God's relation to mankind. Two of the four statements in *The Confession of 1967* relative to the Bible follow (emphasis mine):

> 9.29 The Bible is to be interpreted in the light of its witness to God's work of reconciliation in Christ. The Scriptures, given under the guidance of the Holy Spirit, *are nevertheless words of human beings*, conditioned by the language, thought forms, and literary fashions of the places and times *at which they were written. They reflect views of life*, history, and the cosmos which were then current. The church, therefore, has an obligation to approach the Scriptures with literary and historical understanding. As God has spoken the divine word in diverse cultural situations, the church is confident that God will continue to speak through the Scriptures in a changing world and in every form of human culture.

> 9.30 God's word is spoken to the church today where the Scriptures are faithfully preached and attentively read in dependence on the illumination of the Holy Spirit and with readiness to receive their truth and direction.[1]

Notice the italicized words. *Are nevertheless words of human beings* and *they reflect views of life* according to the writer's understanding of what was happening around him. The Bible is not understood to be God's very breathings (1 Timothy 3:16). This makes statements by the Apostle Paul in epistles he wrote merely expressions of his understanding of life during his time on this earth.

It was not until years later when I read the Auburn Affirmation of the United Presbyterian Church in the United States of America (UPCUSA) that it made sense why my minister answered my question of the inspiration of the Bible as he did. Here is what I found when I read the Auburn Affirmation. Here is the section concerning the interpretation of the Scriptures (emphasis mine):

> With respect to the interpretation of the Scriptures the position of our church has been that common to Protestants. "The Supreme Judge," says the Confession of Faith, "by whom all controversies of religion are to be determined, and all decrees of councils, opinions of ancient writers, doctrines of men, and private spirits, are to be examined, and in whose sentence we are to rest, can be no other but the Holy Spirit speaking in the Scripture". (Conf. I, x). Accordingly, our church has held that the supreme guide in the interpretation of the Scriptures is not, as it is with Roman Catholics, ecclesiastical authority, but the Spirit of God, speaking to the Christian believer. Thus, our church lays it upon its ministers and others to read and teach the Scriptures as the Spirit of God through His manifold ministries instructs them, and *to receive all truth which from time to time He causes to break forth from the Scriptures.*

> *There is no assertion in the Scriptures that their writers were kept "from error."* The Confession of Faith does not make this assertion; and it is significant that this assertion is not to be found in the Apostle's Creed or the Nicene Creed or in any of the great Reformation confessions. *The doctrine of inerrancy, intended to enhance the authority of the Scriptures, in fact impairs their supreme authority* for faith and life, and weakens the testimony of the church to the power of God unto salvation through Jesus Christ. We hold that the General Assembly of 1923, in asserting that "the Holy Spirit did so inspire, guide and move the writers of Holy Scripture as to keep them from error," spoke without warrant of the Scriptures or of the Confession of Faith. We hold rather to the words of the Confession of Faith, that the Scriptures "are given by inspiration of God, to be the rule of faith and life." (Conf. I, ii).[2]

Boldly, the Auburn Affirmation speaks against the idea of the Bible being inerrant because its authors do not use the word inerrant in the biblical text. Certainly, we find in 2 Peter 1:19–21 the biblical teaching the words of prophecy are not fundamentally the words of the human author, they are the very words of God. Because the words of the human authors were ultimately what the Holy Spirit intended them to be, by denying the doctrine of inerrancy one denies the perfection of the Holy Spirit. Once the canon is closed, no longer will men be moved by the Holy Spirit with respect to receiving new revelation on equal with what is in the 69 books of the Bible we Protestants hold together.

Back to White and the doctrine of justification as I was learning it through his networking[3]. At some point during the late 1960s, Jack introduced me to Dr. Norman Shepherd. I remember pleasant conversations with him about biblical theology. I had Dr. Johannes Geerhardus "J.G." Vos for Bible 101 at Geneva College. I was interested in his father Geerhardus Vos's work *Biblical Theology*. Seeing how the message of the Bible relative to salvation grows out of Genesis 3:15 captured my heart. This was the way White preached. This was the way Shepherd preached. It was remarkable to watch the protoevangelium work its way throughout the Old Testament and into the New Testament when the promised seed/offspring of the woman crushed the head of the serpent/Satan by remaining on the cross, shedding His blood for the remission of sins and cleansing of sinners elected before the foundations of the earth, going to the grave to be raised on the third day, the Christian Sabbath/Lord's Day, to be exalted to the right hand of His Father where He presently sits governing the affairs of men and nations, so that at His resurrection and coronation He and the Father sent the Holy Spirit to apply the salvation Jesus accomplished. In 2000, Shepherd wrote a book entitled *The Call of Grace: How the Covenant Illuminates Salvation and Evangelism.*

Before going any further with Shepherd's impact on my understanding of justification, it is to be noted that in 1994 a document of which Dr. White played a role in formulating during his time as President of Geneva College and an officer in the National Association of Evangelicals entitled *Evangelicals and Catholics Together* saw the light of day. Noteworthy signatures included Catholic Richard John Neuhaus and evangelical Charles Colson. The list goes on. This was an effort to take Jesus's words recorded in John 17:11: "And I am no longer in the world, but they are in the world, and I am coming to you. Holy Father, keep them in your name which you have given me, that they may be one, even as we are one."

Because of Jack's networking, he was constantly meeting men and women of faith. He knew Richard John Neuhaus and Charles Colson and many other "big name" Christians, all of whom shared a commitment to see the fragmented body of Christ live in more harmonious ways. He even worked with Roman Catholics praying for another reformation which would lead to greater cooperation in spreading the gospel the world over. More than that, White desired to see faithful members of the visible church (while White embraced the teaching of the *Westminster Confession of Faith* that the Roman Catholic church is apostate) confess together the gospel. He recognized genuine believers in the Lord Jesus Christ whose lives manifested a vibrant relationship with the Triune God, and he sought dialogue and written affirmations of oneness in Jesus Christ in hopes of *advancing the vision*.[4]

I still remember being a fraternal delegate to the General Assembly of the Orthodox Presbyterian Church (OPC) the year *Catholics and Evangelicals Together* was published, feeling compelled to speak to the fact that Dr. John H. White, President of Geneva College, an institution of higher education under the oversight of the Reformed Presbyterian Church of North America, was involved in the production of such a statement. While I do not remember my remarks perfectly, I believe I said something like:

> *Surely many of you fathers and brothers in the Orthodox Presbyterian Church are scratched your heads in bewilderment when you learned Dr. White helped draft what we now know as* Catholics and Evangelicals Together. *I can assure you Dr. White's understanding of the reformation's SOLAs is rock solid, he is ever praying, as we all ought to be praying, for the visible oneness of the Church of Jesus Christ, His Bride. Perhaps through such an endeavor as this, the Holy Spirit would bring about genuine reformation within the Roman Church. After all, it is only through collaboration with those within the Roman Catholic Church, some will be brought to understand the gift of faith they enjoy is not unto the infusion of righteousness, but the imputation of righteousness.*

When I sat down, I remember putting my head face down on the table in front of me weeping. I was compelled to speak favorably of the one whom the Lord used to draw me to himself and who spent many hours disciplining me. We are all prone to believe such an action would not *advance the vision*, but we won't know the impact of that document and the subsequent document had on biblical ecumenicalism until the new heaven and new earth is ushered in at the glorious return of Jesus.

It was during the years immediately following *Catholics and Evangelicals Together* that White and I had conversations related to the doctrine of justification. We both embrace the reformation's *SOLAs*, especially *sola fide*. Being a math major, I often thought mathematical formulas. During those conversations with White, he would often quote Dr. Gerstner. The quote which suck with me, which I have shared on many occasions when talking with others about justification is: "You know, Bruce—Gerstner would say, if a thief says he is a Christian because he believes in Jesus Christ unto salvation; if that thief does not stop stealing, he is not justified." Some would say that this borders on heresy. It sounds on the surface as though faith plus works; i.e. believe Jesus to be one's Lord and Savior AND stealing no longer equals justification. I remember reading the various formulae offered which depicted one's justification as it relates to one's faith and works. It was at the dedication of the Dr. John H. Gerstner's library within McCartney library on the campus of Geneva College that I picked up a small card produced by Dr. Gerstner explaining the different views of justification in the Christian world.

> *Justification by Faith Alone (Romans 4:5)*
> *(1) Works → justification — faith (Liberalism)*
> (2) *Faith → justification — works (Neo-Orthodoxy)*
> *(3) Faith → justification — works (Antinomianism)*
> *(4) Faith + Works → justification (Roman Catholicism)*
> *(5) Faith → justification + works (Reformed Theology)*[5]

Now that I have this description of justification by faith written by Gerstner, I am encouraged because instead of using the word *justification* in the formula, I used the word *salvation* in the formula. The → (yields or produces) in my formula went exactly like Gerstner's Reformed theology formula.

My formula: salvation → faith → justification + works. Since "justification is an act of God's free grace, wherein He pardons all our sins, and accepts us as righteous in His sight, only for the righteousness of Christ imputed to us, and received by faith alone."[6] I put salvation first because God's elect are chosen before the foundation of the cosmos. Because God foreordains those who will believe unto eternal life before creating all that exists; our salvation is secured in eternity past. The Holy Spirit does His work of regeneration[7] so that the faith instilled in the regenerate person is exercised in embracing/receiving Jesus as the propitiation[8] for our sins. Since Jesus's blood cleanses the repentant sinner of sin, so we who believe on the Lord Jesus Christ are adjudicated righteous in God's sight because Jesus's righteousness is imputed to our account. Justification is enjoyed experientially when the sinner believes on or in Jesus the Christ, so that he believes Jesus. When faith is exercised unto one's justification, justifying faith will manifest itself in righteous living (James 2:17). We know from Ephesians 2:8–10 faith is a gift of God resulting in the newborn person finding their delight in obeying the Law of God.[9] Had White not networked with Dr. Gerstner, I would not have realized the way I was formulating salvation with respect to justification was so similar to what I read on the three inches by two inches card setting for his formula of justification I picked up at the dedication ceremony of his library being donated to McCartney Library on Geneva College's campus.

Following graduation from Geneva College, I entered the Reformed Presbyterian Theological Seminary with my spiritual father's encouragement. I entered seminary seeking to understand the Bible better and the Reformed faith more clearly. I wanted to be a math teacher and basketball coach. During my senior year of college, I took an independent study course which gave me the opportunity to write a paper entitled "What is Christian Education?" J.G. Vos had published a tract on Christian education, which I read. I also read a work by Dr. Cornelius Van Til entitled *The Dilemma of Education*. It was what I learned from this Van Til piece that I wanted to speak in person with him if the way became open. It did, and once again, because of White's networking, it would be Rev. Henry W. Coray, an Orthodox Presbyterian Church minister and author of the book *The Son of Tears: A Novel on the Life of St. Augustine*, who would introduce me to Van Til.

Here is how it happened. Coray visited College Hill RPC at White's invitation to preach and teach one Lord's Day. That is when I met him, though it was a week or so later that I was invited to spend a weekend at Westminster Theological Seminary in Philadelphia, Pennsylvania. When I arrived on the campus of the seminary, I went to the library to look for Van Til and, much to my surprise, Coray was walking in the hall in the library. We remembered each other and he asked me why I was in the library. I told him I was looking for Van Til, so he took me to the professor's office and kindly introduced us. Thank you, White. The Lord granted me two hours with Van Til as he invited me to accompany him on his walk around Machen Hall. What a delightful two hours! Van Til was a gracious gentleman, theologian, apologist, and pastor. I learned it was his practice to go to hospitals during the afternoon on the Christian Sabbath. His compassion for the frail and ailing impressed me.

Back to justification and my spiritual father's networking. It was during the summer between my middler and senior years at RPTS that I accepted a summer internship with Dr. Ed Robson, minister of the Reformed Presbyterian Church in Syracuse, New York. I soon learned the location of the church building was in a poorer neighborhood of Syracuse. How impressed I was by Pastor Robson's ability to relate with the folks in that neighborhood. His passion for the lost and the ease with which he engaged folks walking along the sidewalk challenged me to be ready to engage anyone with the hope of sharing the good news of Jesus Christ. Along with occasionally exhorting the saints of the Syracuse RPC on the Lord's Day, I learned how to "preach" on the radio. Oh, it was White who encouraged me to intern with Robson. It was through observing Robson's shepherding of the flock and reaching out to the lost that I decided upon entering my senior year, I would do so with my eyes open to becoming a teaching elder. The questions I raised my senior year were significantly different than those I raised as a freshman and a middler.

Because I was a seminary student as a communicant member of the Reformed Presbyterian Church under the care of the Presbytery of the Alleghenies, I took exams conducted by the Presbytery toward licensure to receive a call as a teaching elder. One of the exams was in the area of exegesis. Students had to demonstrate the ability to work with the Hebrew and Greek texts of the Bible. I was assigned an exegesis paper on Ephesians 4:17–24, particularly verses 22–24, especially focusing on the image of *putting off* the old self and *putting on* new self.

> 17 Now this I say and testify in the Lord, that you must no longer walk as the Gentiles do, in the futility of their minds. 18 They are darkened in their understanding, alienated from the life of God because of the ignorance that is in them, due to their hardness of heart. 19 They have become callous and have given themselves up to sensuality, greedy to the practice of every kind of impurity. 20 But that is not the way you learned Christ – 21 assuming that you have heard about him and were taught in him, as the truth is in Jesus, 22 to put off (ἀποθέσθαι from ἀπάτη) your old self, which belongs to your former manner of life and is corrupt through deceitful desires, 23 and to be renewed in the spirit of your minds, 24 and to put on (ἐνδύσασθαι from **ἐνδύω**) the new self, created after the likeness of God in true righteousness and holiness.

It is clear in this passage the apostle Paul is talking about two ways of life. He speaks of the way Gentiles live in general. Those who are not born from above walk in the futility of their minds, alienated from life in God, greedy in impurity due to their hard heart and sensual desires. When we are honest with ourselves, this perfectly describes us before we repent and receive Jesus, right? We live impure lives. The degree of impurity varies between individuals. But does our new life in Christ demonstrating we wear a new garment? Have we indeed *put off* our old self? Have we *put on* our new self?

The verbs translated *put off* and *put on* are middle aorists in the Greek. Grammars tell us the action of the verb is being performed by the subject of the verb. Being an aorist points to an action without reference to duration; i.e. is it continuous or momentary? What we can say of these two verbs is they imply something someone does at some time in his or her life. Because this is action done by the believer, generally we speak of this as an aspect of sanctification. We already saw justification is an act of God. Turning again to the Shorter Catechism: What is sanctification? Sanctification is the work of God's free grace, whereby we are renewed in the whole man after the image of God, and are enabled more and more to die unto sin, and live unto righteousness.[10] One might think of sanctification in two ways. First, God's free grace renews the whole man after God's image. That seems like a one-time work of God. It reminds us of the apostle Paul's teaching in Galatians 2:20. What does he say about those who are born from above? "I have been crucified. It is no longer I who live, but Christ who lives in me. And the life I live in the flesh I live by faith in the Son of God, who loved me and gave himself up for me." Once again, it appears when Jesus died on the cross, all who were given to Him as He hung on the cross died with Him. Is this not the old self of whom Paul writes in Ephesians 4:22–24? Again, a once-and-for-all act with reference to the Christian's life, Paul enjoins "the saints, the faithful in Christ Jesus" (Ephesians 1:1b) "to put off the old self" and "to put on the new self."

Have you stopped and considered why Paul nearly always addresses his readers by referring to them as saints (ἁγίοι, the plural of ἅγιος)? The ἅγιος is the holy one or the set apart one. In Ephesians, the ἁγίοι are those who have a new self—the old is passed and the new has arrived. Isn't this what Paul is saying to the Corinthians in his second letter? "Therefore, if anyone is in Christ, he is a new creation. The old has passed away; behold the new has come."[11]

It was through my study of this passage I was introduced to *Principles of Conduct* by Dr. John Murray, Systematic

Professor at Westminster Theological Seminary in Philadelphia, another friend of White. Because of these seemingly punctiliar actions taken by a believer or being subject to as a believer, Murray began talking about a definitive aspect to sanctification.[12] It made sense to me in light of the passages presented that something more than being justified happens as one exercises the gift of faith which accompanied being born from above. The newly justified sinner is also set apart, made holy, becomes a new creation, sets aside the old way of life and enwraps one's self with the new garment stitched for us by our Lord and Savior as He takes up residence within us. Some have observed, the believer will be no more holy than at the time of their being justified; who rightly may be called *saints*. Thus, Paul writes "to all the saints in Christ Jesus who are at Philippi, with the overseers and deacons…to work out your own salvation with fear and trembling."[13] Of course, Paul presses the point as "we work out our own salvation," we do so remembering "it is God who works in you, both to will and to work for his good pleasure."[14]

For further study, I offer a brief critique of Dr. Shepherd's views of evangelism in light of the covenant of grace as set forth in the book mentioned earlier. I recall hearing Shepherd speaking at a conference saying something to this effect: When a person is united to the triune God through the covenant of grace, that person enjoys holiness (100% of their sanctification). If by that statement, Shepherd means the Christian will be no more sanctified in the eyes of God than when justified by grace alone, through faith alone, in Christ alone; in other words, Christians are saints—definitively sanctified, personally I am satisfied. Now the believer must work out their salvation—progressive sanctification.

Again, to my way of thinking, this makes sense. Where Shepherd falls prey to criticism, it seems to me, is that he seems to speak of a person not being able to say they are justified unless works of righteousness accompany faith. Again, so far, so good. Where things become tenuous is when talking about the covenant child who has been baptized according God's mandate, such that believing parents present their infant children to the sacrament of water baptism in the name of the Father, and the name of the Son and the name of the Holy Spirit. That child is included in the covenant of grace. That being the case, that infant is sanctified, set apart unto the LORD. Does that child enjoy Christ's righteousness imputed to them because of baptism? If so, won't it be by the child living more and more in obedience to the commands of God, thus showing their justification OR being understood as justified. What role does faith play? What role does works play? Well, that's for another day…

Notes

[1]Online copy of the *Confession of 1967*. The italicized words are to emphasize where *the Confession* understands the Bible to be more human than God-breathed. Hence, it is subject to interpretation according to the culture in which it is preached. All the while, the reader must read in hope of the Spirit causing truth to *break forth from the scriptures.*

[2]Auburn Affirmation from an online source. The italicized portions are to demonstrate when the Auburn Affirmation was adopted, the foundation of the reliability of what is read being true is suspect. It is with error, because human authors wrote it. 1 Timothy 3:16 indicates the very words contained within the Bible are the out-breathings of God.

[3]One reason Jack was given to networking, it seems to this author is *The Covenant of 1871*. This was a covenant drafted and adopted in the May 27, 1871 meeting of the Synod of the RPCNA in Pittsburgh, PA. Section 4 reads: "That, believing the Church to be one, and that all the saints have communion with God and with one another in the same Covenant believing, moreover, that schism and sectarianism are sinful in themselves; and inimical to true religion, and trusting that divisions shall cease, and the people of God become one Catholic church over all the earth, we will pray and labor for the visible oneness of the Church of God in our own land and throughout the world, on the basis of truth and of Scriptural order. Considering it a

principal duty of our profession to cultivate a holy brotherhood, we will strive to maintain Christian friendship with pious men of every name, and to feel and act as one with all in every land who pursue this grand end. And, as a means of securing this great result, we will by dissemination and application of the principles of truth herein professed, and by cultivating and exercising Christian charity, labor to remove stumbling blocks, and to gather into one the scattered and divided friends of truth and righteousness."

[4]It was during a lunch together that Kim and I enjoyed with Jack and Mary, I was reminded of Jack's desire to see faithful members of the visible church live their lives in the market place such that the Mediatorial Kingship of Jesus would fill the entire earth. He confessed he would have to take an exception to the *WCF's* equating the kingdom of God with the visible church. Abraham Kuyper's *Stone Lectures* greatly influenced both Jack and me to think this way. *Thank you, Jack!*

[5]A 3-inch by 2-inch card remains in my possession.

[6]*Westminster Shorter Catechism* Q & A 33.

[7]John 3:1–8

[8]1 John 2:2

[9]1 John 5:1–5, Ephesians 2:10

[10]Shorter Catechism Q & A 35.

[11]2 Corinthians 5:17

[12]Murray, John *Principles of Conduct*, Photolithoprinted by Grand Rapids Book Manufacturers, Inc. Grand Rapids, MI, original printing, January 1957, fifth printing, October 1974. p. 214–219.

[13]Philippians 1:1b, 2:12c–13 (ESV)

[14]Philippians 2:13 (ESV)

CHAPTER TEN

B.B. Warfield and the *Autographa*

Jeff Stivason

In a recent journal article, Richard Brash argued that "present-day evangelical discussions of the 'originals' of Scripture typically focus on the *autographa*…"[1] What is more, Brash contends for the influence of Old Princeton in this regard, especially the likes of B.B. Warfield and A.A. Hodge. However, he asserts that this way of understanding the "originals" is not in keeping with Reformed orthodoxy of the 17th century.[2] In other words, according to Reformed orthodoxy, in distinction to Old Princeton, the "originals" of Scripture are not the *autographa* but are simply the Greek and Hebrew documents.

Brash is not alone in pointing up the difference between Old Princeton and the Reformed orthodox. Richard Muller, before him, wrote that there is a "tendency in many recent essays to confuse the two views."[3] What is more, Muller goes so far as to say that Old Princeton's view of the *autographa* "is a logical trap, a rhetorical flourish, a conundrum designed to confound critics—who can only prove their case for genuine errancy by recourse to a text they do not have (and surely cannot) have."[4] Muller begs the obvious question. What was Old Princeton's view of the *autographa*? Did the Princeton theologians think of their position as a mere "rhetorical flourish" or a "logical trap" to dissuade liberals from getting too close for comfort or did they actually believe their argument, which again begs the question what was their argument?

The purpose of this article is set forth in broad strokes Benjamin B. Warfield's view of the *autographa*. Further, I will demonstrate that Warfield's view is in keeping with the text of the Westminster Confession of Faith on the matter of immediate inspiration and providential preservation. I will begin by briefly explaining Warfield's view of the immediate inspiration of Scripture. Second, I will explore Warfield's understanding of God's providential preservation of the text of Scripture and its confluence with Confessional teaching. And finally, we will see what, if anything, Warfield can contribute to the current theological discussions regarding the originals.

Warfield and Immediate Inspiration

At the outset it will be important for us to have a working understanding of what the term "immediate" means. The etymology of the word helps us to understand the theology of the word. It is a word made of a verb (*mediates*) and a prefix (*in*) meaning "without anything in between" or "without anything in the middle." Thus, when we say that God works immediately we are not referring to the pace of God's work, rather we mean that He works without an intermediary or mediator. He works without anything in between.

But what does that mean? After all, the production of Scripture is a long process of varied divine activities featuring providence, grace and miracles all of which are to be taken into account when we speak of God's pure word.[5] So, why is an additional immediate operation of God which we call "inspiration" necessary? Perhaps the easy answer is that Scripture teaches immediate inspiration in passages like 2 Timothy 3:16 and 2 Peter 1:20–21. However, that still leaves the question open. For instance, if God providentially prepared the author of Scripture and endowed him with the intellectual breadth and acuteness required of him to pen the exact words and sentences and paragraphs that God wanted him to pen, then why is there a need for immediate inspiration?

Warfield offers a two-fold answer. First, according to the Princeton theologian, even if there was divine guidance—and there was—that guidance can only bring a man to the height of his own abilities. Or to put it another way, inspiration endows the books written under the Spirit's bearing "a quality which is truly superhuman; a trustworthiness, an authority, a searchingness, a profundity, a profitableness which is altogether Divine."[6] In other words, immediate inspiration endows Scripture with a divine rather than simply a human character.

Second, inspiration provides Scripture with a quality whereby this divine word is spoken "immediately to each reader's heart and conscience."[7] Thus, inspiration teaches that the Scriptures are not simply a heightened human awareness but God's utterance. But in addition, there is the immediacy of that word brought to bear upon the reader. In other words, the reader hears "the Divine voice itself speaking immediately in the Scriptural word to him."[8] Thus, coterminous with God's efficacious call and the Spirit's resurrecting activity, the regenerated person immediately hears the voice of God inherent in the inscripturated word.

However, theological immediacy is not always understood. Thus, when A.A. Hodge and B.B. Warfield collaborated on the now-famous article, "Inspiration," for *The Princeton Review* in 1881 they found themselves experiencing friendly fire. An editorial surfaced in *The Presbyterian* in which the writer confused providence and inspiration. Even worse, the editorial accused Hodge and Warfield of being guilty of teaching the confusion! Warfield straight away took pen in hand to say, "The article carefully defines inspiration to be, *not* 'providential leading.'"[9] Though providential leading is not absent the process, it is also not the immediate inspiration of the Confession and it is certainly not that of the Bible.

Warfield and the Preservation of Scripture

The careful reader of the Westminster Confession will notice that the preservation of Scripture is not described as "immediate." Instead the Confession speaks of God's "singular care and providence" in the preservation of Scripture.[10] What is more, "for the better preserving" of God's truth God determined "to commit the same wholly unto writing."[11] Thus, writing and copyists copying the writings was the means whereby God providentially preserved His truth.

At this point, let us pause and think about a distinction that Warfield is making. According to the Princeton theologian, the Bible is "immediately" inspired but it is "mediately" preserved. In other words, God chose immediacy when inspiring Scripture and mediacy in its preservation. To put it another way, God breathed His word out such that men were carried along by the Spirit in their writing but in the preservation and transmission of the text He chose scribes to copy His word from one generation to the next. God chose to preserve his word mediately.

With that in mind let us think together about what the mediate preservation of a text actually means. Whether you are dealing with Shakespeare's works or the Bible, the most basic distinction one can make in a discussion regarding the act of copying an original text is one that Warfield makes in two different ways and in two separate works. In his long-forgotten manual on textual criticism, *An Introduction to the Textual Criticism of the New Testament*, Warfield argues for the *ipsissima verba* or the "very words" of a particular work. According to Warfield, "the text of any work is concisely defined as the *ipsissima verba* of that work."[12]

However, soon after Warfield introduced an important distinction. There is a difference "between the text of a document and the text of a work."[13] Thus, a work can have but one text and "its *ipsissima verba* are its *ipsissima verba*, and there is nothing further to say about that."[14] Nevertheless, a work may exist in several copies and each copy has its own *ipsissima verba.* In other words, Warfield is making a distinction between the original ("a document") and the copies of the original ("a work").

Warfield makes this distinction even clearer in an article he wrote for *The Independent* in 1893 titled, "The Inerrancy of the Original Autographs." There he spoke of the *autographic codex* and the *autographic text.*[15] The *autographic codex*, for example, is the original piece of papyrus on which Paul wrote the letter to the Romans. However, multiple churches cannot all be in possession of one *autographic codex* or the original letter, so copies or *apographs* were made. These *apographs* are not the *autographic codex*, nor can they be, but they do contain the *autographic text*. Perhaps an example might help to clarify.

Warfield illustrates his point using Shakespeare's *Hamlet*. There is but one *autographic codex* of Shakespeare's *Hamlet*, that is, the one that Shakespeare actually penned, the *codex* that Shakespeare authored. However, since the printing press there are numerous *apographs* or copies of Shakespeare's *Hamlet*. What is more, the printing of many copies also has a way of producing many print errors. Thus, we may no longer have the *autographic codex* of *Hamlet* but through the study of the printed copies we are able to reconstruct, that is, eliminate scribal or printer errors and so have the *autographic text* of *Hamlet*.

In a way similar, God has preserved his truth. Yet, the issue of mediate providential preservation raises three crucial questions with which Warfield must deal. First and often asked is the question, do we have the *autographs*? This was the question Dr. Henry Van Dyke was asking in Warfield's day and it was this question to which Warfield felt obliged to answer in his article "The Inerrancy and the Original Autographs." Warfield wrote, "Thus, we have heard a vast deal, of late, of 'the first manuscripts of the Bible, which no living man has ever seen,' or 'Scriptures that have disappeared forever,' or 'original autographs which have vanished'" of which men claim to have no knowledge.[16] The liberals of Warfield's day argued that we do not have the *autographs* and many conservatives today might agree.

However, Warfield's response was simple. If it is the case that we do not possess the *autographs*, then we have no way of knowing what was actually in the *autograph* and we have no way of knowing if what we have in our Bibles today approximates what was in the *autograph*. Thus, we are to be pitied greatly among men. Not surprisingly, and in Warfield's quick-witted way, he rebukes the critics saying that we must stop speaking "as if it were the autographic *codex* and not the autographic *text* that is in question."[17] Warfield states the case even stronger in his 1894 article in *The Presbyterian Messenger.* He writes, "[it] is as truly heresy to affirm that the inerrant Bible has been lost to men as it is to declare that there never was an inerrant Bible."[18] Therefore, laments Warfield,

> If our controversial brethren could only disabuse their minds of the phantom of an autographic *codex*, which their excitement has raised (and which, apart from their excited vision 'no living man ever seen') they might possibly see with the Church that the genuine text of Scripture which is 'by the singular care and providence of God' still preserved to us, and might agree with the Church that it is to it alone that authority and trustworthiness and utter truthfulness are to be ascribed.[19]

Thus, according to Warfield, we do have the *autographic text* though we may not have the *codex*.

The second question has to do with the *apographs* or the copies; what distinguishes the Bible as we have it from the *autographic text*? According to Warfield, "Just scribes' corruptions and printers' errors; nothing else."[20] In Warfield's humorous way he writes, "What! Are we to believe that no man until our wonderful nineteenth century, ever had acumen enough to detect a printer's error or to realize that liability of hand-copied manuscripts to occasional corruption?"[21] What is more, "Everybody knows that no book was ever printed, much less hand-copied, into which some errors did not intrude in the process..."[22]

Thus, for Warfield, it was common sense to think that if we have at least two hand-copied texts it would be necessary to engage in the practice of textual criticism or textual reconstruction. To put it differently, mediate preservation does not free the church from her duty of studying the texts but rather requires her to diligently pursue the genuine text of Scripture and free it from apparent discrepancies caused by fallible scribes and printers.[23]

This raises our third question. If the Westminster Confession teaches that the Scriptures have been "by his singular care and providence, kept pure in all ages" then how may we speak of even apparent discrepancies? First, let us notice how seriously Warfield takes this assertion. He writes,

> It has not been uncommon to say, for example, that all that the Confession means is that the Scriptures have been, in the providence of God, kept 'measurably pure,' or, as it is otherwise phrased, 'adequately pure,' 'pure enough to serve the purposes for which they were given. The Confession, however, does not say 'measurably pure,' or 'adequately pure'; but 'pure' without qualification of limitation.[24]

Warfield could not be clearer. What is more, he affirms along with the Confession that the preservation of the Scriptures in their purity is of as vital importance to the Church as their original inspiration.[25]

The natural question is begging to be asked: How can we affirm their purity and talk about scribal and printer errors? According to Warfield this is a red herring. For the Princeton theologian, the Confession does assert the preservation of Scripture in absolute purity, "but it does not assert the "absolute purity" of the 'seventeenth century editions,' or of every copy, or of any copy of Scripture."[26] Such an assertion is not to be found in the text of the Confession. The Westminster divines "recognized the fallibilities of copyists and typesetters; and they looked for the pure text of Scripture not in one copy, but in all copies."[27] Warfield reminds his readers, "'What mistake is in one copy,' they declared through one of their number, 'is corrected in another.'"[28]

Warfield and Present-Day Discussions

When reading Warfield on the Confession one immediately gets the sense that this man knows the theology of the divines who sat in those venerable chairs which produced the fullest flower among Reformation symbols. Therefore, there are some important lessons we can draw from reading Warfield on the Confession. First, some Protestant Scholastics may well have imported the idea of extant copies into their understanding of the "originals" whereas Warfield would have only allowed for the *autograph*. Yet, Brash admits that "some of the Reformed orthodox did make the conceptual, heuristic distinction between the *autographa* and the *apographa*..." Thus, it is difficult to argue for a scholarly consensus that would argue decisively one way or another for a "confessional position" on the matter.

Second, Warfield reminds us to exercise great care when considering a practical univocity between the *autographa* and the *apographa*. Perhaps Warfield's strongest argument against such a position would be his assertion that the Westminster divines looked for the pure text of Scripture, not in one copy, but in all copies.[29] To argue otherwise argues against common sense. As Warfield contends, "Of course, every man of common sense from the beginning of the world has recognized the difference between the genuine text and the errors of transmission, and has attached his confidence to the former in rejection of the latter."[30] It is clear that despite some who ignored scribal and printer errors or minimized them, there were differences in the *apographs* that could not be denied. What is more, the Confession does not assert the absolute purity of any one copy. Rather the Word of God is to be sought in all of the copies. This is the position of the Confession.

Third, Warfield reminds us that the *autographa* is not logical trap, a rhetorical flourish or a conundrum designed to catch unsuspecting liberals. It is the *text* that the writers of Scripture penned while being born along by the Holy Spirit that we might have God's word. What is more, this infallible and inerrant text belongs to the Church today in the copies her posterity has kept safe and absolutely pure through God's providential preservation that we might hear the immediate voice of our God in the reading and hearing of them, for indeed, the Bible is the infallible, inerrant and authoritative word of God.

Notes

[1]Richard F. Brash, "*Ad Fontes!—The Concept of the 'Originals' of Scripture in Seventeenth-Century Reformed Orthodoxy*," *WTJ* 81 (2019): 123–39.

[2]Ibid.

[3]Richard A. Muller, *Post-Reformation Reformed Dogmatics: vol. 2, Holy Scripture: The Cognitive Foundation of Theology*, (Grand Rapids, MI: Baker Academic, 2003), 414.

[4]Ibid.

[5]Benjamin B. Warfield, *The Inspiration and Authority of the Bible* (Philadelphia: Presbyterian & Reformed, 1948), 156.

[6]Ibid., 158.

[7]Ibid.

[8]Ibid.

[9]Archibald A. Hodge and Benjamin B. Warfield, "Inspiration," ed. Roger R. Nicole (Grand Rapids: MI: Baker, 1979), 74.

[10]Westminster Confession of Faith 1.8.

[11]Ibid. 1.1.

[12]Warfield, Benjamin B., *An Introduction to the Textual Criticism of the New Testament* (London: Hodder and Stoughton, 1886), 1.

[13]Ibid., 2.

[14]Ibid., 2.

[15]Benjamin B. Warfield, *Selected Shorter Writings*, ed. John E. Meeter (Phillipsburg, NJ: P&R Publishing, 2005), 2.583.

[16]Ibid.

[17]Ibid.

[18]Ibid., 2.590.

[19]Ibid., 2.584.

[20]Ibid., 2.583.

[21]Ibid., 2.585.

[22]Ibid., 2.582.

[23]Ibid.

[24]Ibid., 2.591.

[25]Ibid., 2.590.

[26]Ibid., 2.592.

[27]Ibid.

[28]Ibid.

[29]Ibid., 2.592.

[30]Ibid. 2.585.

CHAPTER ELEVEN

Let Nations Come Rejoicing: The Impact of the Reformation on the Development of Psalters

Sharon L. Sampson

Introduction

One Lord's Day morning, John arrives late and quietly sits down in the last row of St. Peter's Cathedral in Geneva, Switzerland. He has heard much lately about reformation. As a priest who has given his life to the church, these changes are unsettling. He fears the instability they might bring, yet he has come to learn more. He thinks particularly about music, because in Geneva, the whole congregation sings from a newly composed psalter. Must the Psalms be translated into other languages and set to new music? Should the whole congregation sing? Are these questions important, and will these ideas continue to spread? He makes a mental note to seek answers from some of the men here in Geneva and turns his attention back to the service.

The Psalter in the Bible

The word "psalter" simply means, "a collection of psalms" or, more specifically, "the Book of Psalms of the Old Testament and Hebrew Scriptures." Many people would acknowledge familiarity with the Psalms, and Psalm 23 may well be one of the most familiar passages in the Bible, even to non-Christians. Few people would be familiar with the word psalter, despite its similarity in spelling. Even fewer people would view the Psalms as God's ordained book of praise, although both the Old and the New Testaments testify to them as the songbook for God's people throughout the millennia.

In the Old Testament, the Psalms are used for praise and worship. In one example, "King Hezekiah and his officials ordered the Levites to praise the LORD with the words of David and of Asaph the seer. So they sang praises with gladness and bowed their heads and worshipped" (2 Chron. 29:30, NIV). The "words of David and of Asaph" in this verse refer to the Psalms written by these two men.

In the New Testament, the Psalms are also used for the singing of praise. Following the Last Supper, Matthew 26:30 states, "And when they had sung a Psalme, they went out into the mount of Olives" (1599 Geneva Bible). While many more examples could be given, these are provided to establish that the singing of Psalms is supported by biblical example in both the Old and the New Testaments.

The Psalter in the Pre-Reformation Church

The Early Church Fathers also maintained the importance of the psalter in worship. Ted Postma cites the writings of Jerome, Chrysostom, Basil of Caesarea, and Athanasius which "give us a glimpse into the early church's awe of the Psalms and of the sufficiency of the Psalms."[1] He also notes, however: "The early church struggled to stay on a path that continued to favour the Psalms as songs for worship. Godly theologians, such as Augustine, and various church councils sought to contain and restrain the use of uninspired hymns. The Psalter was promoted and defended."[2]

During the Middle Ages, worship music changed with the arrival of Gregorian chants and other innovations, which led to "words drowned by words and professional confusion."[3] While the Psalms were still sung during this time,[4] increasingly, the congregation was less involved in doing so. The Council of

Constance in AD 1415 decreed, "If laymen are forbidden to preach and interpret the Scriptures, much more are they forbidden to sing publicly in the church."[5] Gradually, both the Scriptures and the opportunity to sing in worship were removed from the people of God.

The Psalter in England

As the Reformation dawned, however, both Word and worship returned to the people. Scripture and song moved into the vernacular, and the music of worship moved away from the patterns of the past. "The Christian Church, from the beginning, used the Book of Psalms as the basis of its praise. Until the Reformation, prose was the literary medium employed,"[6] since the Psalms would have been sung or chanted directly from the Greek or Latin texts. As Scripture was translated into the vernacular, however, prose gave way to metrical renderings of Psalm texts. This work took place all across Europe, but the efforts in England had far-reaching impact, both at home and abroad.

In England, this shift in medium was due, in large measure, to the influence of the popular ballad meter.[7] "In England it was fashionable to set most everything to rhyme—morality, history, philosophy, or literature."[8] The most prominent Englishman associated with this method is Thomas Sternhold, who initially wrote his versifications for private use. In summarizing Sternhold's technique, Weir says,

> He depended heavily upon Coverdale's prose for his basic structure, but he adapted freely to his own style, indulging his love for striking images and his penchant for alliteration, even to the point of occasional wild and erratic idiosyncrasies. The resulting paraphrases are eminently singable stanzas of ballad-like verse which bear a resemblance, but only a very general resemblance, to the prose from which they originated, and which carry the stamp of vigorous originality which Sternhold gave them.[9]

Sternhold's work became foundational for future psalters, which had varying emphases on the importance of poetry versus translation. This early tug-of-war was evident as Weir contrasts the work of others with Sternhold's more loose approach to translation. While acknowledging that other Reformers "encouraged more and more accurate translations of the Hebrew and the Greek parts of the Bible,"[10] he also notes that "any experienced translator of poetry and song lyric could have told him [Whittingham] and his helpers that striving for mere verbal accuracy works against the integrity of form and emotional tone in the new language."[11]

Nonetheless, the work continued, and the Marian exiles carried their Psalms with them as they fled to avoid persecution. They found temporary homes in places like Strasbourg and Geneva, where many Reformers were wrestling with issues of worship and song.

The Psalter in Strasbourg and Geneva

As Glass emphasizes, "Psalm singing was a consequence of the Reformation. It carried the devout believer straight into the presence of his Maker and Deliverer, without the intervention of priest or Creed, and enabled him to shout in triumph."[12] Why the Psalms? As previously noted, Psalm singing was established in the Bible as the means of worshiping God. Postma supports this idea by saying: "The importance of singing the Psalms was understood within the context of *sola scriptura* and the Spirit of using Scripture to bear witness of Him."[13] The Reformers understood the importance of singing the Psalms, and the task before them was twofold: they had to be translated into the vernacular, and they had to be set to music. In God's Providence, He provided many men with knowledge of Scripture and knowledge of music who were living in Strasbourg and Geneva at just the right time.

While the contributions of men like Martin Bucer, Clément Marot, and Theodore Beza could be extensively studied, one name rises above all others in connection with the Protestant

Reformation and his impact on psalmody. That man is John Calvin. As Patrick Millar expresses, "Calvin arrived in 1536 [in Geneva], and by his powerful mind and resolute spirit became the chief architect of the Reformed Church."[14] While his influence touched many areas of society and the church, his views on singing the Psalms and the development of the Genevan Psalter certainly impacted the church far beyond Strasbourg and Geneva.

Initially, Calvin's petitions to the Geneva council regarding the singing of Psalms did not appear to gain immediate traction; his time in Strasbourg beginning in 1538, however, provided a French congregation and an opportunity to pursue a psalter in French.[15] He was also exposed there to the work of Bucer and Marot.[16] Calvin eventually returned to Geneva and published his Ecclesiastical Ordinances in 1541, which emphasized the importance of singing. Calvin's concern for psalmody was rightly twofold, including both the text and the tunes used to sing those texts.

For Calvin, the text of the Psalms was to have primary importance. He says in the *Institutes*, "We must, however, carefully beware, lest our ears be more intent on the music than our minds on the spiritual means of the words" (III.XX.32).[17] This high priority given to the text is in contrast to Sternhold, and in keeping with Whittingham, both mentioned earlier. Speaking of the completed Genevan Psalter of 1562, Ker says,

> We can claim that no version has ever been made which adheres so closely to the Scripture. It proceeds on the principle of giving every thought in the original, and nothing more; and in this it has succeeded to an extent which is marvelous, and which can be realised only by one who has tested it through careful comparison. It meets with some stones of stumbling and suffers some dislocation of words, by adhering to the line laid down; but there is abundant compensation in the life and energy, the picturesqueness and colour, which it preserves by close contact with the old Hebrew soil.[18]

While maintaining the subordination of tune to text, Calvin was not opposed to music. In his "Letter to the Reader," he says,

> For a linnet, a Nightingale or a Popinjay will sing well, but it will be without understanding. But man's proper gift is to sing, knowing what he says; after understanding must follow the heart and the affection, something that can only happen when we have the song imprinted on our memory never to cease singing it.[19]

Unlike what had happened in England, Calvin made no effort to match Psalm texts with melodies associated with street songs. While various forms of the psalters appeared over a number of years, the completed Genevan Psalter of 1562 offered "a remarkable collection of 130 distinct meters and 110 different melodies written specifically for the Psalms."[20] Confirmation of the impact of this work came from the opposition, as the psalter's "reforming tendency is shown by its being promptly added to the List of Heretical Books forbidden by the Church of Rome."[21] A printer from Antwerp named Plantin had his psalter copies burned solely on the basis of the tunes, because they were Calvinist melodies.[22]

Thus, Calvin's approach to publishing a psalter for use by the congregation in worship gave first priority to accurate translation, and second place to the music which should undergird the text. Ross J. Miller in his work, *Calvin's Understanding of Psalm-Singing as a Means of Grace*, affirms the impact of both on the church. "The Psalm tunes as well as their texts came to have considerable authority in Reformed circles."[23]

The Psalter in Scotland

Following the death of Queen Mary in 1558, the exiles returned home, and Calvin's circle of influence expanded. By 1560, not a single English family was left in Geneva.[24] The religious climate was less favorable in Scotland than in England,[25] and the Scottish church focused on issues of doctrine and ecclesiastical polity rather than rushing to produce its own psalter, as England was doing.[26] Scotland was content with the Genevan Psalter.

This contentment is not surprising, since John Knox returned to Scotland with both affection for Geneva and firm conviction regarding worship. He called Geneva "the most perfect school of Christ that ever was on earth since the days of the Apostles,"[27] and Patrick notes:

> His [Calvin's] severe ideas were entirely to the mind of Knox, who accepted the view, among others, that nothing but what was biblical should be used in public worship. This meant that at a stroke the Reformed Church cut itself loose from the entire mass of Latin hymns and from the use of hymnody in general, and adopted the Psalms of the Old Testament as the sole medium of Church praise.[28]

Timothy Duguid affirms this Genevan influence upon Knox and others, which led the Scots to "view each Psalm as unique and thus deserving a unique tune."[29] In the 1564 edition of the psalter, Patrick notes the careful selection of music and the avoidance of secular style and folk song.[30] A clear connection is established between the work in Geneva and the first complete psalter published in Scotland; Young affirms this connection when he says that "it [Scottish Psalter] linked them [the Scottish people] to Geneva—the cradle of their Calvinistic theology, and refuge of their banished fellow-countrymen."[31]

In subsequent years, there were many psalters printed in both England and Scotland for various reasons, which are beyond the scope of this paper. Duguid pursues many of the details, which indicate real differences in psalm practice and psalter printing.[32] The Westminster Assembly, however, sought overall uniformity, and one of the goals was thus a unified psalter.

Like its dealings with other theological issues, the Assembly's work on a psalter was neither quickly nor easily accomplished. Similarly, it is neither quickly nor easily summarized.

Dr. Wayne Spear provides a brief summary of the result of the work for Scotland:

> The Assembly advocated the exclusive use of the biblical Psalms in praise. With this as the only approved manual for praise, the assembly produced a metrical Psalter containing only the 150 Psalms. The Assembly's Psalter was later revised in Scotland and became the Scottish Psalter of 1650.[33]

This final approved psalter was "to be the only Paraphrase of the Psalms of David to be sung in the Kirk of Scotland."[34]

It is important to note the changes to the music of the newly revised psalter. While, as previously discussed, Calvin's Genevan Psalter employed a wide variety of meter and tunes, the Scottish Psalter of 1650 did not continue in the same tradition. According to Patrick, the people needed simplicity in verse and music. While he admits this decision "banished from use the most splendid of the Reformation melodies," the Psalms in simple meter were easier to memorize. He adds that the common people had great affection for this psalter.[35]

While the Scottish Psalter of 1650 may have moved away from being as closely tied to Geneva in terms of variety of meter and tunes used, Roy Mohon notes, "The genuinely British Psalter now known as the Scottish Metrical Version is a reliable translation which has not taken liberties with the text to secure metrical arrangement. Linguistic, exegetical and theological considerations have not been ignored."[36] Lynas and Wright have said, "The Scottish Metrical Version...is really and essentially Scottish, built upon the foundations laid by John Knox and the Scottish Reformers."[37]

The Psalter in the Post-Reformation Church

The psalters of the English and Scottish churches had influence beyond their borders, especially in America in the Post-Reformation era. The immigrants brought their psalters, but the issues of text and tune and the impact of hymnody followed them.

One example of the ongoing issues of faithful texts and acceptable music comes from Rev. F. M. Foster, who laments: "Neither the majority of the people, nor the majority of the Synod [1765, Presbyterian Church in the United States of America], appear to have been burdened with scruples as to fidelity to the original tongue; but were satisfied with a 'free, easy and smooth' versification."[38] Regarding music, he says, "Usually those who want change argue for a version that will be popular and which admits of 'better music.'"[39] In addition to the on-going issues mentioned here, the reality of hymnody creeping into the church over the centuries is well-established. Anyone familiar with church music knows that most churches abandoned the Psalms, until few denominations remained which continued to sing them at all.

The Psalter of the Bible

Should the psalter still be used today? Despite the decline in Psalm singing, the biblical warrant remains. The Apostle Paul exhorts the church to "sing psalms, hymns and spiritual songs" (Col. 3:16, NIV). Dennis Prutow points out that the words "psalms," "hymns," and "spiritual songs" refer to compositions within the Book of Psalms, adding that Paul "thus outlines the content of congregational singing."[40] This admonition for the church to sing the Psalms has not changed with the passage of time.

Since ancient times, the Psalms have been God's book of praise for His people. Because the Psalter calls all nations to sing praise to God, Dr. C. J. Williams affirms the biblical mandate to translate the Psalms into every language. He points out that the structure of Hebrew poetry actually lends itself to such translation. The first responsibility is accuracy of translation from the original Hebrew. [41] Derek Kidner's views are similar:

> It is a striking fact that this type of poetry loses less than perhaps any other in the process of translation. In many literatures the appeal of a poem lies chiefly in

> verbal felicities and associations, or in metrical subtleties, which tend to fail of their effect even in a related language. But the poetry of the Psalms has a broad simplicity of rhythm and imagery which survives transplanting into almost any soil.[42]

Williams further adds that after providing a faithful translation, the church should seek advice on how to sing this text in the best possible way without changing it.[43]

Conclusion

Many years later, another John arrives early one Lord's Day morning and quietly sits down in the front row. He notes that the first Psalm selection is Psalm 67C, which is a call for the nations to come rejoicing. He reflects upon the Reformation and the men who strove to compile faithful psalters for the people to sing praise to God in their own languages. In particular, he thinks of John Calvin in Geneva and many in Scotland, who labored for faithful translations supported by music that the people could sing. As the congregation begins to arrive, he sees the announcement in the bulletin about the new psalter revision committee forming soon. He makes a mental note to remind his fellow presbyters that they must labor faithfully in the same way as these Reformers, and he turns his attention to the sermon he will preach today.

Notes

[1]Ted J. Postma, *Psalmody through the Ages: A Survey of the History of Psalmody* (Ontario: Free Reformed Publications, 2005), 33.

[2]Ibid., 43.

[3]Ibid., 47.

[4]Michael LeFebvre, *Singing the Songs of Jesus* (Fearn, Ross-Shire: Christian Focus Publications, 2010), 21.

[5]Postma, *Psalmody through the Ages*, 47.

[6]Millar Patrick, *Four Centuries of Scottish Psalmody* (London: Oxford University Press, 1949), xiii.

[7]Ibid., 12.

[8]Henry Alexander Glass, *The Story of the Psalters: A History of the Metrical Versions of Great Britain and America from 1549 to 1885* (London: K. Paul, Trench, 1888), 8–9.

[9]Richard B. Weir, "Thomas Sternhold and the Beginnings of English Metrical Psalmody" (PhD diss., New York University, 1974), 66.

[10]Weir, "Thomas Sternhold", 221–222.

[11]Ibid.

[12]Glass, *The Story of the Psalters*, 3.

[13]Postma, *Psalmody through the Ages*, 50.

[14]Patrick, *Four Centuries of Scottish Psalmody*, 9.

[15]Calvin, *The Piety of John Calvin*, 176.

[16]Postma, *Psalmody through the Ages*, 59.

[17]Ibid., 60.

[18]John Ker, *The Psalms in History and Biography* (Edinburgh: A. Elliot, 1886), 207–208.

[19]J. R. de la Haye, *The Impact of Metrical Psalmody upon Reformed Spirituality (with Special Reference to the Free Church of Scotland)*, (Lampeter: University of Wales, 1999), 69.

[20]Joel R. Beeke, and Anthony T. Selvaggio, eds., *Sing a New Song: Recovering Psalm Singing for the Twenty-First Century* (Grand Rapids: Reformation Heritage Books, 2010), 21.

[21]Glass, *The Story of the Psalters*, 6.

[22]Postma, *Psalmody through the Ages*, 67.

[23]Ibid.

[24]Patrick, *Four Centuries of Scottish Psalmody*, 35–36.

[25]Timothy Charles Duguid, "Sing a New Song: English and Scottish Metrical Psalmody from 1549–1640" (PhD diss., University of Edin-

burgh, 2011), 116.

[26]Ibid., 123.

[27]Bruce L. Shelley, *Church History in Plain Language* (Nashville, TN: Thomas Nelson, 1995), 260.

[28]Patrick, *Four Centuries of Scottish Psalmody*, 9.

[29]Duguid, *Sing a New Song*, 276.

[30]Patrick, *Four Centuries of Scottish Psalmody*, 50–51.

[31]Thomas Young, *The Metrical Psalms and Paraphrases: A Short Sketch of Their History with Biographical Notes of Their Authors* (London: C. Black, 1909), 50.

[32]Duguid, *Sing a New Song*, 247.

[33]Wayne R. Spear, *Faith of Our Fathers: A Commentary on the Westminster Confession of Faith* (Pittsburgh: Crown & Covenant Publications, 2006), 113.

[34]Philip Von Rohr Sauer, *English Metrical Psalms from 1600 to 1660: A Study in the Religious and Aesthetic Tendencies of that Period* (Freiburg i. Br.: Universitätsdruckerei Poppen & Ortmann, 1938), 48–49.

[35]Patrick, *Four Centuries of Scottish Psalmody*, 114–115.

[36]Roy Mohon, *Make His Praise Glorious: A Defense of the Book of Psalms as the God Given Manual of Praise, in Response to "The Praises of God in Psalms, Hymns & Spiritual Songs" by Dr. Kenneth Dix* (Eaglescliffe: WMP, [1999?]), 37.

[37]S. W. Lynas, and J. Renwick Wright, *The Scottish Metrical Psalter, Its Story and Influence: Addresses Delivered on the Three Hundredth Anniversary of its Authorization by the Church of Scotland on the 23rd November 1649* (Belfast: Graham & Heslip, 1949), 3.

[38]F. M. Foster. *History of the Decline and Extinction of Psalm-Singing in the Presbyterian Church* (New York: [n.p.], between 1900 and 1920?), 5.

[39]Ibid.

[40]Dennis J. Prutow, *Public Worship 101* (Pittsburgh: RPTS Press,

2013), 462–463.

[41]Clayton J. Williams, interview by author, Pittsburgh, January 8, 2015.

[42]Derek Kidner, *Psalms 1–72* (London: Inter-Varsity Press, 1973), 4.

[43]Williams, interview, January 8, 2015.

References

Beeke, Joel R., and Anthony T. Selvaggio, eds. *Sing a New Song: Recovering Psalm Singing for the Twenty-First Century.* Grand Rapids: Reformation Heritage Books, 2010.

Calvin, Jean. *The Piety of John Calvin: A Collection of His Spiritual Prose, Poems, and Hymns.* Translated and Edited by Ford Lewis Battles; Music Arranged by Stanley E. Tagg. Phillipsburg, NJ: P & R Publishing, 2009.

Church of Scotland. *The Liturgy of John Knox: Received by the Church of Scotland in 1564.* Glasgow: University Press, 1886.

Colligan, J. Hay. *The Geneva Service Book of 1555.* Manchester: R. Aikman & Son, 1931.

de la Haye, J. R. *The Impact of Metrical Psalmody upon Reformed Spirituality (with Special Reference to the Free Church of Scotland).* Lampeter: University of Wales, 1999.

Duguid, Timothy Charles. "Sing a New Song: English and Scottish Metrical Psalmody from 1549–1640, Volume 1." PhD diss., University of Edinburgh, 2011.

Foster, F. M. *History of the Decline and Extinction of Psalm-Singing in the Presbyterian Church.* New York: [n.p.], between 1900 and 1920?

Foster, J. M. *The Book of Psalms, the Divinely Appointed Manual of Praise in God's Worship for the Christian Family, the Christian Nation and the Christian Church.* Boston, MA: [n.p.], 1909.

Fullerton, Roy C. *Psalmody.* Pittsburgh, PA: Reformed Presbyterian Church of North America, Witness Committee, 1950?

Glass, Henry Alexander. *The Story of the Psalters: A History of the Metrical Versions of Great Britain and America from 1549 to 1885.* London: K. Paul, Trench, 1888.

Hall, David W. *The Legacy of John Calvin: His Influence on the Modern World*. Phillipsburg, NJ: P & R Publishing, 2008.

Ker, John. *The Psalms in History and Biography*. Edinburgh: A. Elliot, 1886.

Kidner, Derek. *Psalms 1–72*. London: Inter-Varsity Press, 1973.

Knox, John. *The Select Practical Writings of John Knox*. Carlisle, PA: Banner of Truth Trust, 2011.

_____. *Writings of the Rev. John Knox, Minister of God's Word in Scotland*. Philadelphia: Presbyterian Board of Publication, 1842.

LeFebvre, Michael. *Singing the Songs of Jesus*. Fearn, Ross-Shire: Christian Focus Publications, 2010.

Lynas, S. W., and J. Renwick Wright. *The Scottish Metrical Psalter, Its Story and Influence: Addresses Delivered on the Three Hundredth Anniversary of its Authorization by the Church of Scotland on the 23rd November 1649*. Belfast: Graham & Heslip, 1949.

McFarland, A. J. *The Psalms: God's Authorized Manual of Praise*. Sterling, KS: s.n., 1930?

McFeeters, J. C. *Psalms Versus Hymns: Report on Psalmody Adopted by the Synod of the Reformed Presbyterian Church, Philadelphia, PA, May 27, 1908*. Allegheny, PA: Published by the Committee on Testimony Bearing, 1908.

Miller, Ross James. "John Calvin and the Reformation of Church Music in the Sixteenth Century." PhD diss., Claremont Graduate School and University Center, 1971.

Mohon, Roy. *Make His Praise Glorious: A Defense of the Book of Psalms as the God Given Manual of Praise, in Response to "The Praises of God in Psalms, Hymns & Spiritual Songs" by Dr. Kenneth Dix*. Eaglescliffe: WMP, [1999?].

Murray, John, and William Young. *Minority Report of the Committee on Song in the Public Worship of God: Submitted to the Fourteenth General Assembly of the Orthodox Presbyterian Church*. [n.p.: n.p.], 1947.

Patrick, Millar. *Four Centuries of Scottish Psalmody*. London: Oxford University Press, 1949.

Postma, Ted. J. *Psalmody through the Ages: A Survey of the History of Psalmody*. Ontario: Free Reformed Publications, 2005.

Prutow, Dennis J. *Public Worship 101: An Introduction to the Biblical Theology of Worship, the Elements of Worship, Exclusive Psalmody, and A Cappella Psalmody*. Pittsburgh, PA: RPTS Press, 2013.

Renwick, A. M. *The Story of the Scottish Reformation*. Grand Rapids: Eerdmans, 1960.

Row, John. *The History of the Kirk of Scotland: from the Year 1558 to August 1637, With a Continuation to July 1639, by His Son*. Edinburgh: Wodrow Society, 1842.

Sauer, Philip Von Rohr. *English Metrical Psalms from 1600 to 1660: A Study in the Religious and Aesthetic Tendencies of that Period*. Freiburg i. Br.: Universitätsdruckerei Poppen & Ortmann, 1938.

Shelley, Bruce L. *Church History in Plain Language*. Nashville, TN: Thomas Nelson, 1995.

Slenk, Howard Jay. "The Way toward an English Genevan Psalter." *Reformed Journal* 12, no. 11 (1962): 16–18.

Spear, Wayne R. *Covenanted Uniformity in Religion: The Influence of the Scottish Commissioners on the Ecclesiology of the Westminster Assembly*. Grand Rapids: Reformation Heritage Books, 2013.

______. *Faith of Our Fathers: A Commentary on the Westminster Confession of Faith*. Pittsburgh, PA: Crown & Covenant Publications, 2006.

Van Deusen, Nancy, ed. *The Place of the Psalms in the Intellectual Culture of the Middle Ages*. Albany: State University of New York Press, 1999.

Weir, Richard B. *Survival at the Court of Henry VIII*; *Ballads, Broadsides, & Psalms*; and *How We Began to Sing Psalms*. Recorded at Reformed Presbyterian Theological Seminary, February 18–19, 1975. 3 cassettes.

______. "Thomas Sternhold and the Beginnings of English Metrical Psalmody." PhD diss., New York University, 1974.

Whitley, Elizabeth. *The Plain Mr. Knox*. Fearn, Ross-shire:

Christian Focus Publications, 2001.
Williamson, G. I. "The Scriptural Regulative Principle of Worship." In: *Papers Presented at the 1990 Psalmody Conference.* Flatrock, NC: Bonclarken Assembly, 1990.
Witvliet, John D. "The Spirituality of the Psalter: Metrical Psalms in Liturgy and Life in Calvin's Geneva." Calvin Theological Journal 32, no. 2 (1997): 273–297.
Wode Psalter Project Team. *Singing the Reformation: Celebrating Thomas Wode and His Partbooks, 1562–92.* Edinburgh: University of Edinburgh, 2011.
Wursten, Dick. "Clément Marot, the Learned Poet: Jewish Medieval Exegesis and the Genevan Psalter." *Reformation & Renaissance Review* 12, no. 1(2010): 71–107.
Young, Thomas. *The Metrical Psalms and Paraphrases: A Short Sketch of Their History, with Biographical Notes of Their Authors.* London: C. Black, 1909.

CHAPTER TWELVE

The Pastor as Public Intellectual

Robert M. Frazier

Introduction

The fourth century saw a rise in anti-Christian rhetoric in the Roman empire from notable scholars/intellectuals such as Julian the Apostate and Porphery. In the main, these critiques were rooted in the common pagan claim of the day that Christianity had no place in the public life of Rome, and that its worldview was largely responsible for the unraveling of Roman hegemony in the Mediterranean. In places the anti-Christian rhetoric was hostile. But the claim that Christianity had a no part to play in public life was nothing new in the Roman world. One can think of the criticisms of Tacitus and Pliny for evidence of the intellectual objections in Rome. A reason for these objections is located in the confession of Thomas in the Gospel of John that Jesus was "my Lord and my God." This went beyond a private endorsement of Jesus. The confession had public and political consequences; the title the Caesars increasingly gave to themselves in first century was this title and to assert another was a test to the public authority of the Roman state. In Acts, Herod is challenged by the public ministry of the apostles confronting oppression, and he has James the brother of John killed. There were ebbs and flows of Roman hostility against Christianity including the intellectual variety mentioned above. But there was a renewed animus following Constantine's edict and the dismantling of the Roman empire progressed in the fourth century leading to its invasion by the northern barbarians in 410 and 430 AD.

In the years between the invasions and in light of the intense blame place on Christianity for the demise of the Roman empire, St. Augustine of Hippo wrote his philosophical, theological, and historical apologetic entitled *the City of God*. In it, Augustine contends for two cities: the city of man driven by the *libido dominandi* (lust to dominate) and the city of God characterized by love of God and neighbor. These cities co-inhabit an earthly city (*civitas terrena*) and share a common place, a *publica*, a notion that Augustine explores in *the City of God*. The design of the earthly city is a peace that is peculiar to it that can be shared by pagans and Christians alike; Christians refer this peace to the eternal peace that is to be fulfilled in the restoration of all things while the pagans receive a temporal peace that makes this life good. In a *publica* properly ordered and sustained, the peace of this earthly city is possible albeit it is inhabited by sinners of all strips. Augustine claimed that the then current state of dismantling was the consequence of a disordered dominance of pervasive and perverse power that was its character and form in Christians and non-Christians alike. The *publica* and its good order had been sacrificed on the altar of vice.

The themes of this story might be all too familiar to some as we reflect on the pervasive influence of perverted power in our day. And it is easy for Christians to point the finger and indict unbelievers for this state of affairs in the public realm without personal reference and self-examination. In others, disturbingly both Christians and non-Christians, power is not discerned at all. In fact, in Augustine's view power is a multi-faceted notion much of which is exercised in subtle and covert fashions. In the fifth century as Augustine pens the treatise, the easy road of accusation is not the one he takes like so many Christian pontificators do in this day. No, Augustine calls Christians to bear the responsibility as well as unbelievers and avers complicity on the part of believers, overtly and covertly, by not regarding the public sphere rightly. In fact, Augustine claims that the pastors of the church, the watchmen, as he calls them, reminding the reader of Ezekiel's designation, are especially culpable for the current crisis, (pervasive perverting power covertly exercised), of the temporal peace of the city because they have failed to take up the burden of being what we will call a public intellectual.

In Book One of *the City of God* against the backdrop of comments about God's common grace, Augustine indicts the church and specifically her leaders for failing to discern the perversion of power in the public sphere and for avoiding their responsibilities in this regard. In chapter nine he writes:

> We tend culpably to evade our responsibility when we ought to instruct and admonish them sometimes even with sharp reproof and censure, either because the task is irksome, or because we are afraid of giving offense; or it may be that we shrink from incurring their enmity, for fear that they may hinder and harm us in worldly matters in respect of what we eagerly seek to attain or of what we weakly dread to lose.

The duties he describes, instructing and admonishing or we might say education and rhetoric, are public activities that, in common grace, establish the understanding of "things which may be rightly and innocently enjoyed by good men." He means by good men all persons possessing virtues, the sojourning believer and the unbeliever alike. He locates the chief difficulty behind the failure to engage the temporal peace as "self-interest" or pride, what C.S. Lewis calls the "anti-God attitude." In the public sphere, Christians, in not fulfilling their duty, fail to "love their neighbor as themselves" guarding their "reputations and safety" more than the arduous tasks of instruction, refutation, and persuasion of intellectual errors.

Augustine ends this amazing section by referencing the prophet Ezekiel and his rebuke of the "watchmen" (i.e. prophets) who failed in their public responsibilities mentioned above. Augustine lays the charge that they ignored these duties because of "worldly advantages," things to which they are unduly attached. They ought to be governed by disinterested devotion offered to God. This devotion leads to calling people to repentance and kingdom living, but also to engagement in the public sphere where a temporal peace is possible.

Given the emphasis Augustine places on the *publica* and the duties he attaches to clerics in this regard, we might say that Augustine, as a pastor to pastors, identifies public intellectual responsibilities for the pastor. For Augustine and for a long tradition of the church, the pastor was regarded as a public intellectual and theologian. This might seem strange in the 20th and 21st centuries. Historically, there are reasons why this is the case. But in this short essay we cannot explore these. In this chapter, I want to spell out a theological framework for understanding the pastor as public intellectual against this Augustinian background. In doing so, I will avoid adopting the dominant conceptions of public intellectual in the literature: organic, pragmatic, or liberal. Although I may draw some insights from these perspectives, I contend that Scripture, theological traditions, and Christian philosophical reflection provide the language one needs to develop the notion of the pastor as public intellectual.

I would like to suggest one final introductory note before I develop a notion of pastor as public intellectual. Each of the dominant conceptions of the public intellectual mentioned above are rooted in a position taken by the German philosopher, Immanuel Kant. His 1784 article "What is Enlightenment?" Kant redefines the place a pastor has in the public realm. In the public realm, the cleric may not participate as a cleric per se; he must set aside his attachment to a theological tradition and, like all those who participate in the public space, must function as an unencumbered rational agent. Let me briefly explore the contours of this argument.

Kant calls for an enlightenment that liberates humans and their institutions from what he calls their "self-incurred immaturity." He suggests that mere obedience without questioning is like one who is a member of a herd of cattle and this is the lot that humans basically have chosen for themselves, especially the religious. To experience liberty, humans must make use of reason and argumentation that anyone in the reading (educated) public can access. Kant says of this that for enlightenment to transpire, one must be empowered to make "the public use of reason in all matters." Consequently, religion, Scripture, and theological traditions must defer to the demands of public reason. Kant's public reason perspective is dominant in discussions of what constitutes the public realm in thinkers such as John Rawls and Richard Rorty; there must be no attachment to grand narratives, theological or otherwise, in the public space.

So, what place might the clergy play in a culture where the public space is defined by public reason and enlightenment? Kant spends much of the essay concerned with the location of religion in an enlightened age. He does so because "religious immaturity is the most pernicious and dishonorable of all." Kant warns of a "society of clergymen" or a "venerable presbytery" because of the oath they take to a "certain unalterable set of doctrines, in order to secure for all time a constant guardianship over each of its members." Further, this clerical commitment is a "crime against humanity, whose destiny lies in… progress." In Kant's view, the pastor ought to function with both public and private reason. Private reason is employed by the pastor as he fulfills his clerical duties like preaching and catechizing. Public reason lays aside those positions and duties associated with the private—he claims that as an educated person, the pastor could not possibly rationally believe those doctrines and realizes that they will change over time—and engages as an intellectual in reassessing those dogmas he has announced to the faithful. As an intellectual, the pastor extracts from the traditions those things that might be practically valuable for fulfilling one's moral obligations, but nothing more. Satisfying one's moral obligations, which he spells out in his various writings on ethics, is at the core of how one lives in a just public space. Although the cleric is a public intellectual in evaluating and arguing for justice and moral goodness, he functions in the private realm, that is the ecclesiastical realm, in catechizing and worship while he acknowledges that these structures are rationally indefensible to public reason. Hence, the cleric cannot function in the public realm qua pastor informed by the tradition and authority of church or Scripture.

The impact of Kant's views has been great, overtly and tacitly. It helped produce an intellectual skittishness among clerics that led to a retreat from the public realm (a sharp public/private divide), or a retreat to anti-intellectualism, or a turn to the pastor as administrator, or an elevation of the pastor-as-technocrat as we see so often today, or the pastor-as-therapist, or a host of other emphases that accept the definition, at least tacitly, given by Kant. The result in that public space for Christians and clerics is disembedded from the Triune God and this is captured by Václav Havel and Aleksandr Solhzenitsyn in the following quotes:

> During those centuries the orthodox faith became part of the very patterns of thought and the personality of our people, the forms of daily life, the work calendar, the priorities in every undertaking, the organization of the week and of the year. Faith was the shaping and unifying force of the nation. (Solhzenitsyn, The Templeton lecture, 1983)

> We have so hopelessly ceded our humanity that for the modest handouts of today we are ready to surrender up all principles, our soul, all the labors of our ancestors, all the prospects of our descendants—anything to avoid disrupting our meager existence. We have lost our strength, our pride, our passion. We do not even fear a common nuclear death, (perhaps we will hide in some crevice) but fear only to take a civic stance. (Solhzenitsyn, "Live Not by Lies")

> The loss of this respect (for attachment to God) always leads to loss of respect for everything else-from the laws people have made for themselves, to the lives of their neighbors and of our living planet. The relativization of all moral norms, the crisis of authority, the reduction of life to the pursuit of immediate material gain without regard for its general consequences- the very things Western democracy is most criticized for-do not originate in democracy but in that which modern man has lost: his transcendental anchor, and along with it the only genuine source of his responsibility and self-respect. (Havel, "Forgetting We Are Not God")

In light of these introductory comments, I would like to offer a model of the pastor as public intellectual that addresses the current plight of clerics in the public space and works for the common good. Over against the alternative models of what constitutes being a pastor listed above (therapist, technocrat, and administrator) and against the pastor functioning in lock-step with a political party or leader to the compromise of the integrity of the pastor as mediator of God's redemptive activity, I wish to address three issues that provide such an alternative. If the current conception of the public rooted in the Kantian idea of public reason is found wanting, then we might offer another way of thinking about the public that does not discount reason but treats reason within the boundaries of philosophical and theological thought. In my account, Augustine offers such a position and this account requires practical reason, *phronesis*, for its application within its realm. I will call this the Augustinian framework of the public. Further, we want to offer a different grounding and eschatology than the one offered by Kant. His foundation is in unencumbered reason and an eschatology of steady progress toward enlightenment. I, along with a host of others, have argued against the idea that humans can be such reasoners in my book entitled *Responsible Belief*. The alternative grounding I suggest is rooted in the common grace covenant and its continued providential superintendence by God. This foundation is explicitly disclosed in the Noahic renewal of the creation covenant and is binding for all human cities and nations. So, I offer an Augustinian framework rooted in the biblical and theological tradition of the Noahic common grace covenant that serves the common good. But I contend for one final aspect of this model. I need to address the kind of public intellectual that is the cleric. The function of the pastor as public intellectual is located in the place that the prophets, in the Old and New Testaments, play as covenant mediators (Noahic common grace for the common good foundation) and as educators, rhetoricians, and logicians in the public space.

The Framework: Publicness in St. Augustine

Augustine's notion of a public develops throughout *City of God* culminating in a well-known passage found in Book XIX, chapter 24, a counter-claim to the idea of publicness in Cicero. But to view this passage without considering the passages that lead up to Augustine's discussion of Cicero, provides, in my view, a truncated conception of the public. His more robust notion of the public comes about from looking at passages up to and beyond Book XIX, ones in which the notion of the *societas* or *civitas* are discussed and in considering, albeit briefly, some other passages in which the components of the public life are asserted.

The Peregrinatio

Augustine is clear about identifying the current situation of the people of God as peregrination. From the opening pages of the treatise to its end, God's people are identified as sojourners and aliens with resident responsibilities in this *saeculum*.[1] In the preface, Book I, Augustine promises to consider the status of the member of the city of God as "stranger among the ungodly"[2] during this age. In the last book of *the City of God*, Augustine contends that in accepting this pilgrim status, "the city of Christ (does not) fight against its godless persecutors for temporal salvation" even though many would have supported them doing so.[3] To explore this theme I will cite several of the peregrination references found in *the City of God* that especially apply to the question of the public realm.

In Book I, chapter 29 Augustine contends that God's people "enjoy their earthly blessings in the manner of pilgrims, and they are not attached to them, while these earthly misfortunes serve for testing and correction."[4] In Book V, chapter 18 Augustine extols the Romans whose virtues have made it easier for pilgrims to walk toward its "own country." As for Christians, they should live with a "quality of the citizens of God's City during their earthly pilgrimage. They must live a life according to the spirit and not according to the flesh, that is they must live by God's standards, not man's."[5] The earthly city falls prey to the standards of the flesh and, hence, the people of God must be on constant guard against this perversity. In this sojourn, the virtue of humility is especially prized. Augustine avers, "that is why humility is highly prized in the City of God and especially enjoined on the City of God during its pilgrimage in this world."[6] The Christian is sustained by hope which is the "longing for this reward (eternal peace)" and because of which Christians must live "devout lives, guided by faith, during this troublesome pilgrimage."[7] Consequently in this age, the people of God are identified as sojourners who enjoy earthly blessings common to all, model humility and godliness in the hope of eternal felicity and who appreciate the temporal, although imperfect, virtues of the unbelievers in their midst who preserve something of a proper temporal order.

The Intermingling of the Cities

In this age (*saeculum*) the City of God and the City of Man are intermingled and interwoven and only in the *eschaton* will they be severed. Until the *eschaton* God's elect are sojourners and pilgrims in intermingled public squares and whose lives are benefited when the public realm is sustained by a proper exercise of power, or proper authority as one might say. Augustine discusses and uses the point of peregrination (*peregrinus*) throughout *the*

City of God to foster an understanding of the believers' plight but also to make them aware of their responsibilities in this realm. As such, it provides the background to his discussion of the shared space in the public realm of the two cities.

The peregrinated people of God are interwoven with unbelievers in this age. Interestingly, there are several places in *the City of God* where this idea of intermingling occurs. I will mention three because Augustine sets his task of refuting the charges against Christendom in the context of these. The first is found at the end of Book I, a passage that frames Augustine contention about the progress of power and the complicity of the church in that progress. Augustine suggests that God has permitted God's enemies to survive the invasion of Rome for God's own purposes. One purpose might be evangelism. The "pilgrim City of Christ the King" must "bear in mind that among these very enemies are hidden her future citizens" and that "she must bear hostility"[8] until "she finds them confessing the faith."[9] It is on account of these "predestined friends" that "those two cities are interwoven and intermixed in this era (*saeculo*) and await separation at the last judgment."[10] One might claim that evangelism, in the long run, is enhanced by the proper execution of a public in which believers acknowledge the interconnectedness of the two cities. This suggests that there is an *ordo* (order) that is proper to the public space although vitiated by sin. Augustine continues that understanding the "origin, development and end of those two cities," albeit intermixed, facilitates the purposes of evangelism and proper order ensuring that "the glory of God" will shine "brightly."[11]

In books XV through XVIII Augustine provides a biblical and historical account of the origin and development of the two cities. He ends Book XVIIII with another clue to understanding the purposes of God in permitting the interweaving of the cities. He has written about the "mortal condition" of the two cities "which are mingled together from the beginning to the end of their history."[12] Augustine writes of this intermingling as a time when "both cities alike enjoy the good things, (of the temporal order), or are afflicted with the adversities of this temporal state, but with a different faith, a different expectation, a different love, until they are separated by the final judgment, and each receives her own end, of which there is no end."[13] Notice a few things about this series of quotes. First, the intermingled public realm is terminal; it has a mortal condition. Its eschatology is vapid. Also, Augustine points out that the intermingled public enjoys good things in the temporal realm and is afflicted in it as well. The enjoyment of temporal goods is a feature of the shared public existence of the two cities. Finally, notice the priority given to perspectivalism in the passage; each group holds a different perspective on the significance and meaning of the enjoyment and affliction of the age and this contributes to the eschatological execution of justice and the permanent state of the existence of each.

At the end of Book XVIII Augustine claims that in Book XIX he will explore the ends of both cities. The City of God has as its end eternal felicity, eternal peace. The City of Man has as its end eternal hostility and quarrelsomeness. In the interim of intermixedness, there is a temporal condition of peace which frames the proper order of the public realm. This is variously identified as the "earthly peace," temporal peace," or "domestic peace." This temporal peace is crucial to the public realm; it is hindered and devastated when perverse power (*libido dominandi*) is pervasive in a society. About this earthly peace Augustine writes, "Meanwhile, however, it is important for us also that this people should possess this peace in this life, since so long as the two cities are intermingled we also make use of the peace of Babylon, although the People of God is by faith set free from Babylon, so that in the meantime they are only pilgrims in the midst of her."[14] The pilgrim people of God take action to procure this peace because "in her peace is your peace- meaning, of course, the temporal peace of the meantime, is shared by good and bad alike."[15] Temporal peace is of common interest to both cities in this realm and the pilgrim citizens of God take certain actions to foster its development; temporal peace has a utilitarian purpose for the pilgrim, it enhances their pursuit of eternal peace with God. These three (evangelism, enjoyment of the temporal goods and values of this realm of existence, and temporal peace) are cited as reasons for the mingling of the pilgrims with unbelievers.

Publica

I will now explore the common location of the intermingled cities discussed earlier. Pilgrims and unbelievers together occupy this realm and Augustine laboringly articulates how this location is to be understood. Let us proceed to consider the ways in which Augustine uses *civitas* and *publica* in defining this realm.

Augustine's first stab at defining publicness is found in Book I, chapter 15. He discusses Marcus Regulus as a model of the virtuous spirit, one which should give the pilgrim an incentive to pursue "true virtue" which can bring happiness (felicity) to a community. He continues, "For the source of a community's fellowship is no different from that of one man, since a community is simply a united multitude of individuals."[16] The word translated united is the word *concors*. *Concors* entails like-mindedness, oneness of thought, so to speak. Augustine's contention is that a public is single-minded about virtue being its unifying element. Without virtue, even of an incomplete and limited variety, there will be no public. With virtue, publicness ensues. Notice in the passage that Regulus is identified as virtuous and whose example encourages in the pilgrim the awareness of the value of virtue for this age. The common life of the public rests on the fellowship of virtue, friendships of virtue, and its enhancement in the public realm. According to Augustine, Rome, in the days of its success, valued virtue which, in turn, fostered *concors*.

Further, Augustine identifies a public as a "fellowship of men" who have some kind of common bond.[17] On page 762 he describes this bond as something that derives from a common nature, i.e. humankind's shared features. In the second passage, Augustine suggests that this common fellowship can be distorted by people who look for "worldly advantages" over others, which leads to a dividedness in society. Together these passages assert that publicness be viewed as a bond or union that occurs because humans share similar features. Augustine believed that humans were created social beings and this drives them into publics. This fellowship in common bond is a commonwealth. In Book V, chapter 15, virtuous Roman rulers are commended for not taking into "account their own material interests compared with the common good, that is the commonwealth and the public purse."[18] The rightly functioning public is concerned to "promote the wellbeing of the common people."[19] The public is a commonwealth sustained by virtue with pilgrims and unbelievers as its inhabitants emergent from a shared social nature.

Additionally, the public in Augustine is associated with a number of factors derived from a general conception of justice. I have three things in mind. Augustine indicates in Book XIX, chapter 4, in a discussion of the cardinal virtues, that justice is commonly understood as rendering to everyone his due. He writes that "the function of justice is to assign each his due; and hence there is established in man himself a certain just order of nature..."[20] I take this to mean that humans possess, naturally, an idea of justice and this idea corresponds to the nature of things.[21] Justice is a mediating virtue in the public realm such that without justice, the publicness of shared life evaporates. A second claim made by Augustine about a general conception of justice in the public realm is his concern for equality. In Book XIX, chapter 12, he writes, "How much more strongly is a human drawn by the laws of his nature, so to speak, to enter upon a fellowship with all his fellow-men and to keep peace with them, as far as lies in him."[22] Interestingly, this is found in a section in which Augustine is discussing the strong bond of family. The "how much more strongly" refers to the public over against the family structure. The reason he supplies for this strength is that this "fellowship," so natural to human life, is a "fellowship of equality under God."[23] The family has a hierarchical structure whereas the public requires a fellowship of equals. He calls this fellowship of equality the right order of things among them.[24]

One final observation is necessary about justice and publicness. Augustine believed that earthly peace (which was mentioned earlier in the paper) to be achieved required priority be given to establishing laws to maintain that peace. He claims that "the earthly city, whose life is not based on faith, aims at an earthly peace, and it limits the harmonious agreement of citizens concerning the giving and obeying of orders to the establishment of a kind of compromise between humans wills about the things relevant to mortal life."[25] The intermingled earthly city is not based on faith but on a compromise of wills about what is important for temporal existence. The public is the place in which that compromise embedded in laws is forged. Although Augustine is clear that the Heavenly city lives on the basis of faith in an eternal peace secured by the redemptive act of Christ and applied by the Holy Spirit to the believer, the pilgrim does not "hesitate to obey the laws of the earthly city by which those things which are designed for the support of this mortal life are regulated; and the purpose of this obedience is that, since this mortal condition is shared by both cities, a harmony may be preserved between them in things relevant to this condition."[26] The harmony about which Augustine speaks is embodied in laws designed to hold in check human wills by the standard of justice and equality. Further this harmony permits the Heavenly City, on pilgrimage in this world, to "call out citizens from all nations and takes no account of customs, laws and institutions, by which the earthly peace is achieved and preserved" and supports and defends these as long as they are not detrimental to "true religion and piety."[27]

The field of justice spoken of above cannot be construed, though, as the absolute condition of the public. Justice, in modern terms, is a necessary condition, but not a sufficient one. One can see this in his examination of Scipio's (Cicero's) view of the commonwealth. Scipio defines a commonwealth on the basis of justice. A public is united by a common sense of "justice" and cannot exist without it. Augustine contends that the absolute sense of justice advanced by Scipio fails to be met in this age because it is hindered in rendering to God what God is due, and because of the disruption of the *ordo naturalis* vitiated by sin. If Scipio's definition is correct and following the requirement to render to God His due coupled with following the natural order has been unmistakably not met, Augustine concludes, that on Scipio's account, there has never been a commonwealth.[28] He avers, "But where this justice does not exist, there is certainly no 'association of men united by a common sense of right and by a community of interest'. Therefore, there is no commonwealth; for where there is no 'people,' there is no weal of the people."[29]

Thus far we might claim that Augustine's view of the public entails that it is a common fellowship between compromising wills of pilgrims and unbelievers who manifest virtuous qualities in the context of partial justice, equality, and law directed toward a temporal peace. Temporal peace is supported by goods, customs and institutions understood through the conditions of the public realm. Authority mediates the public common fellowship for the welfare of all people within it, even the common lot of humans.

Augustine provides one final condition for a public. This is found in the passage alluded to earlier from chapter 24 of Book XIX. On finds in it the definition he offers to replace the idealism and optimism of Cicero. It is my view that this definition clarifies and completes the discussion that has ensued thus far about the public in the City of God. Augustine contends that a "people is the association of a multitude of rational beings united by a common agreement on the objects of their love."[30] Consistent with the rest of the book, Augustine finally draws attention to the organizing and motivating presence of love in forming a public. Notice that all agents in the public equally are considered rational and capable of discerning what they collectively love. It is important to note that Augustine does not use the vocabulary of love employed at earlier points in the essay. He does not speak of *caritas,* or *amor*, or even *cupitas*. He uses the word *diligo*, which means to prize or esteem something or to appreciate the value of something as a good. It seems, then, that Augustine views the public space as the realm in which the collective love of a people directed toward the proper value of things (creational value) provides a location for a temporal, earthly peace to be realized by rational creatures, sojourners and unbelievers alike, who order shared goods, customs and institutions by virtue and the constraints of partial justice, the *ordo iustilas.*

Augustine captures clearly what he has in mind in Book XIX, chapter 13 of *the City of God.* He provides a description of the goods of public life which ought to be shared by all in society. These provide for the temporal peace that results from the aspects of the public life discussed earlier. I will quote the passage in its entirety to get a clear picture of what Augustine has in mind.

> God then, created all things in supreme wisdom and ordered them in perfect justice; and in establishing the mortal race of mankind as the greatest ornament of earthly things, he has given to mankind certain good things suitable to this life. These are: temporal peace, in proportion to the short span of a mortal life-the peace that consists in bodily health and soundness, and in fellowship with one's kind; and everything necessary to safeguard or recover this peace- those things which are appropriate and accessible to our senses: light, speech, air to breathe, water to drink, and whatever is suitable for the feeding and clothing of the body, for the care of the body and the adornment of the person. All this is granted under the most equitable condition: that every person who uses aright such goods, goods designed to serve peace of mortal men, shall receive goods of a greater kind.

Notice some of the natural goods that he has in mind: health, shelter, clothing, education, equitable laws that serve the common good, food, mental health. Further, the accumulation of these natural goods by a few impedes the public peace. The social bond of all humans ought to make them generous and hospitable particularly to the stranger, the poor, the widow, and outcast who are deprived of these goods. Financial control and dominance for Augustine is one of the forms in which subtle power manifests itself and vitiates God's shalomic design. He locates this vitiation in the pursuit of private, individual interest over against the interest of the whole and societies rooted in self-interest foster this vitiation. Augustine claimed rightly that humans are communal "by nature, but quarrelsome by perversion." The cleric as public intellectual ought to guard against such things.

This public space requires, because of humankind's postlapsarian condition and its tendency to vitiation God's shalomic design the presence of some form of coercive power that guards it, restrains sin, and promotes the public good. So government is a part of that good order to promote and preserve the temporal peace that witnesses to the proper love of natural goods. One wonders whether there is a surer foundation that promotes such temporal peace and proper love. My claim is that the Noahic common grace covenant provides such a foundation and is binding on all humans, all descendants of Noah.

The Foundation of the Public: The Noahic Common Grace Covenant.

In light of the above, it seems that a different foundation is necessary for a public that encourages the pastor to function as an intellectual in that realm. We need a replacement for reason as the foundation of the public square. I want to suggest that the covenant renewal enactment in Genesis 8 and 9 between God and Noah and his descendants is a perpetually binding covenant on humankind and supplies such a foundation. I am not alone in this assertion, but join the company of Old Testament scholars who do, like Meredith Kline, Jeffrey Niehaus, W.J. Dumbrell, and Craig Bartholomew. Theologians such as Mike Williams, Michael Horton, Gordon Spykman, and David VanDrunen concur. For example, VanDrunen writes, "What I have called the "common kingdom" is formally established in the covenant that God makes with Noah in Genesis 8:20–9:17. By this covenant God ordains that there be a stable natural order until the end of the world. All living creatures will live within this order, and the entire human race will engage in a variety of cultural activities." (*Living in God's Two Kingdoms*, p. 79) Kline, Niehaus, Bartholomew, and Dumbrell rightly see Genesis 8 and 9 as the renewing of the covenant that God made with humans at creation; it is the perpetual reestablishment of this covenant (except for the feature of the Sabbath) and is binding on all who will come to exist. In *The Drama of Scripture*, Bartholomew and Goheen (p.51) argue "In Genesis 9 God is renewing his covenant in creation and doing so with Noah. The evidence for this relates to the way in which Genesis 9 depicts Noah as the second Adam." Spykman considers this enduring covenant as one side of a coin, so to speak, with the idea of the kingdom as its other. The covenant enacts a relationship and the kingdom lives it out in his view. And as Kline contends in *Kingdom Prologue*, the Noahic covenant entails a common grace order that will continue until the *eschaton* fully arrives. I intend to explore the contours of this creation covenant renewal with the hope of fleshing out its implications for a justification of the Augustinian conception of the public described above.

Although there are a variety of positions on what constitutes common grace, I will try to be as generic as possible in describing its reality. Williams defines common grace as "God's continuing providential care over human life in the world" (Williams p. 91). Kline expands this a bit by claiming that the principle of common grace is "a grace that provides benefits to just and unjust and blesses all of creation in the process" and this informs "the divine government of the postlapsarian world" (Kline, p. 154). I take Kline to be right about this.

In the book, *Kingdom Prologue: Genesis Foundations for a Covenantal Worldview*, Kline first explores the development of the notion of common grace in the early chapters of Genesis. We begin with a look at chapter 3. The context is the fall and the severing of the covenant of creation between God and His images bearers. It is important to note that the account of the fall is one in which a foreign wisdom is offered to replace the foundation of wisdom located in God's command and purposes given to Adam and Eve. The serpent was an image and symbol for wisdom in the ancient world and so it is no accident that Satan takes this form. The contest of wisdom perspectives is the backdrop of the fall and for the rest of human history and directly bears on the debate concerning the essence of a public; one must choose whose wisdom to follow and the perspective adopted becomes a map guiding the condition of justice, virtue, and liberty. In the fall Adam and Eve adopt, believe you may say, an alternative account of their existence apart from God's. As interpretive creatures, their bearings in life depended upon the assent they would give to the accounts of wisdom they encountered. In this context they chose to suppress the truth and in so choosing, deception became a guiding framework and struggle for humanity. Competing wisdoms and the propensity toward deception became the lot of humankind, then and now. But God intervenes with the promise of redemption in Genesis 3:15ff and sets the history of fulfilling this promise in the context of a common grace order.

In the Genesis 3:15–19 account of God's response to Adam and Eve, there are a number of things worth noting. Not only is there the promise of redemption referred to above, but, according to Kline, there is a common curse that presumes a common blessing context for its realization. Notice the continuation of the institutions of the original creation covenant in these verses each bearing the structural integrity of the creation order. The common curse in verse 16 whether directed to the man or woman presumes the blessing of marriage will remain, albeit filled with difficulty. Although birthing may be difficult, birthing continues allowing the blessings of fruitful fulfillment for humans. Man and woman may have to guard against the power and manipulative tendencies they now possess toward one another and yet they are still called to leave and cleave to the other. These common blessings remain in the framework of a common grace universe in which sin is restrained through God's providential order of intervention. In verse 17–19, the blessing of being a laborer in God's creation continues, although now fraught with the struggles associated with the curse. The creation covenantal call to make and nourish continues in the world sustained by common grace. If not, humans would be unable to harvest anything. The common curse is framed by common blessing, the result of God's common grace continuation of His ordered creation. Humans making, tending, creating, and procreating, i.e. doing the things they were constituted to do, is the lot of man even in his postlapsarian state because common grace provides the environment for their flourishing in the public sphere.

Further, I find it interesting to consider Genesis 4 in light of common grace provisions. Cain is driven from the presence of his family because of his murderous act against his brother Abel (he was his brother's keeper after all, just like we are as social creatures by nature), and finds himself the recipient of God's common grace (again not redemptive grace) in building a city in which the conditions of just governance can occur and one in which cultural flourishing will take place. The structure of the city demands social welfare for all, justice, shelter, and protection. Ironically, the very thing that Cain denies his brother is the gift of kindness God extends to him as His just Judge. The requirements for marriage persist although Cain's descendent Lamech usurps power, perverting both marriage and proper just governance in his *polis*. These are obligations he bears as leader of the city, but self-deceptive self-interest is the wisdom he adopts, thus, the city moves away from its proper structure and its institutions are badly distorted. Notice that even though this occurs, the blessings of humankind's call to build culture finds fulfillment in Lamech's sons: Jabal the shepherd, Jubal the musician, and Tubal-Cain the smithy. In these two accounts, in common grace marriage persists, government continues, goods are loved, justice is enacted, and the productive and interpretive components of human life are manifested. Humans are still bound by the stipulations of the creation covenant although in their fallen state, and it is common grace that allows them to gain any blessing and avert complete annihilation. Even in the flood complete annihilation is averted because God's grace saves a family from the destruction of the curse, the deserved outcome for the thoroughness of sin, power, and evil in human life.

The common grace framework of God's providential care is particularly evident in the renewal of the creation covenant with Noah. This account begins after the flood in Genesis 8:20 and continues to chapter 9:17. There are three clear sections in the account: 8:20–22, common grace will preserve the beauty of the created order in the face of the sinfulness of humankind; 9:1–7, the renewal of the creation order and human responsibility for it; and 9:8–17, the covenant extends to all that is, making explicit the conditions of the creation covenant to the world order. In response to the pleasing aroma of things that God made good in the sacrifice offered by doxological man (worship of some kind drives human existence), God declares that humankind's perpetual sinfulness will not override His grace in sustaining and keeping the creation. It and its order will endure until it is no more. This is the promise given by the Sovereign Lord. Notice again the eschatological ordering of the promise; until the present order is replaced by the new heavens and new earth, the yearning creation has for itself expressed in its groaning is assured of resolve which is accomplished through the reconciliation of Jesus in His death and resurrection. (Romans 8, Revelation 21, and Colossians 1.) This groaning is evidence of the centrality of hope as the confident assurance of the promise of a reliable and trustworthy agent which characterizes proper existence in the current state of the yet and not yet. The creation focus of Genesis 1 is pronounced again; it is good, intrinsically so, declares the God who made it. Its goodness will persist; it is as if God is declaring in grace, "I promise to sustain this goodness." The beauty of its substance will give record of and disclose the beauty and perfection of the one who made it. This covenantal arrangement is the backdrop of the great Psalms that announce and confess the goodness of creation like Psalm 104 and how God made these with wisdom as in Psalm 111.

In the second section of the Noahic account, the connection with the creation covenant becomes clearer. There is parallel language in both accounts such as be fruitful and multiply and fill the earth. Responsibilities found in the creation account are reaffirmed for humankind such as guard the created order and nourish it. Humankind's image is reaffirmed; although sinners, humans still bear God's image and likeness, virtue is possible, and that has natural implications for rights, justice, and governance. There remains a proper law-like structure and creaturely adherence or deviation from it is the test. In the section before us, God, as the sovereign Lord, adjusts the structure of His design ever so slightly to accommodate the postlapsarian state of humankind. For example, the animal world responds to humans with fear unlike their original sense of trust in humans. The diet of humans adjusts as well. The city is a special concern because of humankind's propensity to usurp power as a consequence of sin and so justice is emphasized as definitive for the polis. The section ends with the call again to be fruitful and multiply and to abound on the earth.

As I indicated above, in the third section what was implicit in the creation account is made explicit in the Noah account. This is necessary because of the fall. God declares that the covenant extends to animals and the created order itself. This leaves no doubt about God's commitment and concern for the whole of what he has made. Animals and the creation are to be viewed, as Wendell Berry suggests in "Gift of the Good Land," as the gift of God who cherishes these and binds Himself in oath to them. As the grand interpreter, He grants meaning to the rainbow; it is the sign of this perpetual devotion of God and the promise He makes to sustain it. This bow attests to humans that they are under-shepherds of the one who supremely loves and cares for His creation. God declares, "When the bow is in the clouds, I will see it and remember the everlasting covenant between God and every living creature of all flesh that is on the earth" (Genesis 9:16). Noah and his descendants are called to remember, as well, that God has established this covenant; it is a sovereign covenant that will last forever, and which depends for its fulfillment on God's oath. It is a covenant that emphasizes the centrality of the significance of the good and the essential place that justice plays in the public realm.

The binding character of the Noahic common grace covenant is clear as one explores other parts of the Scriptures. I suggest a few. In terms of creation, we have many Psalms and other passages that celebrate its order as a blessing to all humankind and that wisdom will attend those who fear God and understand it rightly. We see this attending to creation rightly with wisdom in the commendation that God declares toward the work of Hiram, a non-Israelite who helped in the building of the temple and palace under Solomon. He is pronounced wise. Those who study astronomy in the birth narratives are identified too as wise. The wisdom of the Egyptians and Babylonians is attested to in Scripture as valuable. These persons fulfill parts of the Noahic covenant while failing to attest and defer to the ultimate source of wisdom, God who made them.

We might look as well at the issues of justice and governing present in the prophetic evaluation of the nations of the world, including Israel. The book of Amos guides us at this point. In chapters 1:1–2:3, Amos cites, in the form of a lawsuit, the various transgressions of the nations. The standard of condemnation reflects the stipulations of the Noahic covenant. Here are a few examples. Damascus followed a policy of violence in its governing structure including assassinations of legitimately ruling leaders thus violating the edict against murder in the city. Moab carries whole communities into exile, ignoring the rightful boundaries of neighboring city-states. Tyre is indicted because they did not remember the covenant of kinship that is that all are descendants of Noah. All of these are traceable to the stipulations of the covenant made with Noah, his descendants, and all of humankind and which are still binding on humankind.

Abraham was an exile and sojourner in his own country even though he was promised redemption and that he would be a blessing to the nations, Hebrew 11. The Noahic covenant monitored his activities just as it did his descendants whether living a nomadic life in Canaan or a settled life in Egypt. In Israel's exile from the Promised Land, the conditions of the Noahic covenant prevailed just as it does for the people of God redeemed in the New Testament. Recall that Peter calls us sojourners in his first letter. In chapter one, Peter calls the church to live in "reverent fear" because God will judge all humans "impartially," according to their deeds. In chapter two, he writes, "I urge you as aliens and exiles to abstain from the desires of the flesh." He follows this reminder of the alien status of the believer with the imperative to engage in conduct in life that is honorable, i.e. virtuous, so that non-believers will see the excellence of their lives. The Christian is to live by the standard of conduct imposed on the nations, that is according to the stipulations of the Noahic covenant with the acknowledgment that their redeemed life makes this effectual.

We see in the ministry of Jesus constant concern for justice and mercy, the goods of life like health and shelter mentioned earlier, and for the condition of virtue in the life of believers. He viewed this as a condition of the heart, the basic source of love and its orienting power (Mark 7). Further, in Acts 17, Paul preaches to the intellectuals at Athens and refutes the Epicurean and Stoic philosophers present in the Areopagus. It is interesting to note that the beliefs these groups held had, in Paul's mind, an adverse effect on the public space. He commends the knowledge they possess to a degree because it attests to the covenant God who made all things. Then in a remarkable statement, Paul claims that God has allotted all nations "their existence" and set the "boundaries" of their place and rule. As doxological agents these nations "grope for God" and the structures they create are commensurate with that status. He then asserts that the establishment of these things is evidence that in God "we live and move and have our being." In other words, the common grace, common good structure is rooted in the reality of God's being; it has metaphysical roots. Paul states the same sort of thing in Colossians One where all of the universe is held together and has its existence in the Wisdom/Word, the Eternally Begotten Son of God. Another way to understand this for the believer is that as we love the Lord with our whole heart, mind, and strength, they will affirm the goodness of the common grace covenantal framework of the public. As a sojourner, our lot is to be governed by the intimate relationship that we have as a member of the covenant of redemptive grace with the Triune God and as faithful bearers of his image with all humankind in fulfilling the covenant of common grace established through Noah. Our membership in the former enables us to be a blessing in the latter, thus the blessing believers bring to the nations is not only the message of salvation in Jesus Christ, but the doxological labor they engage in fulfilling the Noahic covenant that brings a kind of "temporal peace" to the non-believer (Augustine, *the City of God*, book XIX). The duty of the Christian is to teach all, believers and non-believers, to love things according to the worth they possess in God's design, and to labor for all to experience the kind gifts of God socially, politically, and creationally.

Let me supply one more example of the exilic status of the believer called to satisfy the conditions of the Noahic covenant of common grace. I take this from Jeremiah 29, identified earlier by Augustine. There was a first wave of exiles from Judah to Babylon in the last couple of years of the seventh century, BC. All of the significant cultural leaders of Judah were a part of that exile. Jeremiah writes to them in about 597 BC encouraging them to consider the implications of their exile and commanding them to do a number of things. Forebear with me as I cite a number of verses from this interesting and well-known text.

> Jeremiah 29:5ff:
> Build houses and live in them; plant gardens and eat what they produce. Take wives and have sons and

> daughters; takes wives for your sons and give your daughters in marriage; multiply there and do not decrease. But seek the peace of the city where I have sent you into exile, and pray to the Lord on its behalf, for in its peace you will find your peace.

Jeremiah goes on to tell them to guard against false prophets and their attempts at imposing a deceptive wisdom, given the propensity of humankind to deceive one-another. This is followed by the assertion of God's providential care which provides the elect with a "future and a hope." If we consider these verses, we notice the parallels to the Noahic renewal of the creation covenant expressed in the commands given to the exiles. They are called to be fruitful and multiply; to engage in the institution of marriage; to seek with diligence the temporal peace of the polis and its community; to imitate God by laboring in the created order with some stability that comes about by establishing roots. All of these entail understanding the culture in which they find themselves and fulfilling the demands of the proper order of the creational covenant in their exiled state.

God, binding Himself in oath to the conditions of the Noahic covenant and framing the postlapsarian history of humankind by common grace, provides us with a way of understanding how it is that the ungodly engage in acts of beauty, knowledge cultivation, and truth development over the spheres of the covenant arrangement. Augustine acknowledges this in *the City of God*, book XXII. He writes:

> Who can adequately describe, or even imagine, the work of the Almighty? There is, first, this capacity for the good life, the ability to attain eternal felicity, by those arts which are called virtues, which are given solely by the grace of God in Christ to the children of the promise and of the kingdom. And besides this there are all the important arts discovered and developed by human genius, some for necessary uses, and others simply for pleasure. Man shows remarkable

> powers of mind and reason in the satisfaction of his aims, even though they may be unnecessary, or even dangerous and harmful; and those powers are evidence of the blessings he enjoys in his natural powers which enable him to discover, to learn, and to practice those arts. Think of the wonderful inventions of clothing and building, the astounding achievements of human industry! Think of man's progress in agriculture and navigation; of the variety, in conception and accomplishment, man has shown in pottery, in sculpture, in painting; the marvels in theatrical spectacles, which man's contrivances in design and production have excited wonder...For all the medical resources for preserving or restoring health; all the seasonings or spices to gratify his palate or tickle his appetite. Consider the multitudinous variety of the means of information and persuasion, among which the spoken and written word has the first place; the enjoyment afforded the mind by the trappings of eloquence and the rich diversity of poetry; the delight given to the ears by the instruments of music....How abundant is the stock of knowledge of natural phenomena! It must be remembered that we are now speaking of the natural abilities of the human mind, the chief ornament of this mortal life."

Augustine attributes this to God's power for preserving the natural order He made so that it "would not fall into wretchedness." Toward the end of this section in book XXII, Augustine claims that the "beauty and utility of the natural creation" given to humankind is the result of "divine generosity," common grace to all without regard to whether one is saved or not. Calvin echoes this as well when, in the *Institutes*, he claims that it is appropriate to "contemplate God's works" since humans are spectators of God's "glorious theater." Suffice it to say that it is God's common grace that enables the goodnesses we see all about us to persist.

The Pastor as Public Intellectual: Prophetic Function

As I indicated in the introduction, Augustine thought of the pastor as having a prophetic role to play in the church and in the public sphere. Further, the Augustinian conception of the public as justice, liberty, virtue, and the proper quest and love for the order of creation granted us an alternative conception of the public to Kant's which is tacitly held in contemporary discourse about the public. The common grace covenantal foundation provides the undergirding necessary for the framework of the public discussed in part one. We return in this last part to the pastor as public intellectual and the function of mediator he bears for the public commonly graced sphere discussed above. The failure of his duties in this area contributed to the vitiation of a good design for a temporal public order in ancient Rome, and dare I say, contemporary public life. As such, the public realm and its political and social life were overwhelmed by the pervasive and perversive manifestations of the *libido dominandi*, the lust for power. The argument so far has sought to establish a particular framework for the public rooted in a proper love for the basic goods of creation, virtue, justice, and liberty explored in Augustine's *the City of God*. I then asked if there was biblical warrant for such a view and contended that we find this in the Noahic covenant renewal in the Book of Genesis as it is sustained in common grace as the foundation for the public. This covenant structure is binding on all humans and is enjoyed by all alike through God's providential care. The prophetic function is necessary to educate, persuade, and refute in the public sphere so that its good framework might be achieved and its foundation clarified. In other words, to function as a public intellectual. In this last section, I wish to suggest the contours of a prophetic model and its consciousness and passion and to do so by articulating a unique concept of an intellectual rooted in the Christian tradition. [31]

Abraham Joshua Heschel in his two volume work on the prophets avers "to us a single act of injustice is slight, to the prophets a disaster; to us injustice is injurious to the welfare of the people, to the prophets it is a deathblow to existence; to us, an episode, to them, a catastrophe, a threat to the world." In many ways this quote captures the spirit of what I would like to suggest. The pastor as prophetic intellectual stands aghast at the vitiation of the public with its basic goods necessary for life, and its justice, rights, and freedom. The prophetic intellectual is indignant at the exploitive economic arrangements that favor few, or political behavior of leaders as they pollute the framework of temporal peace for all as common good. The prophetic intellectual is appalled at the church's indifference, or *acedia*, and its sometimes overt complicity in violations of peace in the public space. The identification of a pastor with the agenda of political parties muffles the role and function of the pastor as public intellectual because his allegiance is wedded to a party or ideology and not the foundation and framework of public life as discussed above. This leaves culture, public, and church open to the unraveling of its good order of temporal peace. As such, there may be a revisiting of Rome's demise as our own.

There are two main areas of the prophetic public intellectual I would like to explore. I draw these from an examination of the prophets in the Old Testament with a specific look at Amos. I will call the first of these the consciousness of the pastor/prophetic public intellectual. In particular, this area is concerned with the perspectives that the prophetic public intellectual possesses as he engages in an analysis of culture and public life. I will cite a number of passages that demonstrate this case and how these give one an insight into the mind of the prophet. The second area of concern engages the pathos of the prophets. We might call them pathetic: filled with pathos in confronting the vitiation of God's good design in both church and public. This awareness and passion should be characteristic of the people of God, especially the clerics, in all ages as we wait in hope for the full restoration of the heavens and the earth at the coming of the Son of God. Until then, the Holy Spirit equips the church and particular leaders in the church (pastors) to carry on the prophetic task. And, it seems to me, that it is heightened in the believer as they recognize that it is in the Triune God that we live, and move, and have our being. Let's continue with an exploration of the first of these two characteristics: perspectival consciousness.

The first aspect of the perspectival consciousness of the prophetic intellectual is an awareness of the covenants and the covenantal structure of the Scriptures. Again my references will come primarily from Amos and a few from Hosea. Amos references the binding nature of the Abrahamic covenant in 9:12 in a discussion of how Israel failed to be the blessing to the nations embedded in her call through Abraham. Three other Abrahamic redemptive covenant applications are present in prophetic consciousness as well. The Mosaic covenant structure looms large in the Book of Amos. For example, Amos 2:7 is a reflection of Deuteronomy 23:17–18 where the concern is for the poor and treating them well, without oppression. In Amos I find at least 13 direct citations from the Mosaic books (Exodus, Leviticus, Numbers, and Deuteronomy) most of which concern the treatment of the poor, the common good, justice, and loving the good things of creation aright. In both Hosea and Amos, the theme of the Davidic covenant is present and formative. In Amos 9:11–12 the promise of the Davidic covenant is extended and required of the nations who are blessed because of Abraham's election. In other words, these nations and their leaders bear duties that emerge from the description of authority associated with David. I take it to suggest that public and political leadership bears responsibilities similar to what we find in kingship attached to David and expressed in passages like 1 Samuel 12. Political authority is defined over against the abuse of power, *libido dominandi*, that was discussed earlier. The king shall not rule to foster his own interests (the common interests of all are the primary concern); there will be no economic exploitation (a prominent theme in Amos and Hosea); there will be no political oppression to advance one's own agenda (consider power politics and gerrymandering today); and no disregard for the poor, the alien, the outcast, the widow (hospitality and welcome to the sojourner). Psalm 101 captures David's understanding of his covenantal duties as authority by claiming that he will walk with virtue, will honor the good and true, will rebuke those who slander others and who live arrogantly, and will not practice deceit. These prophetic intellectuals, who provide the model for pastoral public concern, were mediators of the covenants that God made with humans including the Noahic common grace covenant discussed earlier.

In the prophets the common covenants for all descendants of Noah are present as well. For example, in Hosea 6 we find the writer referencing Adam's failures and associates these with several cities of evildoers. God renews the covenant with Noah made initially with Adam and its focus on the cultural mandate and the quest for knowing God. Also, Amos repeatedly mentions the violations of the covenant of kinship (everyone is bound by common descent) by the city/nations he condemns. The covenant presumes the common familiar structure of all descendants of Noah. This is why one does not slander others and promote racism and bigotry; the other bears the image of God too and this shows the common bond that Augustine discussed. In Amos 5 and then again in chapter 7, the writer mentions the broken covenant of creation again which is renewed in the Noahic configuration mentioned earlier. When one thinks of the mind of the prophets, covenant awareness both of the redemptive Abraham sort and the Noahic expressions are prominent.

It is important to note that these prophetic public intellectuals understood that their message was not their own but came from the God who reveals Himself in nature and in Scripture. They understood that their freedom and ability to speak and address the concerns of the public and the church resulted from their submission to the truth. The medieval theologians understood truth as giving form to particulars in the created order. To be severed from truth, leaves the public life floundering. Unlike the post-Lockean understanding of truth residing in the mind of man, these intellectuals understood that truth is located in the God of the covenant who discloses truth in reality.

The prophetic consciousness extends to two other aspects of the mind. I briefly mention these. It seems to me that the prophets manifest as part of their intellectual perspective what we might call a memorial understanding. In other words, they know the history of Israel and the surrounding nations. We see references to the patriarchs, the exodus, the pre-monarchial era in Judges and the sojourn in the wilderness. And their consciousness was characterized contextually by a studied awareness of the societal and political environment of their day. They understood the conditions of exploitation economically and otherwise. And this awareness extended to the nations surrounding Israel as well. The perspective of these prophetic intellectuals included, then, a historical understanding and a social and political knowledge contemporary with their writing.

I also suggested that there was a pathetic aspect to the prophets that enabled them to be unearth the pollution of God's good creational design in public life. A first component of this pathos was that the prophetic intellectual possessed a sensitivity to evil. Three manifestations of that sensitivity to evil were: a sensitivity to ideological distortions; a sensitivity to systematic oppression, politically and economically; and a sensitivity to complacency, what I earlier called *acedia*. Let's explore some of the ideological distortions in Hosea and Amos.

There are at least four types of ideological distortions I would mention. The first concerns the ideology of violence. In Amos 1, for example, the Ammonites are rebuked for their violent and oppressive acts committed against women. Moab is condemned for their acts of violence against Edom. Another type of distortion is economic or what we might call the ideology of affluence. Affluence as a form of power oppresses the poor and needy, and disregards the stranger, Amos 4. God promises in response to the affluence of the powerful class to "tear down their summer homes." The problem of litigation, litigating without regard to justice, is an issue raised by a variety of the prophets including Isaiah who includes the ideology of litigation as indicative that a nation has entered into a covenant with death. This ideology abhors the one who speaks the truth (Amos 5:10–11). One final ideological distortion occurs when religion is used in the service of the powerful. God, according to Amos, takes no delight in festivals when religion is the pawn of power. It keeps the religious believer docile and agreeable to those in power so that the religious are easily manipulated by empty promises and the like. Each of these is a form of power as force (violence), financial (affluence), or story (religion in the service of the powerful or litigation).

A second kind of evil that the prophetic intellectual was sensitive to were those that emerged from systematic oppression. The opening chapter of Amos lists a series of nation/cities that engaged in oppressive activities. In verse six, the prophet cites Gaza who has carried whole communities into slavery. A little later Tyre is condemned because they too carried away communities into exile. The oppression of Moab destroyed the capacity of Edom to defend itself and to have shelter. The oppression exercised by Israel was rooted in pride and fostered an animosity toward the alien. The oppression manifest by the Israelites is recorded in the encounter between Amos and Amaziah, the priest of Bethel (Amos 7). Amos reveals the pervasive oppression of Jeroboam and religious complicity in it. Amaziah rebukes him and tells him to go back where he came from. Amos responds by criticizing the harlotry of the political, religious, and social structure.

A final sensitivity to mention is the complacency, *acedia*, that is characteristic of the powerful in the public realm. In chapter six, Amos condemns those who are "at ease in Zion, those who are made to feel secure on Mount Samaria." The lie on "beds of ivory" (affluence) and sing idle songs while they feast and others starve. *Acedia* is the absence of care and the docility that arises from it. In Martin Luther King Jr's "Letter from a Birmingham Jail" he claims that the great source of his discouragement stems from the "white moderate" who do not feel intensely enough the evil of slavery that they will act or what we've been calling the sensitivity to evil and oppression.

Although one might say that these suggestions concern what is often called *realpolitik*, that is the way that power functions politically in the public space. So what sets this apart from other positions on what constitutes a public intellectual? The prophetic intellectual presumes that he is a mediator of a well-designed public life that has been vitiated by those who engage in politics and public life as *libido dominandi*. *Realpolitik* thinks of the public space as the location of power without regard to an order that is good. The model I propose suggests the goodness of the public as designed and covenantally sustained. It seeks to unearth the beauty and excellence of that design and bring to light the ways in which power brokers and structures skew its goodness. It supposes that this goodness is embedded in truth, rectitude, and justice and the concern that all humans enjoy the fruit of its excellence. In light of this, the prophets Hosea and Amos manifest another type of pathos. That pathos is zeal for Yahweh's honor. They are indignant with any perspective that is idolatrous, or manifests an insipid religiosity, or melds together aspects of powerful ideologies with religion that masks the core of what is good and true and beautiful. The prophetic intellectual sees these as failing to render to God what is due to God and in the final analysis is a failure to love God with one's heart, soul, mind, and strength.

Finally, the pastor (guarding and watching the flock of his congregation and loving neighbor as self in functioning prophetically for the public sphere) must be an agent of wisdom and prudence. Wisdom entails an excellence in deliberation about public affairs that culminates in actions that promote the morally good. In our case, the good of the public sphere is the purview of concern for the pastor. As we look around today at the public space and pastors' involvement in it, too often we see the complicit promotion of a political party that seeks to demonstrate what we have called *libido dominandi*.

Or so that some agenda that has been defined as Christian by the powerful might be enforced. Pastors have too often become pragmatic, justifying silence because Christian concern is being legislated in some way. As such, the pernicious nature of religion as an agent of political power muffles the zeal that is necessary to promote a peaceful *civitas terrena* enjoyed by believer and non-believer alike.[32]

Notes

[1]There are about 60 references to the cities of pilgrim status throughout *the City of God.*

[2]Augustine, *The City of God*, p. 5.

[3]Ibid., p. 1031.

[4]Ibid., p. 41.

[5]Ibid., p. 566.

[6]Ibid., p. 573.

[7]Ibid., p. 744.

[8]Ibid., p. 45.

[9]Ibid.

[10]Ibid., p.46.

[11]Ibid.

[12]Ibid., p. 842.

[13]Ibid.

[14]Ibid., p. 892

[15]Ibid.

[16]Ibid., p. 25.

[17]Ibid., p. 608.

[18]Ibid., p. 204.

[19]Ibid., p. 880.

[20]Ibid., p. 854.

[21]It is important to keep in mind the priority of the concept of order for Augustine. In both *On the Usefulness of Belief* and *On True Religion*, Augustine contends for a proper order in the way in which folks come to know. In his work *On Order* Augustine maps out further the place of providence and predestination in the scheme of things. Throughout the Augustinian corpus, there is an order that is natural, *ordo naturalis*, that has been radically affected by sin. The order that Augustine has in mind in the passage cited above is the order by which God will judge the volitional acts of humans; in kindness and grace God supplied the principles of justice to negotiate this present realm and hence the public.

[22]Augustine, *The City of God*, p. 868.

[23]Ibid.

[24]Ibid., p. 869.

[25]Ibid., p. 877.

[26]Ibid.

[27]Ibid., p. 878

[28]Augustine discusses this in chapter 21 of Book XIX.

[29]Ibid., p. 890.

[30]Ibid.

[31]It is important to note that I am not claiming that the whole of the duty of the pastor is bound up with functioning as a public intellectual. The pastor preaches redemptively to his congregation, administers the blessed sacraments to believers, shepherds the flock under his care, and a host of other things. My concern is that the important aspect of rightly affirming the public sustained by common grace in the Noahic covenant has been sacrificed and clerics jump on the bandwagon of ill-conceived political brokering by the powerful.

[32]It is with great honor that I contribute to this volume in recognition of Dr. John White's contribution to the kingdom. I have known Jack since the early '70s and his life and ministry have greatly impacted my life. I am joyful to call him my friend and mentor.

CHAPTER THIRTEEN

Leadership Authority Under God

Maureen O. Vanterpool

Leadership is an elusive phenomenon that human-centered theories fail to explain adequately and, in my view, that is because they do not place God at the apex of the leader-follower relationship. Human-centered leadership theories can be traced back to the ancient Greeks, when Plato described the ideal leader as a Philosopher-King. In Plato's theory, superior intellect was the primary criterion for leadership.[1] Starting in medieval times, hereditary monarchs in Europe embraced the doctrine of the Divine Right of Kings, asserting that they had a God-given right to absolute authority, with no accountability to anyone. Political revolutions caused the divine right doctrine to crumble by the late 18th century.[2] Divine Right was a human-centered theory, with a thin veneer of being God-centered. The true nature of leadership continues to be elusive.

In the present age, any mention of God in public discourse raises objections by many in the United States and elsewhere in the world. Since the early 20th century, scholars have attempted to define leadership from a perspective rooted in humanistic psychology. After exhaustive research, Joseph Rost organized definitions of leadership into two main categories, the Industrial Paradigm and the Postindustrial Paradigm.[3] The Industrial Paradigm includes several theories that view leadership as good management: The Great Man theory describes leaders as personalities to be imitated. Group theories assert that leaders attain status from their role and contributions within the group. Trait theories identify general characteristics of leaders.

Behavior theories identify specific functions that leaders perform. Situational theories stress the importance of contextual factors. The Postindustrial Paradigm includes theories that view leadership as intending change. Excellence theories emphasize higher level effectiveness. Transformational theories emphasize values such as collaboration, diversity, and consensus decision making. While all of these theories help leaders to gain insight, they do not go far enough. In many ways, they seem to be based on the false assumption that human beings are the ultimate authority in all things.

The purpose of this work is to break the news to leaders, that God is the ultimate source of leadership authority and that they are accountable to him for how they exercise that authority. God declared in his word through the Apostle Paul, "…for there is no authority except that which God has established."[4]. This Scripture carries immense significance, because it applies to all leaders, not just believers. Therefore, all leaders are accountable to God for how they exercise authority. The principles of the model introduced here apply to all leaders, from heads of state on down.

This work addresses the following topics: What is Authority? A Model of Leadership Authority Under God, Abuse of Authority, Crises of Leadership, and Two Examples of Biblical Leadership. Those who do not believe in the God of the Bible and even some who do, may reject these ideas. To be sure, God's authority and His right to empower leaders does not depend upon human affirmation. I invite readers to approach this work with an open mind, prepared to raise questions and to seek answers from Scripture for yourself.

What is Authority?

Table 1 compares and contrasts common dictionary definitions, scholarly definitions, and theological definitions of authority. Notice that the dictionary and scholarly definitions indicate limitations on authority within a specific context or situation, while the theological definitions portray authority as unrestricted.

Dictionary Definitions	Scholarly Definitions	Theological Definitions
"Power to influence or command thought, opinion, or behavior; freedom granted by one in authority: right." "Power to act especially over others that derives from status, position, or office."[5]	"Authority involves the rights, prerogatives, obligations, and duties associated with particular positions in an organization or social system. A leader's authority usually includes the right to make particular types of decisions for the organization"[6]	Power, freedom, right. "Prerogative, warrant, license."[7] (Elwell 1996). "Unimpeded, permission."[8]

Table 1: Comparison/contrast of dictionary, scholarly, and theological definitions.

The New Testament uses the word "authority" 102 times, according to *the Westminster Theological Wordbook of the Bible.*[9] Such an extensive use of the word gives an indication of its significance. As the ultimate source of all authority, God confers authority as He chooses.

A Model of Leadership Authority Under God

None of the scholarly sources I reviewed focused on the idea that a leader derives authority from God and is accountable to

God for how they exercise that authority. Drawing on biblical truths, I assert that leadership, in whatever context and at whatever level it occurs, involves a divine element as well as a human element and that the divine element is superior to the human element. Due to a felt need, I set out to develop a biblically inspired hierarchical model of leadership, as illustrated in Figure 1. This three-tiered model of leadership is God-centered: (1) God is sovereign over all creation; (2) God establishes a leader's authority; and (3) God's word is to be obeyed by leaders and followers. These truths are evident throughout Scripture.

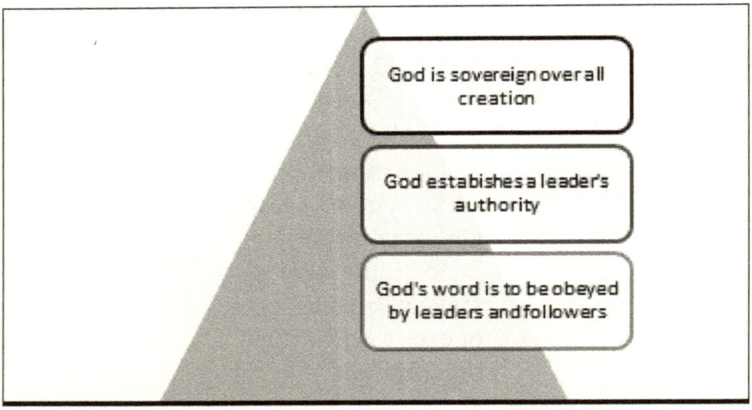

Figure 1: Leadership Authority Under God, illustrating a hierarchical relationship between parties in the leader-follower relationship.

This model grew out of my commitment to provide a biblical perspective to students in the Master of Science in Organizational Leadership (MSOL) program at Geneva College. The predominantly human-centered culture of most organizations notwithstanding, this model could be followed by leaders who choose to do so in any organization. That is because the principles of the model are to be lived, rather than preached.

Following is an elaboration of the components of the model, with emphasis on the concepts of sovereignty, authority, and obedience that get to the heart of leadership from a biblical perspective. This model is both hierarchical and integrated, with God at the top and also within each level. Notice the subtle differences in human-centered definitions from the dictionary as compared to God-centered definitions from theological references.

God is Sovereign Over All Creation

From a human-centered perspective, sovereignty is a term commonly used in reference to a government such as a republic or a monarchy, or the jurisdiction over which the government rules. For example, the sovereignty of a nation implies that it views attempts by other nations to exercise control over its internal affairs as acts of aggression. The definition of sovereignty in Webster's Dictionary includes, "supreme power…freedom from external control…autonomy…controlling influence."[10] When the term sovereign is used as a noun, it often refers to a monarch.

From a God-centered perspective, theological references define the concept of sovereignty as an attribute of God. Walter Elwell[11] defined sovereignty in terms of God's complete freedom. Grenz, Guretzki, and Nordling[12] defined sovereignty as, "The biblical concept of God's kingly, supreme rule and legal authority over the entire universe…Divine sovereignty is emphasized especially in the Augustinian-Calvinist tradition, where it is paradoxically contrasted with human responsibility." Jesus Christ testified to the sovereignty of the Father as he taught his disciples, "This, then, is how you should pray: Our Father in heaven, hallowed be your name, your kingdom come, your will be done on earth as it is in heaven…" (Matthew 6:9–10). God the Son made a definitive statement of the Father's sovereignty for the edification of His disciples through the ages.

Several of God's other attributes distinguish divine sovereignty from human sovereignty. Elwell identified a number of attributes used to describe God. For example, the triune God is one, eternal, holy, omnipotent, omnipresent, omniscient, righteous, self-existent, and unchangeable.[13] These are by no means the only attributes of God, but these typically are reserved to describe God and not human beings. However, by God's act of redemption through Christ's death on the cross, believers are called to share in God's holiness and righteousness (1 Peter 1:14–16; 2 Corinthians 5:21).

Acknowledging that the sovereign Lord is at the top of the hierarchy is the starting point to gaining a fuller understanding of leadership authority. Human-centered ideas about leadership that fail to recognize God's authority, in effect, disregard His sovereignty. Nevertheless, there are biblical examples in which God accomplished His purpose through leaders such as Pharaoh of the Exodus, who refused to acknowledge his sovereignty (Exodus 5:1–14:31). Another vivid example is the account of Nebuchadnezzar. The Babylonian king finally acknowledged God's sovereignty after God removed the king's authority and let him spend time living like a wild animal (Daniel 4:18–37). Nevertheless, God's authority is not dependent upon human acknowledgment.

God Establishes a Leader's Authority

Romans 13:1b reiterates, "The authorities that exist have been established by God." In a commentary on the subject of authority, John Calvin stated in his *Institutes of the Christian Religion*, "...It has not come about by human perversity that the authority over all things on earth is in the hands of kings and other rulers, but [it came about] by divine providence and holy ordinance."[14] Leaders must be clear about the source of their authority.

God's Word is to be Obeyed by Leaders and Followers

Obedience is the highest expectation God has of humanity. Scripture states, "Observe the commands of the Lord your God, walking in obedience to him and revering him (Deuteronomy 8:6). With specific reference to the leader-follower relationship, the full text of Romans 13:1–2 reads,

> [1]Let everyone be subject to the governing authorities, for there is no authority except that which God has established. The authorities that exist have been established by God. [2] Consequently, whoever rebels against the authority is rebelling against what God has instituted, and those who do so will bring judgment on themselves.

Portions of that passage of Scripture lays out God's expectations for followers, which is to submit to leaders.

Other passages of Scripture lay out God's expectations for leaders. For example, the Apostle Paul listed several spiritual gifts that believers receive, and he described how to use those gifts. He stated, "...if it [the spiritual gift] is to lead, do it diligently..." (Romans 12:8). By extension, that admonition applies to all leaders, since their authority is established by God, whether they are believers or not. Furthermore, God expects leaders to care for and nurture followers, according to Christ's command to the Apostle Peter, when He said, "Feed my sheep" (John 21:17).

Trust is essential to obedience. In order for leaders and followers to be obedient to God, they must trust in Him. Trust is a pivotal factor in human relationships as well and when the trust between human beings is rooted in trust in God, the bonds of the relationship should be stronger. As Scripture indicates, "Trust in the Lord with all your heart and lean not on your own understanding; in all your ways submit to Him and He will make your paths straight" (Proverbs 3:5–6).

James M. Kouzes and Barry Z. Posner identified trust as something not to be taken for granted.[15] They suggested that leaders must first demonstrate trust in others in order to gain their trust. Followers perceive such leaders as trustworthy. People who cannot trust others cannot lead others effectively and according to Kouzes and Posner, they can end up doing all the work themselves. Followers perceive such leaders as less deserving of trust. Without trust, followers may rebel against leaders, which is contrary to God's Word. Leaders also may be disobedient to God's word by abusing their authority and mistreating followers.

Abuse of Authority

Throughout the course of human history, there are many examples of abuse of authority. For example, the Medici family ruled ruthlessly in Italy in the late 15th to early 16th centuries. Their heinous abuses were celebrated and justified by Niccolò Machiavelli in his well-known work, *The Prince.*[16] Through the ages, his ideas have been so despised by others that the term *Machiavellian* is still used to describe ruthless leaders. The most notorious example of abuse of authority in the 20th Century was Adolph Hitler's murderous rule over Germany and conquests of other nations. Hitler and the Nazi party killed an estimated six million Jews, and about another six million people, comprised of Polish, Czech, and Russian citizens.[17] The Nazi concept of a "master race" was diametrically opposed to God's word. The Genesis account of the creation indicates, "So God created man in His own image, in the image of God He created him; male and female He created them" (Genesis 1:27). Furthermore, God decreed through the Apostle Paul, "There is neither Jew nor Greek, slave nor free, male nor female, for you are all one in Christ Jesus" (Galatians 3:28). When one group considers itself superior to another group, conditions are ripe for abuse of authority.

This begs the question, what should be done about tyrants who abuse authority? Some people take the position that nothing can be done, possibly because they are afraid of risking their own necks. Some take the position that nothing should be done, possibly because they share the sentiments of the tyrant or they are protecting their self-interests. Others take positions of undermining, revolt, or other forms of violent rebellion against their leaders.

I take the position expressed by John Calvin—that persons in authority are obligated to curtail abuses by others in authority. Calvin made a clear distinction between persons with lesser authority duly protecting the people from tyrants, vs. random individuals rebelling in their own strength. Calvin referred to the people with lesser authority as "constitutional defenders of the people's freedom."[18] In fact, Calvin asserted that if lesser authorities overlook tyranny, "they dishonestly betray the freedom of the people, of which they know that they have been appointed protectors by God's ordinance."[19]

Curtailing abuse of authority is a point that is highly significant for leaders who occupy positions of lesser authority. Such leaders are not free to look the other way when followers suffer at the hands of unjust leaders from above. To reiterate, it is my view that the principles that apply to heads of state apply equally to leaders at all levels. Therefore, while followers are to submit, they also are to look to other persons with authority who are obligated to God to be a source of help. According to Scripture, "Where there is no revelation, people cast off restraint…" (Proverbs 29:18). In effect, when leaders with lesser authority fail to speak truth to power, we find ourselves in a crisis of leadership.

Crises of Leadership

"Crisis of leadership" is a phrase coined by James McGregor Burns, who received the Pulitzer Prize and the National Book Award for his now classic work titled, *Leadership*. Burns attributed the leadership crisis at the time of his writing to mediocrity and irresponsibility. For him, moral development was central to the kind of leadership that is transforming, in which "leaders and followers raise one another to higher levels of motivation and morality."[20] He believed that transforming leadership, as he called it, would help people avert the crisis of leadership. I assert steadfastly that crises of leadership are due to human-centered approaches to leadership that remove God from the apex of those relationships.

Throughout the world, there are numerous crises of leadership evident as I write this. Complaints against leaders include abuse of power, unjust policies and practices, corruption, financial crimes, sexual impropriety, and illegitimate ascension to office, to name a few. Citizens of various countries have taken to the streets in protest. In some cases, the people are calling for censure, resignation, or removal of their leaders. In 2019, there were numerous reports of protests in the following places: Algeria, Czech Republic, Great Britain, Hong Kong, Puerto Rico, Russia, Sudan, Thailand, United States, and Venezuela. In addition to these governments, three of the largest U.S.-based corporations with a global presence, were subjects of employee protests at home and abroad. Those corporations were retail giant Amazon, entertainment giant Disney, and technology giant Google. The Internet was flooded with reports of the protests in credible online news sources such as *The New York Times, The Washington Post, National Public Radio, The Guardian, Newsweek*, and *Time*, to name a few. These crises highlight the broad need to consider leadership from another perspective and I submit this model of Leadership Authority Under God for consideration.

Two Examples of Biblical Leaders

Following are accounts of Moses and Deborah, two leaders in different circumstances. Consider each of these cases in reference to the model of leadership presented here: (1) God is sovereign over all creation; (2) God establishes a leader's authority; and (3) God's word is to be obeyed by leaders and followers. In the accounts of Moses's and Deborah's leadership, there is evidence of faltering that is characteristic of human beings. Nevertheless, they trusted God and led his people faithfully. Each description is followed by analytical statements from Bible commentaries.

Example 1: Moses

Moses was the leader of the Israelites' exodus from Egypt. After a reluctant start, Moses was faithful, as he served the Lord for 40 years leading the Israelites in the desert. It was an overwhelming job, but God provided him with capable help. First, God appointed his brother Aaron as his spokesperson, because Moses was not much of a public speaker. Both his brother Aaron and his sister Miriam played leadership roles with less authority. At one point, God sent Moses's father-in-law, Jethro, to advise him how to delegate authority. This delegation of authority lifted a burden from

Moses when he appointed group leaders to handle day-to-day responsibilities, such as disputes among the people. Eventually, God appointed Joshua as the person Moses groomed as his successor. The Lord used Joshua to lead the Israelites into the promised land. Moses was faithful in many things. Nevertheless, God did not allow him to enter the promised land because he broke faith with God. Moses failed to uphold God's holiness when he struck the rock to provide water for the people, instead of speaking to it, as God commanded at Meribah Kadesh (Deuteronomy 32:48–52). In the context of the model of Leadership Authority Under God described in this work, Moses held God at the apex of the leader-follower relationship, he knew clearly that God established His authority, and he understood that God expected him and the multitude of Israelites to obey his word. Following are excerpts from commentaries on the leadership of Moses:

> Moses was daunted by the mission to which God was calling him but received God's assurance that he would be empowered to accomplish his divinely appointed purpose. God not only prepared Moses to be a leader of His people, but He also gave him the power to succeed in his mission.[21]

> No leader can thrive without teammates, as the life of Moses illustrates...No leader should ever take the journey—or the credit by himself [or herself].[22]

> In our age of lowering moral standards, we find it almost impossible to believe that God would punish Moses for the one time he disobeyed outright. What we fail to see, however, is that God did not reject Moses; Moses simply disqualified himself to enter the promised land. Personal greatness does not make a person immune to error or its consequences."[23]

See the Old Testament books of Exodus, Leviticus, Numbers, and Deuteronomy for the account of Moses's faithful execution of leadership authority under God.

Example 2: Deborah

Deborah was a judge and prophetess in Israel long after they entered the promised land. Unique among women, Deborah was a leader in peacetime and in wartime. She was faithful as she counseled the people, settled their disputes, and prophesied in God's name. After much provocation by the Canaanites, Deborah received word from the Lord that the Israelite army was to go into battle against them. When the Israelite commander Barak faltered, she led the army into battle along with him, because he refused to go without her. Deborah may have been understandably frustrated with him. She prophesied that because Barak faltered, he would not get the honor of the victory. She said that the Lord would hand the victory to a woman. In a surprise twist, Deborah's prophesy came true when the Canaanite commander met his end at the hands of Jael. The song of Deborah, following the Israelites' victory over the Canaanites, left no doubt that she gave God the praise. Deborah held God at the apex of the leader-follower relationship, she had no doubt that God established her authority, and she was sure that God expected her and the warriors of Israel, including Barak, to obey His word. Following are excerpts from commentaries on the leadership of Deborah:

> Her story shows that she was not power hungry. She wanted to serve God. Whenever praise came her way, she gave God the credit. She didn't deny or resist her position in the culture as a woman and wife, but she never allowed herself to be hindered by it either...Deborah's life challenges us in several ways. She reminds us of the need to be available both to God and to others.[24]

> The story of Deborah is one of courage, singleness of purpose and quiet confidence in God's revealed will. As a prophetess, Deborah led Israel with the strength and wisdom that came from a deep relationship with God.[25]

> Those who in God's name call others to their duty, should be ready to assist them in it...Whatever Deborah, Barak,

> or the army had done, the Lord must have all the praise. The will, the power, and the success were all from Him.[26]
>
> The highest calling of any leader is to help other *leaders* reach their potential. Deborah helped Barak achieve his God-given purpose. Leaders who move to this level change their focus from inspiring and leading followers to developing and leading other leaders.[27]

See Judges Chapters 4–5 for the account of Deborah's faithful execution of leadership authority under God.

Conclusion

From the days of the ancient Greeks to the present day, scholars and leaders have attempted to define, describe, and codify leadership qualities and processes. Those efforts gave us partial explanations that include personal characteristics, behaviors, contexts, and a variety of other factors. Even those with the best intentions miss the mark when it comes to acknowledging God's place in the leadership dynamic. I assert that leadership should be God-centered, with God at the apex of the leader-follower relationship and His presence should be integrated throughout the leader-follower relationship.

Notes

[1]S. E. Frost, Jr. *Basic Teachings of the Great Philosophers.* (New York: Doubleday, 1962).

[2]Encyclopedia Britannica. 31 July 2019. Online: https://www.britannica.com/topic/divine-right-of-kings.

[3]Joseph C. Rost, *Leadership for the Twenty-first Century.* (Westport: Praeger, 1993).

[4]Romans 13:1a. All scripture quotations in this work are from the *Holy Bible: New International Version.*

[5]Merriam-Webster. 31 July 2019. Online: https://www.merriam-webster.com/dictionary/authority.

[6]Gary Yukl, Lea*dership in Organizations, 7th ed. (Upper Saddle River: Pearson Prentice Hall, 2010)*·

[7]Walter A. Elwell, Evangelical Dictionary of Bibli*cal Theology. (Grand Rapids: Baker, 1996).*

[8]Geoffery W. Bromiley, ed. The International Standard Bible Encyclopedia. *4 vols. (Grand Rapids: Eerdmans, 1979-1988).*

[9]Donald E. Gowen, ed. *The Westminster Theological Wordbook of the Bible.* (Louisville: Westminster John Knox, 2014).

[10]Merriman-Webster. 31 July 2019. Online: https://www.merriam-webster.com/dictionary/supremepower.

[11]Ewell, 1991.

[12]Stanley J. Grenz, David Guretzki, Cherith Fee Nordling. *Pocket Dictionary of Theological Terms.* (Downers Grove: InterVarsity, 1999).

[13]Ewell, 1991.

[14]John T. McNeill, ed. *Calvin: Institutes of the Christian Religion*, 2 vols. (Philadelphia: Westminster John Knox, 1960, 1489).

[15]James M. Kouzes and Barry Z. Postner. *A Leader's Legacy.* (San Francisco: Jossey-Bass, 2006).

[16]Diane'. *Fifty Major Philosophers: A Reference Guide.* (New York: Routledge, 1987).

[17]Otis C. Mitchel. *A Concise History of Western Civilization*, 2nd ed. (Minneapolis: Burgess, 1976).

[18]McNeill, *Calvin*, p. 1518.

[19]McNeill, *Calvin*, p. 1519.

[20]James McGregor Burns. *Leadership.* (New York: Harper & Row, 1978), p. 20.

[21]Sid Buzzell, Kenneth Boa, and Bill Perkins, eds. *The Leadership Bible (NIV).* (Grand Rapids: Zondervan, 1998), p. 72.

[22]John C. Maxwell, ed. *The Maxwell Leadership Bible: New King James Version.* (Nashville: Thomas Nelson, 1997), p. 87.

[23]*Life Application Bible: New International Version.* (Wheaton: Tyndale, 1991), p. 127.

[24]*Life Application Bible*, p. 387.

[25]Buzzell, Boa, Perkins, Ibid., p. 276.

[26]Matthew Henry. *Matthew Henry's Concise Commentary of the Whole Bible*. (Nashville: Thomas Nelson, 1997), pp. 242-243.

[27]Maxwell, Op. cit., p. 279.

References

Bromiley, Geoffrey W., ed. *The International Standard Bible Encyclopedia.* 4 vols. Grand Rapids: Eerdmans, 1979–1988.

Burns, James McGregor. *Leadership*. New York: Harper & Row, 1978.

Buzzell, Sid, Kenneth Boa, and Bill Perkins, eds. *The Leadership Bible* (NIV). Grand Rapids: Zondervan, 1998.

Collinson, Diané. *Fifty Major Philosophers: A Reference Guide.* New York: Routledge, 1987.

Elwell, Walter A., ed. *Topical Analysis of the Bible.* 5 vols. Grand Rapids: Baker, 1991.

___________. *Evangelical Dictionary of Biblical Theology*. Grand Rapids: Baker, 1996.

Encyclopedia Britannica. 31 July 2019. Online: https://www.britannica.com/topic/divine-right-of-kings.

Frost, S. E., Jr. *Basic Teachings of the Great Philosophers.* New York: Doubleday, 1962.

Gowan, Donald E., ed. *The Westminster Theological Wordbook of the Bible.* Louisville: Westminster John Knox, 2014.

Grenz, Stanley J., David Guretzki, and Cherith Fee Nordling. *Pocket Dictionary of Theological Terms.* Downers Grove: InterVarsity, 1999.

Henry, Matthew. *Matthew Henry's Concise Commentary on the Whole Bible.* Nashville: Thomas Nelson, 1997.

Kouzes, James M., and Barry Z. Posner. *A Leader's Legacy.* San Francisco: Jossey-Bass, 2006.

Life Application Bible: New International Version. Wheaton: Tyndale, 1991.

Maxwell, John C., ed. *The Maxwell Leadership Bible: New King James Version*. Nashville: Thomas Nelson, 2002.

McNeill, John T., ed. *Calvin: Institutes of the Christian Religion*. 2 vols. Philadelphia: Westminster John Knox, 1960.

Merriam-Webster. 31 July 2019. Online: https://www.merriam-webster.com/dictionary/authority.

Mitchell, Otis C., *A Concise History of Western Civilization*, 2nd ed. Minneapolis: Burgess, 1976.

Rost, Joseph C. *Leadership for the Twenty-first Century*. Westport: Praeger, 1993.

Yukl, Gary. *Leadership in Organizations*, 7th ed. Upper Saddle River: Pearson Prentice Hall, 2010.

CHAPTER FOURTEEN

The Unformalizable, Irreducible Primacy of the Person in the Digital Age

Esther Lightcap Meek

I offer this recently presented paper as a sample of the service of scholarship in which I participate thanks to President Jack White's 2004 invitation to join the faculty of Geneva College. It reflects interdisciplinary work at and for Geneva, in philosophy and in humanities, as well as the opportunity to join in the Polanyi Society and other academic ventures. I believe that the essay emblemizes Jack's world-embracing vision, which requires excellence in liberal arts scholarship, practiced in convivial conversation with other scholars, to the end of prophetically blessing the nations. In forwarding the primacy of the person, it bears witness to a distinctively Christian claim and reality.

Introduction

We live as humans in a digital age, a complex reality which this conference has met to explore.[1] In this paper I would like to contribute to the conversation a Polanyi-attuned philosophical reflection especially on the intriguing work of Satinder Gill, our host. Dr. Gill in her research has identified concrete expressions of the personal and interpersonal in what she terms the tacit engagement of humans.[2] Her larger agenda is to do this in order to develop technology to be able to support the "wider bandwidth" of personal engagement. To identify dimensions of the personal in human engagement, she has drawn on the thought of Michael Polanyi, specifically, his account of the bodily rooted functional aspect of tacit knowing. [3] Exploring this fascinating arena, she has identified bodied, interpersonal dynamics that are rhythmical as is music and dance. She and others are exploring art for the humanness missing in technology and science.

Especially since my own work foregrounds the person and the interpersoned, as well as dancelike rhythm and conversation, in my Polanyi-based epistemology, I find it confirming that Gill appropriates Polanyi, and then identifies bodied rhythms of knowing together.[4] Gill's work rightly foregrounds the bodied personal, and rightly exposes the modernist non-person centered epistemology which has fueled technological development. [5] Her discoveries advance the cause of a person-centered and inter-person-attuned epistemology.[6]

However, I wonder whether her project nevertheless leaves ensconced a deep-seated commitment to fundamental modernist philosophical presumptions, presumptions which Polanyi wrote to challenge as wrongheaded and culturally destructive. There is a lingering reductionism: the point of her endeavor may be to reduce personhood to formalizable components for which technological substitutes may be developed. Also, secondly, there is the implicit relegation of science, language, and technology to the domain of exhaustively impersonal, transferable information and communication—over against which art is cast as essentially different, and human. Third, it appears that Gill sustains a kind of embarrassment about the person—as if the notion of irreducible personhood must be rejected as anthropocentric—somehow a product of the very non-person-centered approach modernism has spawned.

I suggest that these implicit presumptions are just what Polanyi identified and challenged in defense of science, humanness, and culture. He demonstrated the fundamental unformalizability of machines, showing that certain necessary unformalizable contributions are irreducibly the affirmations of a person or persons. He challenged the separation of knowledge into impersonal and personal. He understood the need for a root-level redrawing of what we might call, with a hat tip to Gill's wonderful example of the meteorologists noted below, our inner philosophical picture. He offered such a philosophical vision, which includes centrally the irreducible primacy of the person, and also in which technology itself actually flourishes as the personed venture it is meant to be. I believe that these claims of Polanyi, which move beyond the ones Gill has specifically appropriated, would further enhance her project.

Much is at stake in this conversation. Reductionism, dualism, and dismissal of the person, are widespread in the digital age. Our technology is expanding exponentially, and in many ways our humanness appears to be in jeopardy. What is needed is deeper than an interface between the human and the technological. As Polanyi rightly understood, things must be redrawn on a more fundamental, philosophical, level.

In his 1974 classic, *Zen and the Art of Motorcycle Maintenance,* author Robert Pirsig concluded that the problem with technology was not the technology, but rather the technological mindset of the depersonalized persons using it. [7] But he also showed that personhood is fragile and must be accredited and protected. Even if it isn't the machines' fault, a defective philosophy that misconstrues them can and does occasion our mindless addictive surrender of our personhood. Personhood is irreducible; it is however also fragile.

In support of my thesis, I will present a selective synopsis of Gill's claims. I will then present some of Polanyi's claims and show how they bear on this matter. Finally, I briefly identify the claims of other thinkers which I believe are profoundly germane to this discussion, and to the wider concerns of humanness in the digital age.

Satinder Gill's Tacit Engagement

Summing up her book, Satinder Gill writes: "This book explores whether the concept of the *interface* can be located in *dialogue, performance,* and the *tacit dimension of knowledge* within the human system, and thereby expand possibilities for what it could then mean as technology. For this to be possible, I ask what would we need for an interface to support how we relate to each other, in particular, what Polanyi called our *personal act of knowing.*" [8] She explains that, in society's current reflection on technology, in contrast to the emphasis hitherto on the non-person centered—data, efficiency, utility, and automation, which have permeated the idea of interface, she and others want to ask "how to support our relations with each other and share and enable us to impart knowledge and skills when we are distributed in space." She asks specifically, "Yet what does it mean to mediate? What is the difference in the process of mediation when we are engaged in embodied co-present interaction, and when we are communicating via digital means? What then is the relation between mediation and interface?"

Referencing the Polanyi-Carl Rogers dialogue and the idea of part-whole Gestalt relationship, Gill restates her findings in the arts: "In this newly established self where the parts have become whole, trust and truth are established between dancers and with the audience. In art, authenticity creates trust between performer/artist and the performer and the audience/viewer.

"Truth lies in a personal act of knowing which is relational. This is distinct from truth acquired through data and logic." Also she has shown that: "The paradigm of data (of parts) and utility gives primacy to transactional information over that which is relational . . . Music is necessarily relational (rhythm, pitch, melodic) and language is primarily transactional (semantics and grammar)."[9]

Gill's conclusion: "What is clear is that we can better understand what makes for success if we consider how knowledge is performed in our daily lives with others, i.e., knowledge as skilled embodied performance. It is proposed that the key to success is the process of mediation which is a collective act between the participants engaged in it . . . Mediation is not of an individual's body movement and voice but lies within a collective act, whereby the expert recognizes the apprentice's idea as he moves with it, evident in his response of accepting it . . . In the collective moment of mediation, we express our 'know how', that we 'know that', and critically, that we 'know when', simultaneously."

"In conclusion," Gill writes, "it is arguable that any interface that seeks to engage with our personal act of knowing needs to be able to afford us our relational dimension in balance with transaction."[10]

Gill applauds the slow but growing shift to the relational: in computers: a shift from cognition to action; in music: a convergence of arts with digital technology, artists and scientists and technologists "joining hands to find alternative ways to investigate the relation between human and the digital and the mediated human, beyond the dominant concepts of technology as a transactional conduit. This is a shift in paradigm towards what I will term the *relational interface*" (Gill, 130).

Key to Gill's argument are a handful of significant real-life examples. A couple of them tell against technology and showcase her agenda; and a couple showcase her proposed solution. First, she is struck by her experience of a Japanese colleague proficient in communication, whose effectiveness breaks down when using Skype (Gill, 10-12). This is the technological gap which Gill hopes to reduce. Second, she tells a wonderful story of weather forecasters in the wake of highly digitized meteorological data only continue to succeed at effective forecasting by skillfully building an "inner picture" of the weather (Gill, 83). The data prove perhaps more certain but certainly more useless. Also, as she says elsewhere, digitized data has the effect of stripping experts of their confident, artful, expertise, binding them to the data as "the one best way" (Gill, 129).

Two more examples are positive and telling for Gill. One is her observation (and video) of a conversation between a senior and a junior design architect (Gill, 105ff). It is at the moment when their body movements synchronize, in the "parallel co-ordinated move," that a mutuality of understanding has been achieved. The other example features a group, which contains an expert, exploring a problem (Gill, 84-87). [11] There comes a point when someone in the group becomes "a mediator": he/she expresses the problem in such a way that the expert is able to recognize what is to be done, and the group collectively comes to understanding. These two examples epitomize what Gill notices and finds significant; she defines her central notion of "mediation" as the collective moment of integrative insight which they both display—see her definition in the quotes above. This is also how she conceives of a personal act of knowing, of knowing as relational, and of truth as this interpersoned event.[12] This is the tacit engagement beyond interaction for which technology must develop "bandwidth" in order to support human communication.

Now to my concerns. Gill's, even with her wonderful examples, is to uncover components of human interaction that are focally formalizable and thus capable of being technologically reproduced. It may be that her reasoning masks some slippage in her understanding of the term, mediation, when attributed to humans in direct contact, in which it is Polanyi's integrative aha moment, in contrast to, in technology, its designating a technological interface. Her ultimate goal remains to evolve computers to be more compatible with "the human system."

Second, it appears that the terms of Gill's project remain set by a latent defective epistemology and metaphysic. "Technology is here to stay," she comments (Gill, 158). Her question is how we can develop it more so that it will support human communication. Her solution—to draw on the resources of art and even to explore the liminal space between the two realms—observes a dichotomy between the non-human realm of technology and the human realm of art. She suggests that there are two kinds of truth, non-personal and personal, transactional and relational: science, knowledge and truth of one kind, and language, are non-person-centered; knowing and truth are personal only when knowing occurs between persons. And if these two realms are distinct, it appears that in some sense the transactional retains superiority as real knowledge—we remain concerned to communicate information. This epistemic posture comes through in the quotations above.

In connection with both of these matters, I find it telling that Gill's overall project appears to make little progress from beginning to end: her conclusion restates her original inquiry. While it is good to acknowledge the personal in knowing, it is only possible for her to say that a technological interface needs to be developed to support it.

Third, it appears that Gill harbors an ambivalence about the person. I note the following features of her argument. Technology, science, language (including semantics) is personless for her; art is personed and interpersoned. Further, she poses as significant the addition of the epistemic category of knowing *when* (to the common ones, knowing *that* and knowing how); yet she does not add knowing *who* and knowing *with whom*—even though her evidence compellingly suggests it. Additionally, she voices a concern to restrict the personal even in her own solution: we must "shift the position of the human from the center of a picture of progress to being part of nature and being material, where cosmological qualities of *energy* and *matter* become salient." Elsewhere she says: "However, the problem of intersubjectivity is that we assume and judge others according to our own 'self', so what if the problem of a difference of opinion or a misunderstanding lies with our assumption and not with the other? How can we realize our cultural assumptions in a distributed setting?"[13] These passages suggest that she allies the idea of person with modern Western domination, and thus paradoxically with the non-person-centered side of the dichotomy. Then, instead, she finds a more befitting "modesty," paradoxically, in a more non-personal cosmology.

Michael Polanyi's Unformalizability of the Personal

Let us now gather some of Polanyi's work which address Gill's implicit commitments. First, in a short piece called, "The Hypothesis of Cybernetics," Polanyi demonstrates that the idea that there could ever be an exhaustively formalized system of deductive inference (as his Manchester University colleague Alan Turing and others were proposing) is logically flawed. Instead, any such system requires unformalizable supplements. These consist of positive, substantial, essentially and irreducibly personed acts of knowing, understanding and acknowledging. These may be considered "psychological," but they are also logically undeniable and fundamentally operative, if the system is to be one of semantic (true) inference.[14] Consider the following quotations:

"Thus, I maintain that a formal system of symbols and operations functions as a deductive system only by virtue of unformalized supplements. We must know the meaning of undefined terms, understand what is stated in our axioms and believe it to be true, and acknowledge an implication in the handling of symbols by formal proof. These acts of knowing, understanding and acknowledging are not formalized: they may be jointly designated as the 'semantic operations' of the formalized system."

"Formalisation can be extended to hitherto unformalized semantic operations, but only if the resulting formal system can in its turn rely on yet unformalized semantic operations. The elimination of 'psychological elements' by formalization remains necessarily incomplete. The purpose of formalization lies in the reduction of informal functions to what we believe to be more limited and obvious operations; but it must not aim at their elimination."

"The semantic operations attached to a formal system are functions of the mind which understands and correctly operates the system . . . Since a formal system will always require supplementation by unformalized operations, it follows that none can ever function without a person who performs these operations. A formalized deductive system is an *instrument* which requires for its logical completion a mind." [15]

Personal Knowledge contains a closely related discussion, in which he speaks of the tacit coefficient, calling us to the very personed act of accrediting it. The tacit coefficient is both personal and unspecifiable (unformalizable). It alone makes a tool a tool; and this applies not merely to computers, but to a language or to a scientific theory. It is a hazardous, confident, commitment, from start to finish. The personal is essentially and consistently what makes truth and meaning. It alone is what spawns the logical leap involved in new discoveries (*PK*, 257). [16]

In justification, Polanyi cites Kurt Godel's incompleteness proof, and also the work of Alfred Tarski regarding truth. "Tarski has shown that any formal system in which we could assert a sentence and also reflect on the truth of its assertion must be self-contradictory. Thus, in particular, the assertion that any theorem of a given formal language is true can be made only by a sentence that is meaningless within that language. Such an assertion forms part of a richer language than that which comprises the sentences whose truth it asserts."

Polanyi draws attention the logical distinction between persons and machines. "The necessary relatedness of machines to persons does essentially restrict the independence of a machine and reduce the status of automata in general below that of thinking persons. For a machine is a machine only for someone who relies on it (actually or hypothetically) for some purpose, that he believes to be attainable by what he considers to be the proper functioning of the machine: it is the instrument of a person who relies on it. This is the difference between machine and mind. A man's mind can carry out feats of intelligence by aid of a machine and also without such aid, while a machine can function only as the extension of a person's body under the control of his mind . . . The machine can be said to function intelligently only by aid of unspecifiable personal coefficients supplied by the user's mind."

Polanyi explicitly dissents from Turing's conclusion that a machine that deceives us into thinking that it thinks is actually thinking: "According to these definitions of 'mind' and 'person', neither a machine nor a neurological model, nor an equivalent robot, can be said to think, feel, imagine, desire, mean, believe or judge something. They may conceivably simulate these propensities to such an extent as to deceive us altogether. But a deception, however compelling, does not qualify thereby as truth: no amount of subsequent experience can justify us in accepting as identical two things known from the start to be different in their nature." [17]

Polanyi concludes that we must accredit the person and his/her essentially personed acts of understanding, judging, and so on; and he concludes that this calls for an ontology: "Our theory of knowledge is now seen to imply an ontology of the mind. Objectivism requires a specifiably functioning mindless knower. To accept the indeterminacy of knowledge requires, on the contrary, that we accredit a person entitled to shape his knowing according to his own judgment, unspecifiably." [18]

I draw one final quotation from the Polanyi-Rogers dialogue.[19] Carl Rogers laments that science appears to be leaving out the person. Polanyi responds first by citing the Hungarian Revolution, in which Communist citizens awoke to the fact that Communism is essentially not true—and then society's subsequent denial that the revolution had been about truth. For Polanyi this glaringly displays the moral inversion involved in Communism. For the reader it is telling that Polanyi closely associates the totalitarianism ravaging his life and culture with "the mechanistic view of man," about which he says the following: "For the unsatisfactory nature of the same mechanistic conception of man eliminates the responsibility of man, doesn't know the place for it, and has no place for the autonomous intrinsic powers of thought in general — not only responsibility but also the whole of our actions as having meaning. Individuals have no place in the scope of mechanistic interpretation." Polanyi then addresses the need for a revised inner philosophical picture: "As to science, I again think that we must first of all have a pretty good and new idea about knowledge in general, and then we can come to science and put it right. But in the first place, I think we must have a clear mechanism, and that is, at any rate, what I was trying to establish. A mechanism which, without obscurity and without forcing the issue or the conclusions, brings us a way of seeing — a necessary and adequate way of seeing — which does not reduce man to an aggregate of atoms or even to a mechanism but gives us, straight away, an access to him as a person; and when we have that, we can, I think, move on a fairly large scale from man to other things, and also to history."[20]

How do these insights pertain to Gill's commitments? In the Rogers-Polanyi passage we glimpse the philosopher's sweeping agenda: to reshape our "inner philosophical picture." Polanyi is claiming that there is a problem with both mechanization and science as currently understood. Polanyi's solution, in contrast to what I take Gill's to be, is not additive but rather transformative. It involves, not tacking on research from art (presumed to be distinctively human, exterior to (a presumed nonpersonal) science and technology) and a (consequently presumed) space between art and science. Instead it requires a philosophical—epistemological and metaphysical overhaul—to both science and art. His agenda refuses to concede a personless science or technology, but rather seeks to reclaim and rehabilitate them as fully personal, to be what they are and are meant to be.

To say it in a different way, Polanyi refuses to relegate technology, science, and language to Martin Buber's I it, and then go in search of I You. For Polanyi knowledge is I You throughout, technology and science included. In contrast to Gill, Polanyi begins, not by accepting technology as impersonal, but by refusing to accept it as impersonal. I suspect that an improper implicit concession of technology to I it is at least a factor in the way that technology is widely seen now to be threatening our very personhood, rendering us ourselves as robotic.

It's going to take epistemological and metaphysical work that challenges and redraws modernity's assumptions at the most fundamental level. Epistemologically, this will include distinctively and logically the affirmation of the exclusively personal acts of affirmation, appraisal, and understanding as a tacit and unformalizable, robustly personed component of all knowledge of any sort, including technology itself. To this end Polanyi has offered two things. First, he shows the logical defect of overlooking the essential component of irreducible sophisticatedly personal acts in science and technology. Second, throughout his work, he offers a creative alternative epistemology which is difficult to deny in day-to-day life. Both hold a metaphysical implication of the person as an ontologically irreducible reality. Finally, we may infer from Polanyi's concern with Turing's proposals and the overall outlook regarding science, that despite the obviousness of all this, defending the irreducibly personal in this age is an ongoing challenge which must never be allowed to wain—not only in defense of persons, but in defense of science.

Technology and science have been exalted as focal, objective and neutral.[21] They should instead be seen to be tools—intrinsically personal through and through *as* tools in the employ of persons—just as are coordinated body movement and artistry. Rather than reductivistically formalizing and simulating interpersonal dynamics in supposedly impersonal technology, we may do something even better, and arguably more natural: we may catch up the very technology *subsidiarily* as a tool in service to irreducibly personal and interpersonal reality. This renders technology itself personal, as paper and pen are, when it subsidiarily supports a logically prior interpersonal communion and when the interpersonal communion is not reduced to it. One wonderful thing about subsidiaries is that the defining goal is integratively irreducible to it, beyond it, and thus in a freeing way not entirely impeded by its subsidiaries' gaps or failures. So long as the upper-level goal is operative as logically prior and definitive of the activity, even slightly defective subsidiaries—such as technology short of a relational interface—can be indwelt and "forgiven" in the process.

I believe that Polanyi's inner philosophical picture proves more fundamentally germane and helpful to Gill's project than perhaps Gill herself has so far mined it. His philosophical picture not only honors the bodily subsidiary, and that as personal; it also requires commitment to the person as ontologically irreducible and to uniquely personed acts of knowing as fundamentally unformalizable, including the necessary personal accreditation of technology, science, and language.

Other Voices

Thomas Friedman

I would like to introduce briefly a few other bodies of work, with which I am also preoccupied, and which I believe are germane to this important study. First is the cultural reflection of Pulitzer Prize-winning New York Times foreign affairs columnist, Thomas Friedman, specifically his most recent book, *Thank You for Being Late: An Optimist's Guide to Thriving in an Age of Accelerations.22* Friedman thoroughly documents the acceleration of technological innovation (alongside other accelerations in globalization and climate change) since 2007. He accepts it and finds it exciting. But he counsels that in order to thrive in this age, humans must foreground irreducibly human things.

We must anchor in sustainable community values, belonging, mutual respect, culture, character. We must become human again; study the liberal arts; scale the Golden Rule. We should seek to build a platform of trust. We should develop "stempathy"—only one-to-one between humans. We should gather small collaborative groups around a dining table. Friedman's counsel accurately gives expression to the primacy of the person in a way that affirmatively contexts, because it does not idolize, technology. [23]

Sherry Turkle

In her *Reclaiming Conversation: The Power of Talk in a Digital Age*, sociologist Sherry Turkle documents extensively the phenomenon of depersonalization that technology appears to be producing. She writes: "This new mediated life has gotten us in trouble. Face-to-face conversation is the most human—and humanizing—thing we do. Fully present to one another, we learn to listen. It's where we develop the capacity for empathy."

Our society's overuse especially of smart phones "all adds up to a flight from conversation . . . technology is implicated in an assault on empathy." "It means lost practice in the empathic arts—learning to make eye contact, to listen, and to attend to others. Conversation is on the path toward the experience of intimacy, community, and communion. Reclaiming conversation is a step toward reclaiming our most fundamental human values." (Turkle, 7). [24] Her repeated mantra: Technology enchants; conversation cures. "My argument is not anti-technology. It's pro-conversation" (Turkle, 25).

Turkle offers copious examples to document the adverse impact of our devices on human conversation, and the adverse impact of that especially on children, but throughout our lives and society. She is especially concerned with our current desire to talk, not through technology, but *to* technology, as if it were a person. One may think that Polanyi had no idea of such a world. Yet it is Alan Turing's "imitation game" which Turkle explicitly cites (Turkle, 349). Turkle sees our current time as a turning point—an opportunity to reaffirm what makes us most human.

Turkle's work confirms that personhood is irreducible but also fragile. It can be defaced (a telling word!), in this case by a very personal decision to accede to technology in an addictive way. Persons may—and sadly often do—give away their personhood—and not just to technology. And it's going to take an exclusively personed acts—reclaiming, and reclaiming conversation in particular—to protect the irreducibly personal. Arguably, giving away our personhood is endemic to non-person-centered modernist epistemology. [25]

D. C. Schindler

These last two bodies of work represent what I take to be the kind of metaphysics that needs to happen helpfully around personhood in modernity, and thus as helpful to our reflections on technology and humanness. Classical Christian philosopher D. C. Schindler argues that reason is essentially ecstatic.[26] By "reason," he means human knowing, and he is herein offering an epistemic account. Unlike modernist epistemologies, reason must be essentially beyond itself, out there in and with "the other"—with the thing that it longs to know. Knowing, for Schindler, decidedly is not the transfer of information, but rather the intimate interpersonal communion of personal presence with the irreducible other.[27] (Schindler, *Love,* chap. 2) And this is not just a description of knowing other persons; it is an account of all knowing of anything. All knowing is "mediation" in Gill's Polanyian sense: an I-see-you encounter. Honoring the person, rather than dominating and belittling the non-personal, actually supports an intrinsic regard for things (Schindler, *Catholicity,* 54). Schindler offers his proposals in order to challenge directly what he shows to be the immodest false modesty of modernist efforts to limit human reason. For Schindler as for Polanyi, human knowledge has a polar, from-to-and-beyond structure.[28]

In his later work, *Love and the Postmodern Predicament,* Schindler directly addresses the technological mindset of our age. Beginning with Aristotle's assertion that all men by nature desire to know. This desire is a fundamental part of what makes us human: we are made for this contact with an intrinsically meaningful and delightful world. However, "one of the things that specifies modern culture and distinguishes it from the traditional cultures of the world, is the effort to buffer this encounter. Modern culture is largely a conspiracy to protect us from the real."[29] He continues: "We mediate our encounter with the world as far as possible through technology, which is said to 'enhance' it in various ways, but technology in fact always sets the terms for our encounter." "In short," Schindler says, "the energies of the modern world are largely devoted to keeping reality at bay, monitoring any encounter with what is genuinely other than ourselves, and protecting us from possible consequences, intended or otherwise."[30] But this means that this project is radically antihuman as well as anti-reality. Schindler's purpose in this book, "in the face of this project which we are increasingly taking for granted as something altogether normal, is to recall a pre-modern vision of man as ordered to communion with reality." His philosophical anthropology taps the positive relational transcendentals, beauty, goodness and truth, as marking all reality specifically as related to positively by the human person in apprehending the world. What is at stake in the transcendentals, "in short, is the most basic meaning of things and so man's fundamental relationship with the world, with himself and others, and with God." In other words, the urgent problem and its one cure are philosophical. This is an apologia for philosophy, "interpreted here as *an all-encompassing love of the real* . . ."[31]

Although Schindler avers that much more could be said, he makes this general assertion about technology: "The more technology dominates our culture, the less philosophical we are capable of being, which is to say the more remote we become from the real" (Schindler, *Love,* 28). Schindler continues: "If what we have been saying is true, a *focus* on technology is an implicit denial of the transcendentals" and is anti-philosophical. From his point of view, philosophizing around technology is likely to be avoided or underdone.

In contrast to Gill, Polanyi, and Friedman, Schindler is obviously less sanguine about technology. Polanyi was writing just before the technological age in which we now move. Schindler, writing from in our time, prodigiously articulates the classical philosophical tradition latent, I believe, in Polanyi's intuitive philosophical reflections. This sets in relief the remarkable contribution of Michael Polanyi as a premier scientist intuitively developing the natural and necessary philosophical implications of his science. It suggests that a Polanyian/Schindlerian philosophical picture need not be antithetical to technology.

Robert Spaemann

German philosopher Robert Spaemann's essay, "In Defense of Anthropomorphism," helpfully addresses Gill's and others' concerns about anthropocentrism. [32]

Spaemann considers the question, "Is this real?" He poses that the real world is not the world held in common, nor the world of objects (modernist anthropocentrism). We confidently grasp reality on the grounds of anthropomorphism, as follows: I see that you are seeing me and talking about me—that what (who) you are affirming is not my body as object, but my*self*. I am object as subject. I am the object of another's speech. Even Descartes' famous cogito implicitly affirms this. "My subjectivity is an objective reality—and this is what we mean by 'persons': an objective reality that represents a standard by which to measure every true judgment." "Persons are real only in plural, that is, as subjectivities that have become objective for one another. "It is only in the act of recognition that the person is given as person. But this is true of every experience of reality in a certain sense." Not to do so is a moral mistake. You cannot separate ontology and ethics.

Spaemann directly challenges Hilary Putnam's "internal realism": "At this point we must all be metaphysical realists." The experience of our own reality is not to be dismissed as "a special case," but rather installed as the paradigm for the humans' relatedness to all things, human and nonhuman. "The mode of givenness of other persons is the paradigm for the givenness of reality in general." "We attribute reality to things beyond what the encountered object is for us and what we experience of it." This is essentially anthropomorphism. It is unavoidable, as Nietzsche and others saw. But Spaemann emphatically distinguishes it from the anthropocentrism endemic to modernity: objectivism is intrinsically anthropocentrism—it reduces things as well as persons to their functional service to me. This anthropocentrism is what allows the possibility, I note, of Turing's destructively reducing thinking to any functional equivalent which deceives me. In fact, rejecting this anthropomorphism actually leads to the disappearance of the person. Spaemann displays what may go on in the way of offering an account of personhood which bears on technology, modernity, and everything else.

In Conclusion

Our digital age is eliciting timely reflection about humanness, of which Satinder Gill's intriguing and telling work is a specimen. At the same time, technology appears to threaten personhood, and personhood proves to be fragile. In this essay I have argued that the conversation must go forward on a fundamental epistemological and metaphysical level, as Michael Polanyi recognized and endeavored to carry out. While Gill is to be commended for appropriating some Polanyian insights, her project would benefit from a more thoroughgoing appropriation of his inner philosophical picture.

Technology is here to stay. But what better not be with us to stay is the defective epistemology and metaphysics that a modernist philosophical picture harbors. Instead, both humans and technology will be helped if we affirm—a personal act—the personal as irreducible and envision if we affirm technology as thoroughly personed tool. I believe that this will only support and enhance the diligence and insights of Satinder Gill.

Notes

[1]Paper for "Tacit Engagement in the Digital Age," CRASSH Conference at University of Cambridge, Jun 26-28, 2019.

[2]Satinder Gill, *Tacit Engagement: Beyond Interaction* (Springer, 2015). Additionally, Ms. Gill presented via Skype at a recent Polanyi Conference (June 2018): "Rhythm and Tacit Knowing in Embodied Performance."

[3]Gill works with Polanyi's *Tacit Dimension.* She notes also the phenomenal aspect of tacit knowing. And she quotes more than once a passage on p. 49 regarding persons as comprehensive entities (Gill, 28, 31, and elsewhere).

[4]Esther Lightcap Meek, *Loving to Know: Introducing Covenant Epistemology* (Eugene, OR: Cascade, 2011).

[5]Satinder Gill, *Tacit Engagement: Beyond Interaction* (Springer, 2015) 39 – 43.

[6]Gill, *Ibid.*, 47 – 58.

[7]Robert M. Pirsig, *Zen and the Art of Motorcycle Maintenance: An Inquiry into Values* (orig. pub. 1974).

[8]Gill, *op* cit, p127. Regarding Gill's repeated allusion to p. 49 of Michael Polanyi, *The Tacit Dimension* (The University of Chicago Press, 1966): I wonder whether she interprets this passage as speaking collectively: a comprehensive entity is the entire phenomenon of persons in interpersonal conversation. I believe that the text should be read distributively: Polanyi is listing some examples of comprehensive entities. This perhaps supports Gill's puzzling (to me) emphasis that mediation is collective (See n. 8 below.) I wonder whether as a result she deems knowing personal and relational only when it involves persons conversationally, rather than all-knowing being personal and relational. This would be in contrast I believe to Polanyi's work, and in contrast to my own epistemic account.

[9]Gill, *op cit*, 128. In a footnote here she distinguishes her use of "relational" from the relationships between people. As far as I can tell, this is the only mention of this distinction. It leaves me unsure of what she means by relational—and I do not recall that she has defined the term in the text. I wonder if this too suggests an embarrassment regarding the person (see below).

[10]Gill, *op cit*, 130. I have struggled to grasp with confidence a single meaning of "mediation" in Gill's usage. At first it seemed that she was using it to reference Polanyi's subsidiary indwelling of clues (Gill, 29). Of course this includes knowing together in ensemble. But here and elsewhere it appears that she restricts the use of the term to the ensemble setting, to the collective aha moment in the ensemble.

[11]Gill, *Tacit Engagement*, pp. 130, 11-12, 83, 129, 105ff, 84-87.

[12]These examples are the heart of Gill's study. They are also the aspects of her work that especially intrigue me with respect to my own covenant epistemology. In future work I would like to transpose her valuable insights into a key that is concerned with knowing and being simply.

[13]Gill, *Tacit Engagement*, pp.131, 158.

[14]Michael Polanyi, "The Hypothesis of Cybernetics." *British Journal*

for the Philosophy of Science (2[5/8] (1951: May-1952: Feb), 312-15, p. 313.

[15]Polanyi, "Cybernetics," pp. 313, 313-314.

[16]Michael Polanyi, *Personal Knowledge: Towards a Post-Critical Philosophy* (Chicago: University of Chicago Press, corrected ed. 1962), 249-64, pp. 249, 250, 250-51, 256, 257. To the point of Gill's concern about Western anthropocentrism, Polanyi at the outset calls us to accredit far wider cognitive powers than objectivist conception (which also reduces the independence of human judgment), p. 249.

[17]Polanyi, *Personal Knowledge*, pp. 260, 261f, 263.

[18]Polanyi, *Personal Knowledge*, p. 264.

[19]"A Dialogue: Carl Rogers and Michael Polanyi." Recorded at KPBS television, San Diego, California, March 5, 1966 [transcribed from pp. 193-201, Coulson and Rogers (eds.), Man and the Science of Man, 1968] http://www.polanyisociety.org/Polanyi-Rogers%20Dialog-pdf.pdf. Gill also notes and quotes from a version of this dialogue (Gill, 128, 157).

[20]It should be evident that Polanyi is using "mechanism" in two different senses: 1) an inner philosophical picture; 2) a machine.

[21]Since the Enlightenment humans have even aspired to themselves be automata, as Gill notes (Gill, 35-36).

[22]Thomas L. Friedman, *Thank You for Being Late: An Optimist's Guide to Thriving in an Age of Accelerations* (Version 2.0; New York: Picador, 2017) I am interested in his work especially because of my task as coordinator of a core interdisciplinary humanities course at my college.

[23]Friedman, *Thank You for Being Late*, pp. 371-87, 486, 273, 391, 444, 484, 490, 482, 488.

[24]Sherry Turkle, *Reclaiming Conversation: The Power of Talk in a Digital Age* (New York: Penguin, 2015), pp. 3, 4, 7.

[25]Turkle, *Reclaiming Conversation*, pp. 25, 349.

[26]D. C. Schindler, "Surprised by Truth," chap. 2 in *The Catholicity of Reason* (Grand Rapids: Eerdmans, 2013).

[27]D. C. Schindler, "Truth: Knowledge as Personal Presence," chap. 4 in *Love and the Postmodern Predicament: Rediscovering the Real Beauty, Goodness and Truth* (Eugene, OR: Cascade, 2018) This chapter began as a lecture given by D. C. Schindler as the 2015 Dr. Byron I. Bitar Memorial Lecturer at Geneva College.

[28]Polanyi's "indeterminate future manifestations" are akin to Schindler's "ecstatic" nature of reason.

[29]D. C. Schindler, "Love," p. 2.

[30]D. C. Schindler, "Love," p. 3.

[31]D. C. Schindler, "Love," pp. 3, 22, 3.

[32]Robert Spaemann, *A Robert Spaemann Reader: Philosophical Essays on Nature, God, and the Human Person* (ed. and trans. By D. C. Schindler and Jeanne Heffernan Schindler. Oxford: Oxford University Press, 2015), 77-96, pp. 81, 83, 85, 81-82, and on the next page, p. 88.

CHAPTER FIFTEEN

The Rise of 'Artisan' English

Jonathan M. Watt

Introduction

It seems fitting for this linguist to contribute to a volume honoring a man with a global vision for cooperation within Christ's body a paper on the effects of modern globalization upon the most widely diffused *lingua franca* of the modern world, namely, English. The subject is coming under widespread examination these days and has been addressed in such works as Jan Blommaert's 2010 monograph, *The Sociolinguistics of Globalization.* This present article will look narrowly at relevant effects manifested in the orthography of what we can loosely describe as the "English" notes of selected multilinguals who were examined for a study that was presented in a paper at a 2015 conference in Vienna, Austria, titled "Idiolect, Candy Bars and 'Artisan English' Orthography." While its anecdotal information is yet to be quantified, it illustrates how multilinguals in a culturally diverse environment adapt their personal notes in a way that reflects divergent linguistic prompts coming from the past and present environments of their writers, and do so in unexpected interesting ways. When language communities come into contact, they share various features (phonological, morpho-syntactic, lexical and semantic) in both directions, and the more densely concentrated and sustained the contact is, the wider the possibilities for code-switching, blending, development of pidgins, and so forth as discussed by this writer in two previous articles.[1] A prevalent twist to this contact-induced picture of influence is the prevalence of technologically-facilitated interaction, which is now receiving attention in the literature as well.[2] This paper delves into a sub-sector of this latter globalized, contact-induced language influence, coming to a writing effect that I have called *artisan English*, after the emergence of artisan bakeries with their internationalized variations on breads and pastries.

Indeed, not all contact originates *per se* on the page. Oral forms are the basis for all natural language phenomena; spoken discourse is ubiquitous, and spoken language is primary. With opportunities for contact being vast, not surprisingly multilingualism is the most common experience for today's population. However, even those of us in the minority who remain functional monolinguals have passed through dialect stages. Like many others, I had a culturally diverse upbringing that included experiences in four continents before I had completed elementary school. As a fourth-generation Australian by birth, my own dialect was to contour mostly to that of the northeastern United States, albeit with vestiges of my childhood dialects emerging with this or that word. So, I started a running in-class game with my undergraduate students some years ago, as a learning incentive, inviting them to win what I call "the prestigious candy bar award." The first student in any given semester who can catch me speaking a word in the Australian-English dialect of my childhood wins a candy bar of their choice. Dozens of chocolate bars are awarded in any given semester, for the game is challenging but reasonable. The way one uses language is an oral fingerprint, and it betrays their life experiences of moving between language communities in contact.

My linguistic fingerprint, i.e. my idiolect (the way an individual uniquely speaks a language) contains roughly 50 words, as

I have come to discover thanks to that classroom initiative, that betray that background. Whereas a more restricted interaction with American dialect *might* have led to dialect leveling—"the ways in which dialects can lose aspects of their distinctiveness when their speakers come into contact with speakers of other dialects"[3]—in my case, an almost complete shift has taken place. Most people recognize my speech as essentially North American, and only occasionally will someone ask where I come from (usually, they guess Ireland), noticing particulars like the following:

- Certain vowels more typical of British or British-Australian dialect:
  invitation, like /ai-oi/
  east /oist/
  *thor**ough**, **Mc**Donalds* /schwa/
  *straw**berry*** /-bri/
  *am**o**ng, sh**o**ne, everyb**o**dy, fr**o**m, sc**o**ne, pr**o**duce, wh**a**t, M**o**slem* - with lax /o/
  ***aw**ful, **a**lright, **a**ll, w**a**ter* /aw/ instead of tense /o/
  *B**u**ddha* /U/
  *Chris**t**ianity* /t/ rather than /ch/
  Some diphthongizations: *how, now* /hau/
  deity /ei/ not /i/
  *c**u**rrent, w**o**rry* schwa instead of syllabic /r/
- Certain words stressed on first (*cremate, detail*) or second (*advertisement*) syllable
- Aspirated /w/ in *which, what, while;* and aspirated /ks/ in *exit*
- Epenthetic /r/ - usually after *idea* (and some non-prevocalic *r*-lessness before consonants)
- Voiced rather than unvoiced /th/ in *tru**ths**, wi**th***
- Expressions: "*Do* see/think/talk" / "in hospital" / "mum" / "Take a crack at it" / "Give it a go"
- Blended British & American pronunciation: *figure* /fIgr/
- Some British word meanings: *diary* 'day-timer', *goodly* (used as adjective),
  Cheers! (i.e. 'goodbye'), *crèche* ('nativity scene')

These features which periodically make their way into my lectures present my students with a modest range of targets. By themselves, some of these features would be nothing more than American regionalisms or free variation (e.g. *gotten*, disyllabic *Graham*, *vase* as /vaz/ instead of /veis/; *systemic* with lax /e/; and *during* with word-initial /j/; *bubonic* with /by-/). However, most of these are vestiges of an (Australian-)English dialect.

The exercise I have described, and the subject I am about to describe, are made possible by the ability people have to recognize, as well as create, a seemingly infinite variety of language variations that makes even the Chomskyan concept of infinite production appear tame by comparison. The complex recombination potentials of sounds, words and phrasing—magnified by the complexities of situational (and pragmatic) factors—become exponentially diversified (and complicated) by the introduction of multiple language codes. What exists at a restricted level in one's idiolect is only a hint of what is emerging in the world of international English*es* (as the literature usually labels it) as they become subjected to internationalized forces.

Focus of This Study

This study examines a small subset of that global scene, namely, code-switching in written class-related notes made by adult L2 English speakers in connection with post-secondary education in North America. All situations involved English as the medium of classroom instruction. The notes provided by the consultants had been prepared only for their own private reference and study—and this brings in a control not typical of most code-switching studies. My goal is to consider how globalization today is prompting new dimensions to code-switching: while central concepts such as *language*, *dialect*, and *register* remain valid, additional nuances and flexibility in our conception of these linguistic concepts is diversifying, as privatized and particularized uses which I am labeling *artisan English* are now appearing as a result of our marketplace of cross-national interactions. By that term *artisan English*, I am designating variations on English language that are not only reflective of language contact (as described in the literature) but are expressive of unique purposes and cultural linkages specific to the individual user and particular speech/writing act. Artisan English forms, unlike their traditional linguistics counterpart concepts, may be transitional and ephemeral; they are not necessarily functioning at dialect level, but might be considered a register or style. Again, the goal is to see how native language, or second languages influences the *written* English of internationals in the United States, specifically in written materials intended strictly for their own personal use. By narrowing the scope in this way, I filter out some of the social circumstances which normally shape language choices.

In the process, it will be helpful first to identify some of the game-changing factors of modern globalism that are prompting language changes. Second, I will introduce some of the observations discussed in Blommaert's[4] as a framework for examining the personal note samples I have gathered. Third, I shall demonstrate how this *artisan English* paints a new face on certain language contact phenomena.

Globalization and Its (Dis)contents

Definitions of modern *globalization* abound in the literature, among them "the process of becoming global…[and] the state that results from this process."[5] It is producing new forms of inter-dependences, as Thomas Friedman mentions in his description of the process, describing it as the "inexorable integration of markets, nation-states and technologies to a degree never witnessed before…"[6] Blommaert similarly suggests that the term is "shorthand for the intensified flows of capital, goods, people, images and discourses around the globe, driven by technological innovations mainly in the field of media and information and communication technology, and resulting in new patterns of global activity, community organization and culture…"[7] Yet, as he notes, globalization is hardly new, given its counterpart movement in 19th century colonial "geoculture" that had been facilitated by the Enlightenment, capitalism and mass politics; he could as well have made mention of the wide reach of classical cultures, as empires such as Greece and Rome stretched their colonizing hands around and beyond their Mediterranean home base.

Although globalization flashes a familiar face, today it moves faster, broader and more inclusively than ever before, and activates a set of factors that are precipitating unprecedented changes that go beyond those seen before. Nikolas Coupland,[8] for example, identifies such factors as the proliferation and speeding up of communication technologies, global dispersion of service-sector work, diminished trust of authorities, upsurge of individualism and ethnic pluralism, and increased permeability of national boundaries alongside demographic mobility and globally-based conflicts. Communication codes are both expanding and fragmenting in "an evolving set of relationships among languages as their utility values change".[9] One of the new effects is the "compression of time and space…[s]ocial relations, and even forms of intimacy, become possible across distance, but they still have to be negotiated through complex and sometimes restrictive forms of mediation," with the effect that such traditional concepts as "community" and "speech community" are becoming re-envisioned at best, or discarded altogether. My study suggests that the compression of formerly distant points may play a role in the transient artisan forms I describe here.

Such conceptual changes, as discussed by Fairclough, are leading to "a transformation in the spatial organization of social relations and transactions…"; he adds to those the "networks, connectivities and interactions which cut across spatial boundaries and borders crucially include, and we might say depend upon, particular forms (or what I shall call *genres*) of communication which are specialized for trans-national and interregional interaction." Among his examples is CNN news, which is "organized to communicate news in a distinctive (though widely imitated way) which is familiar and easily recognized all over the world."[10] He intentionally distinguishes "processes" from "discourses of" globalization while noting that each influences the other. Fairclough's discussion of Held presents differences between "hyperglobalist," sceptical" (sic) and "transformationalist" classifications (2006:14–26) and how they lead to predictions regarding the course of nation-states, consideration of whether these things are cyclical, and whether or not it all leads to homogenization or regional diversities. Fairclough's stated purposes involve "CDA" (critical discourse analysis).

In Chapter Six ("Globalization from below"), Fairclough describes how individuals may defend themselves against, or take advantages of, the "processes of globalization." He suggests (121) that "Globalization makes available new resources for local action which include new discourses and practices and identities (including genres and styles) in which these discourses are internalized and operationalized." It seems to me that it illustrates what Fairclough (p.123) called "the interpenetration of global and local [which] has been referred to as 'glocalization,'" a "cultural hybridity" which evidences "the mingling of cultures from different territorial locations." He summarizes the features of "intertextuality and interdiscursive hybridity of texts" (168–169).[11]

Mufwene notes that in the face of various stages of globalization, the literature has discussed worldwide evolution of English under three categories: native English (e.g. UK, North America, Australia and New Zealand), Pidgin and Creole forms (e.g. in the Caribbean and Pacific islands), and indigenized English (e.g. India and other former colonies). Though global, English is not evenly distributed.[12] "Outer circle" countries have only about 20 percent of their population speaking it fluently, while its usage as a second language diminishes drastically in "expanding circle" countries (such as Japan and Taiwan, and particularly in their rural areas). Contra Crystal, Mufwene argues that the concept of a WSSE—world standard spoken English—is a misnomer. Instead he proposes: "If WSSE were to arise spontaneously, or could do so at all, it would be the first such evolution toward linguistics uniformity in the history of language spread and contact. The universal trend has been for the prevailing language to diversify, especially in the spoken form, as is made evident by the history of English itself and, before it, by that of Latin. Worse for wishful thinking, even Standard English itself, which is controlled by several institutions, has diversified."[13]

The focused study which follows is located in this internationalized conceptual realm, and the unique and perhaps even strange links such a compact world now offers its speakers.

Language Contact: Global-Style

The subject under discussion involves *language contact* and the essential, related concept of *borrowing*, described by Thomason and Kaufman as "the incorporation of foreign features into a group's native language by speakers of that language: the native language is maintained but is changed by the addition of the incorporated features," They add: "Invariably, in a borrowing situation, the first foreign elements to enter the borrowing language are words."[14] As various recent publications have suggested,[15] the forces and frequency of opportunities to share features have intensified and, as a result, the types of morphophonemic and lexical features being shared has taken on new contours, especially in the realm of orthography, as Mufwene[16] and this study suggests; the latter interacts significantly with these volumes, and with Blommaert's *Sociolinguistics of Globalization*.

The occasions for code-switching, a realm that normally goes hand-in-hand with language contact, appear in some unusual ways as well (to be illustrated shortly). *Code-switching* is the alternation of languages or dialects performed by multilingual speakers within a particular speech act, and since Ferguson's classic study[17] is said to be typified by *situational* or *metaphoric* conditions, the former relating to complex (or even conflicting) demands of the speakers present at the time of the interaction, the latter being for the purposes of poetic effect or humor. Code-switching usually occurs at morphological, lexical or phrasal boundaries. Along with various works by this writer (mostly as it occurs in biblical literature), Bullock and Toribio's

Cambridge Handbook of Linguistic Code-switching[18] is a thorough resource (see relevant essays).

The specific ways globalization is layering and complexifying the world picture has been discussed by Blommaert, who contrasts the established paradigm of *sociolinguistics of distribution* with its "movement in a horizontal and stable space and in chronological time" with what he describes as a *sociolinguistics of mobility* which "focuses not on language-in-place but on language-in-motion," replete with "layered...scale levels..." Whereas horizontal space involves neighborhoods, regions and countries, vertical space is "layered and stratified... in which all sorts of socially, culturally and politically salient distinctions occur." He explains that these "*indexical* distinctions" involve "orders of indexicality" that define belonging, identities and roles (see pp. 37–39 for his discussion of indexicality).[19] For example, migration-related language contact once necessitated "change in the spatial organization of one's life in an enduring way. People left their country and settled in another"—though this is oversimplified, as Paulston's work on "extrinsic language communities" shows, it has typically been the case in the past). Blommaert's work is compatible with many of Fairclough's observations.

The new super-diversity just described results in a different sort of *repertoire*—the codes available to a multilingual—that includes more codes than might be expected, including undeveloped ones which he calls "fragmented," "incomplete" and "truncated." These fragmented repertoire options appear in print as well as speech. They now appear in *stratified distribution patterns* "in which specific language resources are deployed...on particular scale-levels and not on others; what is valid in one situation is not valid in another." This helps define a new paradigm for perception: "The key to understanding this complex pattern is what counts as a language in particular contexts," hence the limits of the traditional patterns of code-switching in which codes are "artefectualized languages" [*sic*]; what is emerging is the fact that outside of particular situations or instances certain "languages have no potential for use. Institutionally they are often not even recognized as languages" (p.12; his discussion of repertoires and competence appears in Ch. 4, pp.102–134).

These factors in turn relate to different conceptions of authority and power. Blommaert points to those centers "to which people orient when they produce an indexical trajectory of semiosis," that is, we orient our communication toward addressees, including a "super-addressee," that "larger social and cultural body of authority into which we insert our immediate practices..." He brings in the concept of p*olycentricity*, the fact that authority centers are more diverse and polyvalent than ever before. Thus, he observes that we live in a "less innocent world of linguistic, social and cultural variation and diversity...and in which complex patterns of potential-versus-actual behaviour occur."[20] Today's world involves "a sociolinguistics of mobile resources, no longer of sociolinguistics of immobile languages." Blommaert consequently identifies three "central concepts" now affecting communication in connection with globalization:

a) *Scales*—given the "destabilizing" of speakers' sense of locality, the horizontal and vertical senses need to be reframed to allow "scale jumping" from the "individual to collective, the temporally situated to trans-temporal, the unique to the common, the token to the type, the specific to the general" (33) in sometimes sudden linguistic movements (see discussion on pp. 32–37).

b) *Ordered indexicality*—"the fact that indexical meanings occur in patterns offering perceptions of similarity and stability that can be perceived as 'types' of semiotic practise (sic) with predictable...directions" (37; discussion continues, 37–39). As an example, he notes that the values and status accorded a dialect or register of a language in one location may be quite differently perceived by speakers of the same language in another location. The order of indexicality identifies culturally-defined and -ensconced power (and inequality).

c) *Polycentricity* involves the fact that "evaluative authorities"

(p. 39) and "interactional regimes" are multiplying; rather than being monocentric, "there are as a rule multiple – though never unlimited – batteries of norms to which one can orient and according to which one can behave…" (p. 40; discussion spans pp. 39–41).[21]

Among the many factors that have influenced the new globalization are rapid transportation and frequency of doing business that, on the one hand, have helped level dialects, but on the other have created more need for quick interactional resources. The enormous frequency of electronic, as opposed to face-to-face, interactions (e.g. via computers and cell phones) has constructed fragmented communication needs such as bare-bones informational conveyance, and thereby has advanced acceptability of communicative shorthand. For example, the English being used by a Chinese internet-based businessman as he communicates with a Canada-based Kurdish refugee will differ from the English used by an Australian high school teenager who texts details of a class assignment to a Turkish immigrant classmate.

I aim to bring some of the text-based work of Mufwene into connection with the globalizing discourse work of Blommaert by looking at a specific form of communication described above, written examples of code-switching done entirely for the benefit and reference of the writer. Some other studies come close to this, including Margreet Dorleijn and Jacomine Nortier's chapter on "Code-switching and the internet" in Bullock and Toribio. They choose that area in part because the language there is "produced as unconsciously as possible,"[22] allowing the potentials of code-switching to occur as freely as possible. Nevertheless, their data relate to communication with others, while mine involve self-directed communication. This narrows by an additional degree the social environment of the communication act, by seeing how writers interact with themselves *without* attempting to satisfy the social conditions of the contact environment. Their notes are reflexive in nature.

All the samples provided below were personal notes made by international students for whom English is their second/tertiary language, and which were taken in English-only lecture settings in the United States at the undergraduate and graduate levels. Given that the "audience" for these notes was none other than the writer, the code-switching (and other phenomena) were not done for the situational or metaphoric purposes. Such work is the subject of certain recent publications, such as David West Brown's *In Other Words: Lessons on Grammar, Code-switching and Academic Writing*, though he addresses code-switching that involves American English dialects and register, while this study is cross-linguistic. In some cases (as will be noted), the code-switching occurs as a function of competence: the individuals wrote in their first language because it was easiest to understand at that point. However, as will be shown in connection with specific data (and based on interviews with the sources, with age listed relevant to the time the notes were taken), other factors come into play, and they coincide to some degree with Mufwene's and Blommaert's research.

Student Note Samples

The following samples (see numbered images, attached) represent a broader set of interactions with my undergraduate and graduate students. Some were monolingual English speakers who periodically insert a word or short phrase from another language (usually Classical Hebrew, Greek or Latin) into their notes, but mostly because an instructor made it a key lecture point. Some American-born students who were raised overseas acknowledged code-switching in class notes using one of their second languages acquired during their upbringing. "Noami" (22, female), for example, reported insertion of Cameroonian Pidgin phrases into her English notes when it seemed "more specific to the actual topic or concept"—even though none of these had any obvious affinity with life in Africa. "Jill" (21, female) said she switches to French "if she is angry or emotional about something, or just wants to be sure it remains private."

These comments were echoed in some of the items reported below (and please note the five facsimile samples provided at the end of this paper).

Sample #1—"John" (41, male graduate student)

John is ethnic Han Chinese and grew up near Beijing, where he completed both the undergraduate and graduate studies which prepared him to do university teaching (which he has done for a decade). His post-graduate studies subsequently commenced in North America. The sample provided here is one of many pages he offered. The mid-page starting with "Matt.23" was the best way he could find to summarize an entire chapter from the New Testament gospel in words that were "easy to write and thinking in Chinese." This sample is L2 competence-related.

Sample #2—"David" (25, male former graduate student, now faculty)

Born in Harbin, David is Han Chinese. After completing his graduate education in engineering in North America, he worked for some years in industry and now teaches engineering at the undergraduate level in the United States. The note samples he provided originated from his graduate studies, and most of his cursive Mandarin notations across the four pages are translations of English using Chinese terminology that he said had been "established" in his memory during undergraduate study in China. They came to mind more quickly than the English terms, even when the latter was in use during the lectures he was giving. Most of his Chinese notes are attributable to speed of language processing, the native tongue obviously being faster than the English and sometimes he simply did not know the English words or idioms for something. However, David made comments that went beyond these routine issues relating to degrees of L2 competency; he said that he finds the Chinese not only a quicker and easier production in his mind ("I hear the word in English but it is faster to write in Chinese") but, since the Chinese expressions "convey more than English words," fewer of them have to be written and "they take up less space [on the page]." Efficiency of expression is, not surprisingly, highly valued, as with this one sample containing Chinese cursive near the top of the page. In this sample, perceptions of the breadth of semantic field became relevant to the choice of code.

Sample #3—"Stefan" (52, male former graduate student, now faculty)

Born in Chile to a family of Sicilian ancestry, Stefan's NL is Spanish, but he reports that his grandmother (with whom he was raised) always mixed Italian with Spanish in domestic conversation. English is therefore his third language. Now a professor of engineering at a college in Pennsylvania, he often makes notes intended for himself after he has given an English lecture, but he does so in a mixture of Spanish and English (as seen in this sample; elsewhere, he says, he has Italian as well). In the first line of the third bullet point, Stefan begins with four English words ("Made the pointe (sic) that") which are followed by six Spanish words, then one English word (ZERO), and then he switches back to Spanish. Similar alterations appear elsewhere in the sample page. Stefan made two interesting comments about his code-switching. One was that he does not know why he switches between Spanish and English at a particular point, since he is fluent in both; the three switches described above seemed random, even to him. His second comment pertained to other notes (which he made following an English engineering lecture, as he reviews what he had just presented in preparation for the next time that lecture is to be given): "If I have to stress something [to myself], I need to use words strongly that show character and passion, therefore I tend to use Italian...because of the Italian character, I have to talk with my hands..." He associates Italian with emotional intensity; for him it is the linguistic equivalent of yellow highlighter. This association of language choice and emotional force accords with the comment by Jill (quoted above).

Sample #4—"Rutsko" (18, female undergraduate student)

Born in Korea but raised in Japan from age six, Rutsko's sample from a communication disorders class not surprisingly reflects her first and second languages (English is L3). Item (a) in the third line is the Korean word for "trinity," chosen because it was "more familiar" than the English word but with a pronunciation that she finds "simpler" than the Japanese equivalent. The Korean word written twice directly below it means "breath," and likewise Rutsko chose that over the familiar Japanese word because it was "shorter and easier to write." Directly below those words and following the English "language" is a Korean interrogative particle, this time used because she finds the syntactic order (i.e. phrase/sentence ending with the interrogative) more comfortable than the English. Other Japanese Hiragana writing appearing in the third and fourth lines (to the right) are translations she again found "easier to write." Item (b) in the sixth line elaborates on the word "symbolic") using a central Korean word flanked by Japanese words; similar glossing in the four lines labeled (c) uses Korean and Japanese Hiragana along with Kanji symbols. Item (d) also contains multiple Japanese-Korean switches explaining "jargen" (*sic*). In short, Rutsko switches languages for a combination of reasons that includes familiarity and ease.

Sample #5—"Kim" (21, female undergraduate student)

Kim is an ethnic Korean who was raised in Japan during her upper elementary and high school years and is currently an undergraduate student at a private college in Pennsylvania. She provided two different sorts of writing samples, one of which contained notes she made while listening to an English sermon given at a majority-Westerner worship service. Language codes that appear on this sheet include English, Korean, Japanese Hiragana and Katakana orthographies, Chinese Kanji, and Greek. For example, at the end of the first line (upper left panel), she writes the Chinese symbol for 'bear' but next uses Katakana for the biblical name "Goliath." In the second line, after "God" she switches to Kanji and then to Japanese Hiragana. In the fifth line, after "Jesus" is the two-segment Korean word for "pray," followed by some Hiragana and then an English abbreviation ("HS" for "holy spirit"). After the English word "inspired" she writes a corresponding Japanese passive verb (meaning 'done', in Japanese) but retains the English word because the Japanese just "didn't feel right" to her in that context. Some of the switches in Kim's notes involve conventions governing the use of Hiragana and Katakana (i.e. since the name "Goliath" is a foreign word, the latter is used). Yet for names of books in the Bible, she routinely prefers the one-word Korean title over the typically two-word Japanese name, or the English—though she is fluent in speaking and writing of three languages. She says that writing efficiency is often the issue, and when asked why other language alterations were made on her samples, she reports either that a word in one language simply came to her faster (something often reported by those who code-switch) and that efficiency was crucial. Often, "Korean is shorter and faster than Japanese Kanji," or conversely, sometimes the Kanji "has meaning that hits my eye with meaning…I choose the language that is faster." Some of her explanations align with Rutsko's, but the sample page reproduced below borders on rabid code-switching (and it may have affinity with the increasing use of English in Japanese as discussed, e.g. in Stanlaw 2014).[23]

Observations and Implications

These samples, and the explanations offered by their writers during interviews (which took place at various times late in 2014 and early 2015), circle back to a concept central to many aspects of code-switching, namely, *competence*. What is unfamiliar is least likely to be written because it takes too long to retrieve. Efficiency is of the essence. However, certain other factors warrant mention:

First, a high frequency of switching even to the point of redundancy seems to accompany some students' desires to understand a concept. Additional words garnered from their native lexicon(s) add precision to the grasp of the newly acquired language. This is hardly new, but this study provides additional anecdotal affirmation.

Second, a number of the consultants connect intense emotion with a particular language—and not necessarily their native language! This means that alongside functional and metaphoric is *affective* code-switching—even amidst a dialogue with oneself. Studies have noted that, under emotional duress, people revert to their native code; this one suggests an intentional aspect to emotive associations.

Third, increasingly rapid communication events with multiple interlocutors in the world today (even in self-directed communication) may prompt code-switching that goes from the rapid to the ferocious. This is Blommaert's movement from "spatial scope" to "scale jumping," and the samples above hint (at least) toward the "polycentricity" he mentions, i.e. "we behave *with reference to* an evaluative authority" (2010:39, italics his; see especially Samples #4 and #5).[24]

Fourth, the question remains open as to the association of language with identity. In a number of previous publications[25] I demonstrated (in part) that code-switching between English and Pennsylvania German in letters written by Old Order Amish writers reflected their community identity; yet the practicalities of speed and efficiency are likely to trump such considerations. The interviews connected with Samples #3 and #5 suggest, but do not confirm, that the writer's associate language with cultural identity.

Fifth, a related question comes in reference to my label of "artisan English," given the fact that Samples #4 & #5 contain more non-English in these "English" notes. As Allen Bell (2014:31–32, referencing Peter Auer) notes:

> [R]esearch into code-switching demands that we begin not with identifying the two languages but with the overall linguistic practices of the speakers. What language they are speaking may not be the important question—may not even be answerable... [since certain

> speakers] often blend their two languages together in ways that make it unclear which language a particular item belongs to—it may be either or both...Language is a social practice, a range of resources on which speakers draw rather than a set of linguistic 'codes'...[26]

Julie Coleman speaks for the field when she observes that even "Standard English is not a well-defined concept in itself; its meaning varies according to geographical location and social context. Slang, of course, is even harder to define."[27] In a world of electron-facilitated ubiquity, her words and those of Daniel Heller-Roazen (speaking of the cant of "rogues and riddlers") apply quite broadly: "In private or in public, those who speak a language retain the capacity to draw from their knowledge of its grammar the elements of a new and cryptic variety of speech."[28] Reaching far beyond the realms of slang and argot, rapidity and diversification are rendering the face of language more malleable, as John McWhorter has done with his metaphor of the "lava lamp." The artisan English notes of 21st century students affirm Hugo Schuchardt's 19th century assertion that "*Es gibt keine voellig ungemischte Sprache.*"

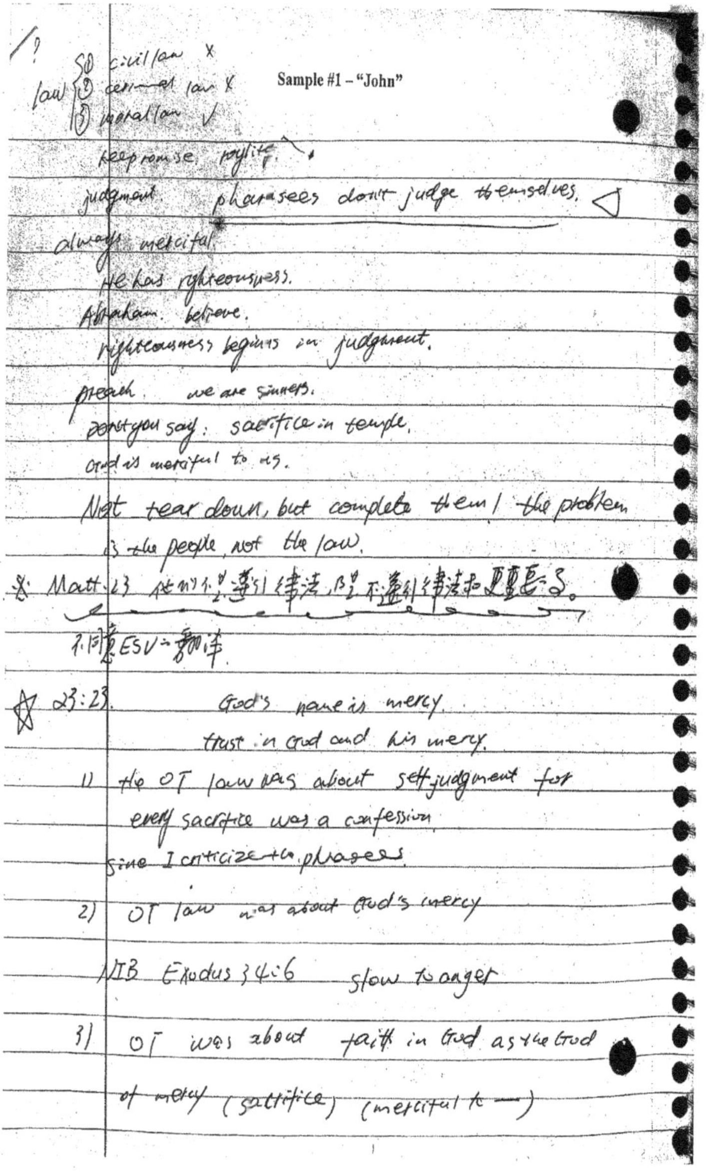
Sample #1 – "John"

/?

law {
① civil law ✗
② cerimal law ✗
③ moral law ✓

keep promise, polite

judgment. pharasees don't judge themselves.

always merciful.

He has righteousness.

Abraham: believe.

righteousness begins in judgment.

preach. we are sinners.

don't you say: sacrifice in temple.

God is merciful to us.

Not tear down, but complete them / the problem is the people, not the law.

※ Matt. 23 你们只遵行律法，但是不遵行律法和更重要的。

不同版ESV的翻译.

☆ 23:23. God's name is mercy.

trust in God and his mercy.

1) the OT law was about self-judgment for every sacrifice was a confession.

since I criticize the pharasees.

2) OT law was about God's mercy

NIB Exodus 34:6 slow to anger

3) OT was about faith in God as the God of mercy (sacrifice) (merciful to —)

Sample #1: "John"

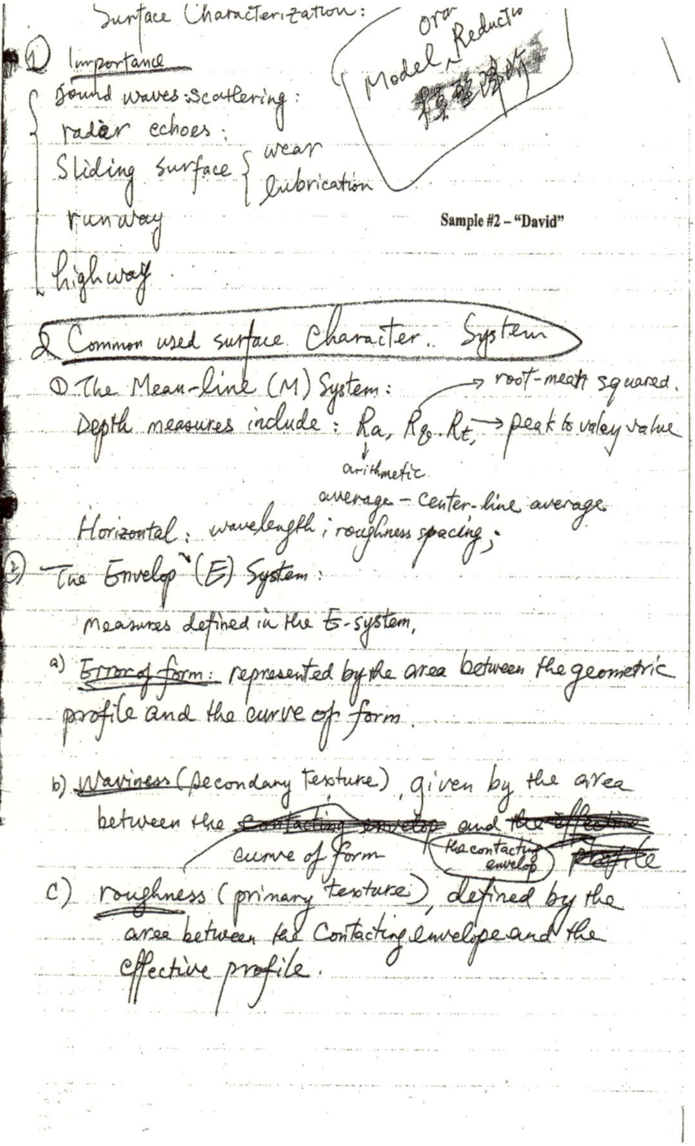

Surface Characterization:

Model Reduction / Order

① Importance

- sound waves: scattering:
- radar echoes:
- Sliding surface { wear / lubrication
- runway
- highway

Sample #2 – "David"

② Common used surface Character. System

① The Mean-line (M) System:

Depth measures include: Ra (arithmetic average – center-line average), Rq (root-mean squared), Rt (peak to valley value)

Horizontal: wavelength; roughness spacing;

② The Envelop (E) System:

measures defined in the E-system,

a) ~~Error of form~~: represented by the area between the geometric profile and the curve of form.

b) Waviness (secondary texture), given by the area between the ~~contacting envelop~~ curve of form and ~~the effective profile~~ the contacting envelop

c) roughness (primary texture), defined by the area between the Contacting envelope and the effective profile.

Sample #2: "Daivd"

Sample #3 – "Stefan"

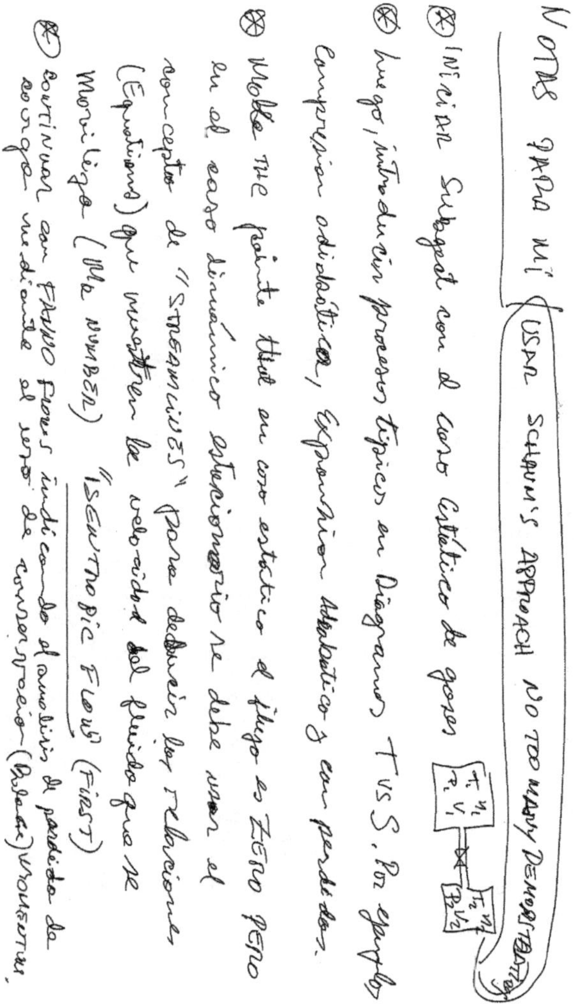

NOTAS PARA MI (USAR SCHAUM'S APPROACH NO TOO MANY DEMONSTRATIONS)

⊗ INICIAR Subject con el caso estático de gases

⊗ luego, introducir procesos típicos en Diagramas T vs S. Por ejemplos compresión adiabática, Expansión Adiabatico y con perdidas.

⊗ Make THE point that en caso estatico el flujo es ZERO PERO en el caso dinámico estacionario se debe usar el concepto de "STREAMLINES" para deducir las relaciones (Equations) que muestren la velocidad del fluido que se moviliza (Ma NUMBER) "ISENTROPIC FLOW" (FIRST)

⊗ CONTINUAR con FANNO FLOWS indicando el analisis de perdida de carga mediante el uso de conservación (Balance) MOMENTUM.

Sample #3: "Stefan"

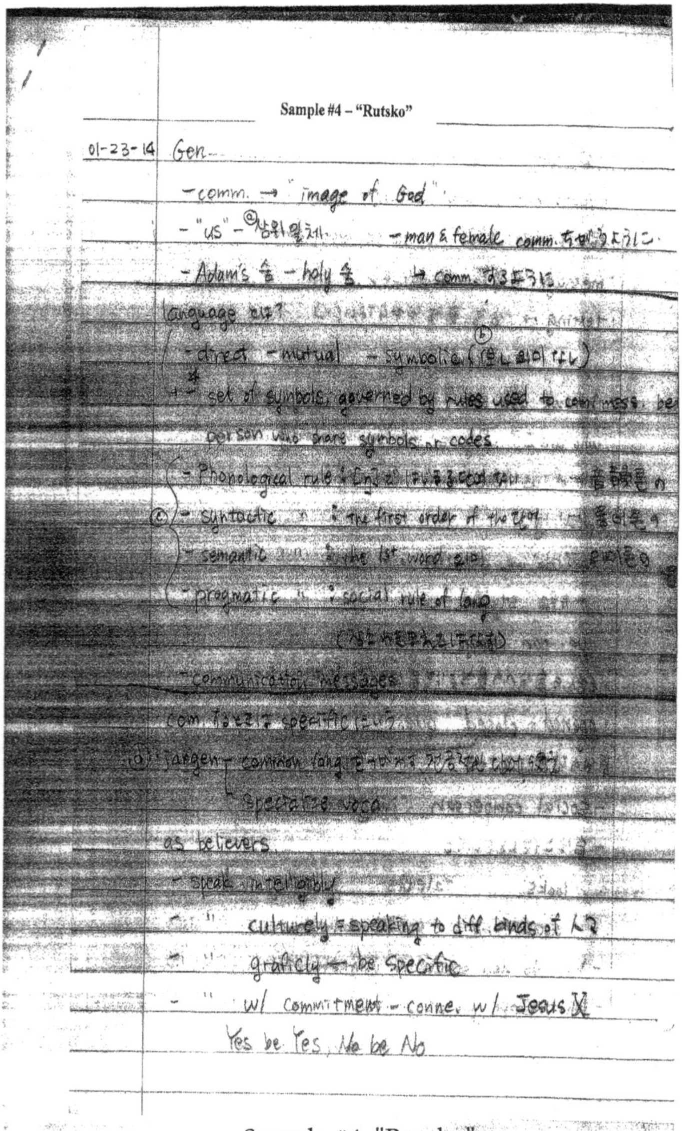
Sample #4 – "Rutsko"

01-23-14 Gen.

– comm. → "image of God"

– "us" – ⓐ – man & female comm.

– Adam's – holy → comm.

language

– direct – mutual – symbolic ⓑ

* set of symbols governed by rules used to com. mess. be person who share symbols or codes.

– Phonological rule

ⓒ – syntactic : the first order of the

– semantic : the 1st word

– pragmatic : social rule of lang.

– communication messages

com specific

ⓓ Jargon – common lang

└ specialized voca.

as believers

– speak intelligibly

– " culturely = speaking to diff. kinds of

– " graficly – be specific

– " w/ commitment – conne. w/ Jesus

Yes be Yes, No be No

Sample #4: "Rutsko"

Sample #5 – "Kim"

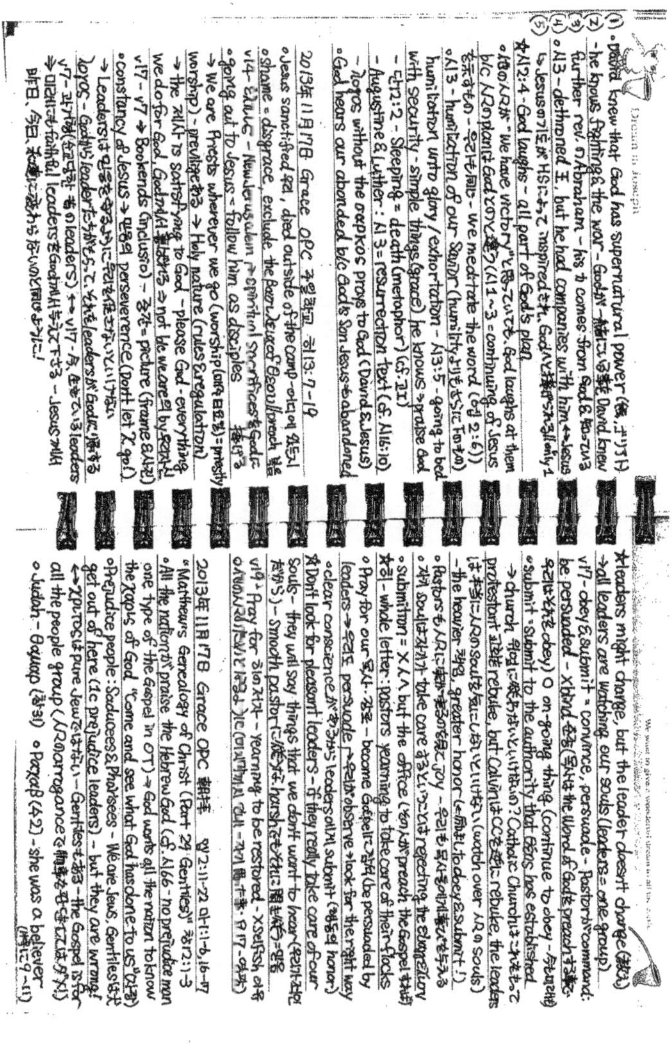

Sample #5: "Kim"

Notes

[1]Jonathan M. Watt, "Some Implications of Bilingualism from New Testament Exegesis." *The Language of the New Testament: Context, History and Development*, Stanley E. Porter and Andrew W. Pitts (eds), 2013. Early Christianity in Hellenistic Context 3. Jonathan M Watt, "The Living Language Environment of Acts 21:27–40," *Biblical and Ancient Greek Linguistics* 4, 2015. 3–48.

[2]Debroah Tannen and Anna Marie Tirester, (eds.), *Discourse 2.0*. Georgetown University Press, 2013.

[3]Barbara Johnstone. "Indexing the Local." Nikolas Coupland (ed.). *The Handbook of Language and Globalization*. Wiley-Blackwell, 2010, p. 387.

[4]Jan Blommaert, *The Socoilinguistics of Globalization*. Cambridge Press, 2010.

[5]Salikoko S. Mufwene, "Globalization, Global English, and World Englishes." Nikolas Coupland (ed.). *The Handbook of Language and Globalization*. (Wiley–Blackwell, 2010), p. 32.

[6]Thomas L Friedmann, *The Lexus and the Olive Tree*. New York: Anchor Books, 2000, p. 9.

[7]Jan Blommaert, *The Socoilinguistics of Globalization*. (Cambridge Press, 2010) p. 13.

[8]Nikolas Coupland, *Op cit*. pp. 2–3.

[9]Ibid. pp. 9, 19

[10]Norman Fairclough, *Language and Globalization*. (London/NY: Routledge, 2006), p. 3 citing Held.

[11]Ibid., pp. 14–26, 121, 123, 168–9.

[12]Salikoko S. Mufwene, *Op cit*. pp. 43–44.

[13]David Crystal, *English as a Global Language*. Cambridge University Press, 1997. Salikok Mufwene, *Op cit*. p. 46.

[14]Sarah Grey Thomason and Terrence Kaufman, *Language Contact, Creolization and Genetic Linguistics*. (University of California Press, 1991) p. 37.

[15]Blommaert, *Op cit.*

[16]Mufwene, *Op cit.*

[17]C.A. Ferguson, "Diglossia." Word 15(1959): 325–340.

[18]Barbara Bullock and A.J. Toribio, *The Cambridge Handbook of Linguistic Code-switching.* (Cambridge University Press, 2009).

[19]Blommaert, *Op cit*, pp. 5–6.

[20]Blommaert. *Op cit*, pp. 9, 12—his discussion of repertoires and competence appears in Ch.4, pp.102–134, 39, 41.

[21]Blommaert, *Op cit*, pp. 43, 33, 32, 37–39, 40–41.

[22]Margreet Dorleijn and Jacomine Nortier's chapter on "Code-switching and the internet" in Bullock and Toribio, *Op cit*, p. 137.

[23]James Stanlaw, "Some Trends in Japanese Slang." In: Julie Coleman (ed.) *Global English Slang: Methodologies and Perspectives.* (London/NY: Routledge, 2014) pp. 160–169.

[24]Blommaert, *Op cit*, pp. 32–37, 39—italics his; see especially Samples #4 and #5.

[25]Jonathan M. Watt, "L1 Interference in Written L2: A Comparison Between the Pennsylvania German and Koine Greek Situations." Werner Enninger *et al* (eds.) *Studies on the Languages and the Verbal Behavior of the Pennsylvania German* II. Stuttgart: Franz Steiner Verlag Wiesbaden GMBH and Watt.1997. *Code Switching in Luke and Acts.* Berkley Insights in Linguistics and Semeiotics 31. New York: Peter Lang.

[26]Allen Bell, *The Guidebook to Sociolinguistics.* (Wiley–Blackwell, 2014) pp. 31–32, referencing Peter Auer.

[27]Julie Coleman, (Ed.), *Global English Slang: Methodologies and Perspectives.* (London/NY: Routledge, 2014) p. 1.

[28]Daniel Heller-Roazen, *Dark Tongues: The Art of Rogues and Riddlers.* (New York: Zone Books, 2013) p. 17.

References

Bell, Allan. 2014. *The Guidebook to Sociolinguistics.* Wiley Blackwell.

Blommaert, Jan. 2010. *The Sociolinguistics of Globalization.* Cambridge University Press.

Brown, David West. 2009. *In Other Words: Lessons on Grammar, Code-switching, and Academic Writing.* Portsmouth, NH: Heinemann.

Bullock, Barbara and A.J. Toribio. 2009. *The Cambridge Handbook of Linguistic Code-switching.* Cambridge University Press.

Coleman, Julie (Ed.). 2014. *Global English Slang: Methodologies and Perspectives.* London/New York: Routledge.

Coupland, Nikolas. 2010. *The Handbook of Language and Globalization.* Wiley-Blackwell.

Crystal, David. 1997. *English as a Global Language.* Cambridge University Press.

Dorleijn, Margreet and Jacomine Nortier. 2009. "Code-switching and the internet." In: Bullock, Barbara E. and Almeida Jacqueline Toribio (eds.). *The Cambridge Handbook of Linguistic Code-switching.* Cambridge University Press. pp.127–141.

Fairclough, Norman. 2006. *Language and Globalization.* London/NY: Routledge.

Fishman, Joshua and Ofelia Garcia (Eds.). 2011. *Handbook of Language and Ethnic Identity.* Vol. 1 & 2. Oxford University Press.

Friedman, Thomas L. 2000. *The Lexus and the Olive Tree.* New York: Anchor Books.

Heller-Roazen, Daniel. 2013. *Dark Tongues: The Art of Rogues and Riddlers.* New York: Zone Books.

Jandt, Fred E. 2004. *An Introduction to Intercultural Communication.* 4th Ed. SAGE Pub. (Particularly Ch.17 - "Identity and Subgroups" & Ch.18—"Multiculturalism")

Johnstone, Barbara. 2010. "Indexing the Local." In: Coupland, Nikolas (ed.). *The Handbook of Language and Globalization.* Wiley-Blackwell, pp. 386–405.

Melchers, Gunnel and Philip Shaw. 2003. *World Englishes*. London: Arnold Publishers.

Mufwene, Salikoko S. 2010. "Globalization, Global English, and World Englishes." In: Coupland, Nikolas (ed.). *The Handbook of Language and Globalization*. Wiley-Blackwell, pp. 31–55.

Omoniyi, Tope. 2010. *The Sociology of Language and Religion. Change, Conflict and Accommodation*. Palgrave MacMillan.

Stanlaw, James. 2014. "Some Trends in Japanese Slang." In: Julie Coleman (ed.). *Global English Slang: Methodologies and Perspectives*. London/New York: Routledge, pp.160–169.

Tannen, Deborah and Anna Marie Tirester (eds.). *Discourse 2.0*. Georgetown University Press, 2013.

Thomason, Sarah Grey and Terrence Kaufman. 1991. *Language Contact, Creolization and Genetic Linguistics*. Univ. of California Press.

Watt, Jonathan M. 1987. "L1 Interference in Written L2: A Comparison Between the Pennsylvania German and Koine Greek Situations." In: Werner Enninger *et al* (eds.). *Studies on the Languages and the Verbal Behavior of the Pennsylvania Germans* II. Stuttgart: Franz Steiner Verlag Wiesbaden GMBH.

Watt, Jonathan M. 1997. *Code-Switching in Luke and Acts*. Berkeley Insights in Linguistics and Semeiotics 31. New York: Peter Lang.

Watt, Jonathan M. 2013. "Some Implications of Bilingualism for New Testament Exegesis." In: *The Language of the New Testament: Context, History and Development*. Stanley E. Porter and Andrew W. Pitts (eds.). Early Christianity in Its Hellenistic Context 3. Linguistic Biblical Studies 6. Leiden: Brill, 2013. 9–27.

Watt, Jonathan M. 2015. "The Living Language Environment of Acts 21:27–40." *Biblical and Ancient Greek Linguistics* 4 (2015):30–48.

CHAPTER SIXTEEN

The Relevance of the Creation to the Gospel Proclamation

Kenneth G. Smith

> "Praise the LORD!
> Praise the LORD from the heavens.
> Praise Him in the heights!
> Praise Him, all His angels;
> Praise Him, all His hosts!
> Praise Him, sun and moon;
> Praise Him, all stars of light!
> Praise Him, highest heavens,
> And the waters that are above the heavens!
> Let them praise the name of the LORD,
> For He commanded and they were created.
> He has also established them forever and ever:
> He has made a decree which will not pass away."
> Psalm 148:1–6 (NASB)

We were on holiday in the West Indies with friends on their 50-plus-foot sailboat. Karl was in the water in the sheltered cove trying to manipulate the anchor. "I can't get it to take hold," he yelled; but after several tries he succeeded. We were firm, secure against overnight drift. He and his wife Joan were by this time experienced sailors and knew the hazards. So my wife and I relaxed.

Over the years of my ministry I have watched Western culture drift. As a boy I went to a one-room schoolhouse in the hills of Vermont. We started each day with ten verses from the King James Bible, read aloud by Mrs. Hutton our teacher, followed by reciting the Lord's Prayer. And then we pledged our allegiance to the United States flag mounted on the wall near the portraits of George Washington and Abraham Lincoln. I'm old enough to recognize the radical drift in America's culture and public schools from this heritage.

I might come closer to home by recalling that before I left for school, we had engaged in family worship, a tradition my folks inherited from their parents, and probably theirs from theirs. It was a tradition handed down the generations; Robert Burns spoke of it in his poem "Cotter's Saturday Night." The family "droned a psalm," read from the Bible, then went to their knees in prayer. This habit was a great influence in early American lifestyle. While we were not living in utopia, still it was the "Depression" era; we were conscious of the Source of our blessings expressed in the lines of "America the Beautiful."

"Our Fathers' God to Thee, Author of liberty, to Thee we sing.
Long may our land be bright with freedom's holy light,
Protect us by Thy might, great God our King."

To those of us who have grown up in Western culture, there has been a steady drift, but today that drift has been aided by stronger winds. As a result of the philosophy of the originators of our public-school system, coupled with the influence in our colleges and universities of the theory of evolution, there has been a growing ignorance of and resistance toward biblical doctrine. And none of these doctrines have experienced more suspicion and rejection than that of "creation." Having preached the gospel for over 60 years, I have sensed not only a drift, but an actual hostile storm against the doctrine of creation. And sadly much of the church has been sucked into this defection.

This rejection of creation has had its influence, even in evangelical circles, so that an "easy believism" has characterized much evangelism. It will become evident that without an understanding of creation, the doctrine and practice of *repentance loses its relevance.* My purpose here is to recognize the place and significance of the doctrine of creation in preaching the gospel of Jesus Christ. Without the doctrine of creation, *salvation* has a hollow ring! So consider some portions of the Scripture which show the foundational truth of creation on which the rest of the gospel rests. Without the doctrine of creation, the message of the gospel, in fact the whole Bible, loses its meaning.

The first text, obviously, is Genesis 1:1. It is a given that no text can be properly discerned without grasping its context. "In the beginning God created the heavens and the earth." What then about the context? It's apparent that as far as this text itself is concerned, nothing is stated before "the beginning." It's obvious then that God was there. And it was in His mind and power to "create." According to the Bible, this was the beginning of *time* and *space.* It was not the beginning of *reality*, for God was *there* and the Bible tells us God is *eternal.* He never had a "beginning," nor will He ever have an end. It's difficult for us to comprehend fully the meaning of *eternal,* for we are *finite.* Let it also be said that it's not *understanding* alone that's in question, it is *belief.* We are in this most basic passage of Scripture told what to believe! It's a declaration, not a conundrum. Let that idea capture your approach to the Bible. The Bible is not a proposition; it is a revelation. It is "true truth," as some have said, and it is to be *believed.* In fact, that is the character of the Bible—it's authoritative, not a proposal!

As messengers of the gospel, when we make such assertions, we meet against great controversy. This fact, moreover, is not new to messengers of the gospel. I am not seeking in this essay to provide the reader with a set of arguments for persuasion. That is not essentially my point, though I certainly use them at times. My point is that it is God speaking; and that's it! I always appreciated hearing Dr. Billy Graham say, "...the Bible says..." He didn't try to defend it. The gospel is a *declaration.* So is the Bible.

Here I must include my appreciation for the College Hill Reformed Presbyterian Church where I worshiped across the street from my alma mater, Geneva College, in post-Navy days. It was sometime later when John H. White was called to be their pastor and countless students, confronted with the claims of Christ, came to submit to His call on their lives. "Jack," as many of us know him, faithfully *declared* the call of God to his listeners. Many former students will testify on the last great day that they were brought to Christ through Jack's faithful *declaring* of the gospel. It's that "declaring," which is how the Bible begins and reads! And no one could listen to such preaching and miss its authority! Let these words sink in to your mind: "In the beginning God created the heavens and the earth."

Today in our Western culture we are sadly adrift without *absolutes.* Of course, that is a direct product of removing the Bible—ultimate authority—from our children's education and our popular culture. It should be no surprise that much of our youth culture is adrift, in fact, it's "at sea." If there are no absolutes, as Francis Schaeffer often pointed out, there is no meaning to anything. Doesn't it become evident that Genesis 1:1 puts everyone and everything in context? The creation is not adrift! As Psalm 19 says "Day unto day utters speech, and night to night speaks knowledge." When you discredit Genesis 1, you put mankind at sea. No moorings! But as we'll see below, mankind does *know better.*

But there's more. Because God made man—not as an extension of some primordial slime but someone in His own image—there was and is personal *being.* We must grieve about today's youth who are committing suicide. Doesn't your heart ache for them? If only they had known the implications of Genesis 1:1! Those first three chapters in Genesis are so fundamental to mankind's orientation and sense of worth! And those words begin with God Himself. And He tells us we have been made *in His image.* There's no suggestion here of man's *evolution* from some kind of "mud!" At first this doctrine of God's creating all things might seem terrifying, but instead it is most comforting.

When today's youth ask, "Who am I?"—and they do—the Bible clearly says, "You're a creature made by God and made after His image." Here we must add that mankind is, unlike any of the rest of creation, *immortal...and eternally valuable.* Genesis 2:7 reads, "Then the LORD God formed man of dust from the ground, and breathed into his nostrils the breath of life; and man became a living being [soul]." Without this understanding, the gospel makes no sense!

I think that this biblical teaching may have been Frances and Edie Schaeffer's great "in" with searching youth at their chalets in Switzerland in the '70s and '80s. These youths were starving for what they did not know, but at L'Abri they were treated with love and dignity. As creatures made by God, they had intrinsic value and worth; and the Schaeffers knew how to love them and answer their many troubling questions. But it was always in the context that they were in the presence of God and the love of His people. Unlike many today, the Schaeffers distinguished between acceptance and approval. They led many to be restored to their Creator and Savior. They did not neglect Genesis 1:1.

Here in a culture that has been challenged to abandon the old truths of the Bible, as the church of Jesus Christ we are called upon to treat these others as the creation of God. Our gospel must address them in a context of love, which means compassionate contact. We live in the "instant" culture—a self-consumed culture as evidenced by their addiction to the screen in their hands and the drugs in their lungs. With all sincerity, we must recognize the cost of such hospitality, often involving the love of strangers. Even though much of our culture has lost touch with who they are, we who have been taken in by Jesus can receive them into our homes—and lives—as God's creation! We live in God's creation. That's our context for life! "In the beginning God created the heavens and the earth."

We must not minimize the significance of this text! And when presenting the call of the gospel, we must simply declare it! While many want to argue about this terse statement, no one has nor can disprove it, any more than they can prove evolution.

When questions arise regarding evolution and its corollaries, I continue to "tell the story," that many have never heard. Later I discuss their questions, but by this time I have delivered the gospel story. And while evolution seeks unsuccessfully to explain our origin, the gospel explains both man's origin and worth! And his destiny. What power there is in this first verse of the Bible! Don't leave it out as though it's unnecessary for the gospel message! Genesis 1:1 puts the rest of the Bible in context!

And so I move to our next text: John 1 and John's introduction to the *Gospel According to John.* What is John seeking to accomplish? He tells us in his conclusion in chapter 20:30–31. "...These have been written so that you may believe that Jesus is the Christ, the Son of God, and that believing you may have life in His name." Many thousands of copies of this gospel are daily being handed out worldwide! Only eternity can reveal how many persons, having read these words in their own language actually have come to faith in Jesus as their Savior!

How does John begin his Gospel? After immediately identifying "the Word" as deity, he says this about Him, "All things came into being through Him, and apart from Him nothing came into being that has come into being" (John 1:3). We should note that before John unfolds to us the gospel of Jesus Christ, he puts what he has to say in the context of Creation. It is abundantly true that our culture does not comprehend this fact. And the gospel, to make sense, must be seen in this framework of reality. Be aware that the Gospel of John when we examine it, puts everything in the context of Genesis 1:1, namely, the reality and doctrine of creation. It was into His own creation that the Son of God came! And it's significant that John makes sure we understand that *beginning* of his Gospel. Creation as the handiwork of God is a vital presupposition behind his Gospel! And John makes it clear that this Person, the Word, was both there and the actual *Agent* of creation. That truth is fundamental to the gospel.

We should also be aware of a truth that must be recognized when presenting the gospel. Namely, the foundation of God's eternal being. God was there *before* creation. God has no beginning. There is a good reason why people hesitate at this point. If this fact is true, then man is accountable. Very early, man is confronted with that accountability. Having been tricked by the fallen angel Satan, Adam and Eve in the Garden of Eden were held responsible for their sin (rebellion) against God and His word. Therefore, they incurred spiritual death and, later, physical death. So, in the meantime, man struggles with a *conscience* out of sync with God's will and purpose. The Bible calls this struggle *sin.*

Fundamental to the question of the doctrine of creation is *fallen* man's efforts to do something about his accountability. It's very evident that if the doctrine of creation is true, then mankind is responsible. We should be aware that if the presuppositions of many evolutionists are true, they leave mankind free and unaccountable. Furthermore, these theorists have a very difficult time as they seek to explain man's failure to be good and to do good. The gospel not only does not deny man's *fallen* nature, but also supplies the "good news" about how this condition can be overcome and peaceful relations with God restored.

We all like a message that comforts our ills and restores hope. After all, "gospel" means *good news.* Consequently, in the attempts to meet our ills many among us have heavily stressed the love of God. To a degree this is commendable. Without the grasp of the doctrine of creation, however, the cost of forgiveness or discipleship has been severely truncated. When Jesus began to preach following His temptations in the wilderness, His first word to His hearers was "repent!" I have often asked myself whether one has no sense of his having been created by God, how could he understand the meaning of *repent?* Or if I am just "a speck of protoplasm floating on a sea of meaninglessness"—then what does one mean by *repent?* Great preachers of the past made it clear that the call of the gospel (*good news*) meant to "repent" for forgiveness. The common understanding then was that people had sinned against God, their Creator, and that they needed to seek His forgiveness! Somehow this understanding has become seriously silenced in many persons' minds as well as from many pulpits. In their senseless minds they want to silence that warning by asking, "what do I get out of it?" In short, they do not *know* God. John lets us know immediately that the gospel begins with God who has made all things. It's in that context that he tells the wonderful story of forgiveness and eternal life in Jesus Christ! And this brings true hope and renewal!

When I served in Northern Ireland in 1971, I became an "evangelist" for the Reformed Presbyterian Church there. I found that when they thought of a series of evangelistic services, they carried over the tradition of the Puritans and their contemporaries. Evangelistic services were established for two weeks: the first week's emphasis was centered on man's sin and need of repentance. The second week focused on Christ and His atoning sacrifice to cover our sins. I was impressed that—like John—they emphasized man's accountability before extending the offer of salvation in Christ.

This need for conviction of sin is imperative if the sinner is going to experience the blessing of eternal life in Christ. We who preach the gospel have no control over what the Holy Spirit does in bringing a person to repentance—with one exception: we still must call sinners to repentance. Dietrich Bonhoeffer, in his *Cost of Discipleship*, clarifies the issue: "When Christ calls a man to follow Him, he bids him come and die." I concur. It is who man is, as the creation of God, that obligates him by this demand. Otherwise he perishes in hell. To obscure this fundamental truth of creation is to denature the gospel of its meaning.

The next text I wish to examine is Acts 17:16ff. The apostle Paul's normal practice in his missionary efforts was to begin preaching in the Jewish synagogues, where people were instructed in the Old Testament, anticipating the coming of the Messiah. Here in Athens, however, as Paul waited for his colleagues' arrival, he first spoke freely in the synagogue; then he was directed then to the market place. His declaration about the Lord Jesus attracted some thinkers and philosophers: *He was preaching Jesus and the resurrection* (v.18). It was these persons who pressured him into providing them with some background to what he was saying. It triggered their interest and curiosity.

The result of this was a gathering at the Areopagus, a rocky hilltop under the shadow of the Greek Parthenon, their heathen temple. It can still be visited today. There in this open forum Paul was asked to explain what he had been teaching. For any of us who work at winning a hearing for the gospel, this proved to be a marvelous opportunity!

Notice that the apostle did not immediately speak of what we describe today as "the gospel." Rather, he began by telling them about the true and living God. He calls attention to their altar dedicated to an "UNKNOWN GOD," and says that he wants to tell them about this God of Whom they are ignorant. Paul begins (Acts 17:24) by telling them of the God "Who made the world." Moreover, he refers to one man from whom all mankind have descended. So, he lays the groundwork for the gospel by building on the doctrine of creation; then God's providence in history, and the coming of Jesus, "a Man whom He has appointed;" then speaks of His death and resurrection. Note carefully how the apostle begins with the creation, takes us to Christ's death and resurrection, and leads us to the final judgment. It's one of the most succinct and comprehensive presentations of the gospel in Scripture!

This approach is very significant. It brings Paul's hearers and us back in principle to Genesis 1:1. He then builds on what theologians would call *common grace* before informing them of the *special grace* to be understood only in terms of the death, resurrection, and final judgment—all administered by the Man Jesus Christ. His resurrection from the dead must have caught their attention.

Many critics have faulted Paul at this point for not preaching a clear invitation to come to Christ. Some even refer to I Corinthians 2:2: "For I determined to know nothing among you except Jesus Christ and Him crucified" as a repudiation of his ministry in Athens, calling it a wrong tack in his preaching. I believe this critique to be a lack of judgment on these critics' part. Perhaps it's their lack of experience. I believe the apostle led his hearers from where they were in their own experience to where they would be confronted with God's call in Christ to repentance. My basis for this judgment is found in verse 33: "But some men joined him and believed, among whom also were Dionysius the Areopagite and a woman named Damaris and others with him."

Though we have no record of a church emerging from that encounter there in Athens -- no epistle to an established church—there were nonetheless some who became believers in Jesus. Note that Paul did not neglect the doctrine of creation. He builds on it, in fact. Furthermore, the Scripture record indicates no quarrel with their grasp of that doctrine. The doctrine of creation unlocks a true understanding of who we are and hence our need of salvation. It's foundational to the gospel itself. Furthermore, it speaks to the *conscience*, which every person possesses.

Reflecting on this, we note that the Areopagus represented the "thinkers" of Athens. So Paul speaks to them about the "unknown" God and that He is the Creator of all things. Here, the apostle is leaning heavily on their awareness that the universe had a beginning. It's this "law written on the heart" to which he appeals before he explains the gospel. He establishes man's obligation to his Creator. I find that this "obligation" is missing from so much of today's so-call *gospel.* Without this fundamental obligation of mankind to *worship* and *obey* His Creator, there remains little logic in the call to "repentance." Repentance is an almost unknown word or doctrine in today's society because much of society has tried to obliterate the truth of Creation. Need I mention the spiritual vacuum in America's public schools? I add to our shame the deep ignorance of today's Church about the Bible's doctrine of creation and its implications!

Now to Romans 1:18ff. This portion of the epistle to the Romans finally explains my thesis. People must come to grasp the doctrine of creation in order to understand and put their trust in the gospel of Jesus Christ. It was largely in this chapter of Romans that Martin Luther had his eyes opened to "grace," the basis of our salvation in Christ. In verses 16 and 17, quoted from the prophet Habakkuk 2 in the Old Testament, the Spirit gave Luther spiritual relief. He had been struggling to find absolution for his soul. This day God opened his eyes to see that man is not saved by his own efforts, but by grace through faith in Jesus! My purpose here is to show that the doctrine of creation underlies that message that gave Luther relief. Moreover, mankind *knows* this!

This text tells us that mankind has been shown that God is and that He holds all people accountable. Modern culture emphasizes the autonomy of mankind. Paul, in this Scripture makes clear a number of truths. We need to review them.

First, man is not *ignorant* of God's reality. Although this is, indeed, a bold assertion, it's very important that we understand it if we are to tell others about the salvation obtained in Jesus Christ. Here we are clearly confronted with mankind's actual rebellion: "For the wrath of God is revealed from heaven against all ungodliness and unrighteousness of men who suppress the truth in unrighteousness, because that which is known about God is evident within them, for God made it evident to them" (Romans 1:18). It's important to understand this; otherwise people will plead ignorance. They may be ignorant of the gospel, but they're not ignorant of their sin and rebellion. Many a missionary who, coming upon tribes who have never heard the gospel, find that they have some sort of "sacrifice" in their paganism to try to cover their sins. To them the gospel of Jesus comes as quite new; yet not so in terms of their knowledge of sin. They have that. The good news for them is that Jesus Christ has made atonement for sinners by His substitutionary death!

Second, verse 20 declares that mankind stands fully informed and accountable for having seen and experienced God's creation: "For since the creation of the world, His invisible attributes, His eternal power and divine nature have been clearly seen, being understood through what has been made, so that they are without excuse." If this not fully grasped by seeing the beauties and mysteries of earth, the Psalmist writes that the "heavens declare the glory of God and the firmament shows His handiwork!" (Psalm 19). Therefore, no one can claim ignorance of God's reality even though he may go to great lengths to try to do so. Many scientists worship this same God Who by His word said, "Let there be...," and "there was." There is no excuse for disbelief. It's contradicted in all creation. Creation is not in conflict with true science.

Let's consider this expression *"they are without excuse."* Does not the fact that our children are being taught in our schools, churches, and universities to believe in organic evolution give mankind an "excuse?" Being taught the foundational views of evolution as true science, does that not contradict this word? Have they no excuse? Certainly as children we are subject to what we've been taught, but maturity also brings with it basic questions about reality. Man has been corrupted by sin so that he does not like to retain the knowledge of God; therefore, man is a sinner! Even though he may assert that has a desire to *know*, by nature man rejects the truth of God.

That, however, is not the end of the story. Having rejected the knowledge of God, man has in the third place chosen to give himself over to the consequences. There is in every person a knowledge of God, even that He is there. But man rejects that knowledge or intuition. Verse 18 says man suppresses the truth. He turns away from his knowing that he has been brought into existence by God and is, therefore responsible to Him. Some like to think of man as "autonomous" or not accountable to God. The Bible, however, teaches no such thing. Man is in rebellion. And unless God intervenes, he will perish!

The picture gets worse. Here in this chapter we find a most vivid picture of fallen man—mankind in rebellion. The Bible's descriptions of mankind's fallen condition get increasingly graphic (v.18 ff.)—fallen mankind's condition concludes with these words: "...And although they know the ordinance of God, that those who practice such things are worthy of death, they not only do the same, but also give hearty approval to those who practice them" (Romans 1:32). So, there is in mankind an awareness; he has a conscience. But his fallen nature remains perverse. Mankind without God and His blessing chooses to do evil. That's his nature. We must remember that the heart of the gospel as heralded by Christ at the earliest stages of His ministry was to call on people to *"repent."* In explaining to people what it means to "repent," I have often said, "If you're driving south and "repent," you turn your car around and drive north." Instead of living in rebellion against God, one turns around toward Him in sorrow, seeking forgiveness. The entire basis on which repentance rests is Creation. Furthermore, man knows this in his heart!

In conclusion, let the reader recapture their own self-image as having been created by God "after His image." This fundamental doctrine—God as our Creator—is foundational in one's comprehending the gospel. There is great comfort in this doctrine for one who is struggling with his self-identity. Today in the West we need to herald again this biblical truth in regard to God and His work of creation. Let it be said that although man *knows* something of this, his tendency is to deny it. His denial, however, is a cover-up to what in his better moments he recognizes as true. Therefore, I return to Genesis 1. The first words of the Bible are unequivocal. They are plain! "In the beginning God created the heavens and the earth." We do not try to "explain" it. We believe it and declare it. True prophets, be they clergy or lay persons, proclaim their message under the rubric: "Thus says the Lord." Today's culture needs to hear those first words of the Bible ringing from our churches: *"In the beginning God created the heavens and the earth."*

Finally, our Creator is not just the God of the West. He is the God of heaven and earth and has been recognized in the historical experience and convictions throughout the existence of our nation. Today we are flooded with pressure to discard the Bible and the restraints contained within its truth. Much of that pressure is coming through the media.

Many seem to acquiesce quietly if not approvingly to the pressure to eliminate any reference to God and His word, the Bible, from all public life. We feel the pressure. Much of it arises from a virtual atheism. It is the Church's task to proclaim the gospel. My message in this paper is an alert to the church. Creation is on the auction block! It is the task of the church to proclaim the gospel of Jesus Christ, always in the framework of creation. Anything less than that is to fail our mission. The full gospel of salvation in Jesus Christ builds on this basic truth. It must not be neglected.

"In the beginning God created the heavens and the earth."

CHAPTER SEVENTEEN

Teaching Ethics to Engineering Students

James S. Gidley

This paper was originally presented at the International Conference on General Education in Applied Universities, May 30–June 1, 2019, Hangzhou, China. The conference was jointly sponsored by Zhejiang University of Science & Technology and Geneva College.

Students of engineering often consider it to be a domain of objectivity and exact calculation, while they think that ethics is a subjective realm of ambiguity. Therefore, they think that knowing how to calculate correct answers to numerical problems is all that should be expected of them. It is true that objectivity lies at the heart of engineering. Engineering students are taught to exclude all personal feelings from their work, and for the most part, this is correct. I sometimes say that I have a PhD in objectivity.

However, entirely excluding the subjective element of ethics from engineering is a dangerous mistake. Two examples will serve to illustrate the point. In the late 1960s, Convair designed the fuselage for the McDonnell-Douglas DC-10 jet airliner.[1] A novel cargo door design, opening outward rather than inward, made it more likely that a cargo door could open suddenly in mid-flight, causing a sudden drop in pressure below the cabin floor.[2] In 1970, Convair pressure-tested the fuselage in a hangar and confirmed earlier concerns that a sudden drop in air pressure in the cargo hold caused the cabin floor to buckle due to the higher pressure in the cabin. The hydraulic control lines running under the floor would be jammed or ruptured, cutting off control of the tail assembly of the airplane.

Convair failed to correct this problem. On June 12, 1972, a cargo door blew out on American Airlines Flight 96.[3] Because the plane was not fully loaded—only 67 passengers were on board—the pilot was able to land the plane safely at Detroit Metropolitan Airport without control of the tail assembly. After this accident, the chief engineer at Convair determined that without sufficient modifications to the fuselage, it was inevitable that this type of accident would occur again, and that the plane would most likely crash. Due to the cost of the necessary modifications, executives refused to act on the engineer's advice, and he let the matter drop.

On March 3, 1974, Turkish Airlines Flight 981 experienced a cargo door failure and lost control of the tail assembly shortly after taking off from Paris.[4] The pilots were unable to control the fully loaded plane, and it crashed. All 346 people on board died. This is an example of what is sometimes referred to as a sin of omission—failing to do something that ought to be done. Convair's engineers knew how to fix the problem; the DC-10 needed adequately sized vents between the cabin and the cargo bays below so that pressure would be rapidly equalized in the event of a cargo door failure. However, the design was not corrected because of the perceived cost.

My second example is more recent. In September 2015, the US Environmental Protection Agency (EPA) cited Volkswagen Corporation (VW) for violating air quality control standards.[5] Volkswagen's engineers had devised a technically competent but unethical design. They designed a number of vehicles with a "defeat device," which would switch the engine into a low-emissions mode only when being tested for emissions but switch to a high-emissions, high-performance mode at all other times. [6]

The deception was not detected until some engineering professors and students at West Virginia University began mounting emission detection systems in vehicles.[7] It was a research project to determine how closely vehicle emissions under actual driving conditions matched the emissions measured by the EPA. When the full extent of the deception was uncovered, VW faced large penalties in a number of nations. In the US alone, VW had to agree to a 14.7 billion dollar settlement.[8] (Bomey, 2016).

This is an example of what is sometimes referred to as a sin of commission—doing what ought not to be done. VW engineers deliberately designed vehicles that would evade emission control regulations, significantly damaging the environment and endangering people's health.

These cases show that engineering is *not* a completely objective domain of exact calculations. The unethical decisions were made by engineers. Only engineers could understand the danger of the cargo door failure on the McDonnell-Douglas DC-10. Executives of the corporation had the authority to make the final decision, but engineers were responsible for the design decisions that led to the problem. In the VW case, only engineers were capable of designing a system that would deceive the emissions-testing methods of the EPA. They made the decision to produce the design. Corporate executives would have been powerless to do so, because they lack the required technical knowledge and skill.

I teach students that design is a series of decisions, assisted by calculations. Consider, for example, a bridge. First, a form must be chosen: shall it be a post-and-beam, an arch, or a suspension bridge? How many piers and spans will it have? What materials shall we use: wood, steel, plastic, or reinforced concrete? If it is steel, what size I-beams shall we specify? If it is reinforced concrete, what cross-sectional dimensions shall we specify, what sizes of reinforcing bars shall we choose, and how many bars shall we specify? None of these decisions is obtained simply as the result of calculating a formula, and many alternative designs are acceptable. Each decision has impacts—some obvious, some subtle—on the cost, safety, utility, and aesthetics of the resulting bridge. Some impacts, such as a structural collapse, are so serious that to choose a design with such an impact is unethical. Making decisions is at the heart of ethics. If engineering is essentially a decision-making process, then ethics is embedded in engineering from beginning to end. Therefore, at Geneva College, I teach ethics to engineers in a course that students usually take in their final year.

It is a great challenge to teach ethics in Western culture today. Many, perhaps most, of our philosophers have given up confidence that there are ethical principles to which we must all agree, and without shared principles, ethical culture is impossible to maintain. As an example of the typical approach taken at most public and private universities in the US, consider this statement by Engineering Professor P. Aarne Vesilind of Duke University: "We may, for example, believe that cheating is wrong, based on moral values. We could also believe that telling the truth is right, and that injury to innocent people is wrong...I would like to suggest that moral values, as contrasted to ethical theories, are personal beliefs that each of us uses to distinguish right from wrong, and these cannot be taught."[9] Notice how Vesilind describes ethical principles: "we *may*...believe that cheating is wrong;" but on the other hand, we may *not*! "We *could*...believe...that injury to innocent people is wrong;" but on the other hand, we *need* not! This is the philosophy that is known as relativism, the notion that each person has his or her own moral principles, which need not and do not agree with anyone else's. But if we cannot agree on such an obvious principle as "injury to innocent people is wrong," then what hope is there for our society?

At the same time that relativism is the dominant philosophy among the educated elite in the West, Western society insists that professionals should act with ethical integrity. For example, all the major and many minor engineering societies have codes of ethics: the National Society of Professional Engineers,[10] the

American Society of Civil Engineers,[11] the American Society of Mechanical Engineers,[12] and many, many more.[13] (IIT CSEP, 2019). Even more pertinently for engineering educators, the Accreditation Board for Engineering and Technology (ABET) requires engineering programs to demonstrate that their students attain seven outcomes, including "an ability to recognize ethical and professional responsibilities in engineering situations and make informed judgments, which must consider the impact of engineering solutions in global, economic, environmental, and societal contexts."[14] All of these standards presuppose that there is a real, shared content of ethics that can be taught. This puts many American engineering professors in the impossible position of having to teach shared ethical standards, when neither they nor their students believe in shared ethical standards.

At Geneva College, we are committed to truths rooted in the historical Jewish ethical and legal tradition, and therefore we continue to hold to objective standards in ethics. Until about a century ago, this was the tradition widely embraced in Western culture. We hold that this tradition is essential to our culture's survival. We are trying to teach our students to follow the ancient paths.

Another obstacle to ethical instruction is materialism, the philosophy that all that exists is matter-energy. This viewpoint is expressed pointedly by Dr. Rodney Brooks, head of a robotics laboratory at the Massachusetts Institute of Technology. According to Brooks, "I believe myself and my children to be mere machines. Every person I meet is also a machine—a big bag of skin full of biomolecules interacting according to describable and knowable rules."[15] To his credit, Brooks admits that he cannot live consistently with his materialistic belief.

It is widely accepted that purely material objects do not have free will. Therefore, if human beings are purely material beings, then we do not make meaningful choices. All human behavior is the inevitable result of biochemical reactions. In the words of E. O. Wilson, longtime professor of biology at Harvard University, all we have left is "the illusion of free will."[16] But at Geneva

College, we continue to hold to the tradition of Western culture, widely held until about a century ago, that human beings are not purely material beings, but consist of a material aspect and a spiritual aspect, that is, a body and a soul. The soul has free will. The soul makes choices that the body puts into action.

Western ethical thinking has identified at least five main elements of ethics: (1) the highest good, (2) virtue, (3) law, (4) consequences, and (5) emotions.

The first element of ethics is the concept of what is good for human beings. Some things are desirable for the sake of something else. For example, a man desires money so that he can buy the things that his family needs and desires. But other things are desirable for their own sake. The highest good (*summum bonum*) must be among the things that are desired for their own sake. Some Western philosophies locate the *summum bonum* in this world, but in the historical Jewish tradition, the *summum bonum* transcends this world.[17] The fictional character James Bond has a family motto, *orbis non sufficit*, which means "the world is not enough." While Mr. Bond often acts unethically, his family motto is correct.

The second element of ethics is virtue or character. The ancient Greek and Roman philosophers, such as Plato, Aristotle, and Cicero, centered their ethical teaching on the character of the person. There are many virtuous character traits, and I do not know if there is an exhaustive list of them. But the ancient philosophers generally agreed that there were four cardinal (primary) virtues: prudence, justice, temperance, and fortitude.

Prudence, or wisdom, is the ability to choose the correct action, given all the circumstances. Prudence was generally regarded to be the most important virtue, because it puts all the other virtues into action. Justice is the ability to render to everyone what is due to them. Temperance, or moderation, is the ability to restrain desire within the proper limits. Fortitude, or courage, is the ability to do what is right in circumstances of danger or risk of loss.

With the rise of Christianity in the West, Christian theologians emphasized the so-called theological virtues: faith, hope, and love. Faith is trusting in the unseen One, based upon valid testimony. Hope is the confident expectation of future good promised to Christians. Love is regarding and treating others as of equal value to yourself. Love is the greatest virtue.[18]

At this point the teaching of Confucius[19] can be compared to that of the Western philosophers. I am only able to read Confucius in English translation, and I have learned enough to know that his sayings can be difficult to understand. Therefore, I ask for your patience in case I have misunderstood him; I would be happy to be corrected. Yet despite the danger of making a mistake, I have decided to comment on the teachings of Confucius to make connections between our cultures.

Confucius's emphasis on humaneness (*ren*) is comparable to the idea of virtue; as he says in *Lunyu*, "If you truly set your mind on being humane, you are not morally culpable."[20] Often his discussions with his disciples return to the question of how a man can develop the humane character of a gentleman (*junzi*): "A gentleman [*junzi*] is fair-minded and generous; he is not partisan or divisive. A petty man [*xiaoren*] is partisan and divisive; he is not fair-minded or generous."[21]

The third element of ethics is law. We could also describe this as rules or duty. Geneva College is committed to the law found in the historical Semitic tradition and summarized in the Ten Commandments. These laws instruct us to do what is right and to refrain from doing wrong.

Confucius often teaches about duty or rules for correct behavior, and at some points he teaches things that are similar to what we cherish in our tradition. For example, he says "Do not impose on others what you do not desire for yourself."[22] He affirms this rule at least two other times,[23] indicating its importance. It is the mirror image of what we call the Golden Rule, "As you wish that others would do to you, do so to them."[24] (Luke 6:31, ESV). Confucius connects humaneness to a great duty: "Fan Chi asked about humaneness. The Master said, 'Love others.'"[25] This corresponds to what we call the second great commandment, "Love your neighbor as yourself."[26]

The fourth element of ethics is consequences. Actions can be evaluated by how much benefit and harm they cause to people. Much engineering work is evaluated explicitly or implicitly in this way. A highway, for example, brings benefits such as the economic value of transporting goods from place to place and the pleasure of those who drive on it. It may also cause some harm, such as the destruction of homes or buildings in its path. In the US, it is not uncommon to evaluate large engineering projects in terms of a benefit-cost ratio, which is an attempt to measure the benefits and harms that will be caused by the project and to decide whether it should be undertaken based on their relative magnitude.

The fifth element of ethics is emotions. Currently in Western culture, emotions are given too much importance in ethics, to the extent that some believe that all ethical statements are merely statements of emotion, a philosophy known as emotivism. In the older Western tradition, however, emotion is considered to be a potential enemy of ethical behavior. We can be enticed to do something wrong by excessive or improper desire. Confucius (2014) also reflects on emotions when he says "When you do not have excessive desires, even if you were to offer rewards for stealing, people would not do it."[27] Thus, when emotion is well-regulated and trained in the proper direction, it can assist us in doing what is right.

While all five elements—and probably more—are important to teaching ethics, in my teaching of engineering students, I have focused primarily on law. There are several reasons to do this: (1) The concept of law is embedded in Western culture. (2) Law is easier to define and to understand, because it tells us which actions are right, and which are wrong. (3) Human laws, enacted and enforced by human governments, cover a large proportion of an engineer's ethical responsibility, and they have an enormous impact on the practice of engineering. I spend at least half of my course teaching how US law impacts engineering practice.

There are four major areas of US law that are particularly important for American students of engineering: (1) product liability law, (2) administrative law, (3) contract law, and (4) intellectual property law.[28] Students typically know little about these topics until they take my course, but most of them will soon be dealing with them in their careers.

Product liability law is concerned with the question of how much responsibility a company has when someone is injured or killed by one of their products. The example of the McDonnell-Douglas DC-10 jet airliner, with which I began this paper, falls into this category. Students often do not realize that their companies can be held responsible for injuries to customers even if the company had good intentions and was not aware that their product was dangerous. With respect to safety, products are expected to be designed up to the state of the art, which means the best that the engineering profession is capable of doing at a given time. If expert testimony shows that a safer method of design existed at the time the product in question was designed, then the company will have to compensate those who were injured by it.

If, on the other hand, the company was in fact aware of a dangerous feature of their product, and there was a way that this dangerous feature could be corrected, and they failed to correct it, then they can be found guilty of gross negligence. In this case, the company must not only compensate those injured by the product; they must also pay an additional penalty, usually much higher than compensation, called punitive damages.

Administrative law comes about in the US when an act of Congress establishes an agency to regulate activities in a particular area. For example, the Occupational Safety and Health Administration (OSHA) was established to protect the health and safety of workers, and it has enacted a wide variety of regulations that have a large impact on engineering. For example: "Trenches 5 feet (1.5 meters) deep or greater require a protective system unless the excavation is made entirely in stable rock."[29]

The second example at the beginning of this essay, concerning emissions from Volkswagen vehicles, is in the domain of administrative law. The Environmental Protection Agency sets the regulations for allowable emissions from motor vehicles. The EPA has a wide array of regulations that have a major impact on many aspects of US industry.

Contract law governs voluntary agreements between citizens, whether they are individuals or companies. Virtually all engineering work in the US is done under contracts. Construction contracts (for buildings, highways, water systems, and many other projects) are particularly complicated, because they typically involve three distinct parties: (1) the owner, who commissions the work and owns it when it is completed; (2) the architect/engineer, who designs it; and (3) the construction contractor, who builds it according to the architect/engineer's plans.

Intellectual property refers to the products of the creativity of artists and designers. Intellectual property law confers an intangible set of rights upon the creators. There are four types of intellectual property in the US: patents, copyrights, trade secrets, and trademarks. A vast amount of the economic value of businesses is tied up in the intellectual property that they own, and engineers contribute greatly to economic development by creating new intellectual property. It is especially important for students going into manufacturing to be aware of intellectual property law.

I will comment on one other ethical topic that I teach my students. As I mentioned earlier, various professional engineering organizations, such as the NSPE, ASCE, and ASME, have codes of ethics. Professional codes of ethics take the form of a series of rules to govern the behavior of individual professionals. These codes are not enacted by government but are the voluntary standards of the engineering profession itself. Professional codes of ethics are relevant to engineers in several ways. (1) In order to practice certain domains of engineering, an engineer is legally required to be registered as a Professional Engineer (PE). In addition to demonstrating technical competence, a candidate must take an oath to abide by the NSPE Code of Ethics to be registered as a PE. (2) Most engineers find it advantageous to belong to at least one professional society in the course of their careers. Members must agree to abide by the society's code of ethics. (3) The codes of ethics express to the public what the engineering profession itself defines as proper behavior to be expected from an engineer.

The ethics codes typically state that the engineer's most important responsibility is to safeguard the health and welfare of the public.[30] In elaborating on this fundamental duty, the codes require things like practicing only in the domain of one's technical competence. But the most difficult aspect of this duty is that the codes require the engineer to oppose their own employer or client if they overrule their professional judgment in a matter affecting the health and welfare of the public. The engineer must work within his company or organization to attempt to change a proposed design to limit the danger to the public. However, if that fails, they must inform appropriate authorities, usual a government agency, that a dangerous design is about to be constructed or manufactured.

This duty is called "whistleblowing." It is relevant to the example of the McDonnell-Douglas DC-10 jet airliner with which I began this paper. The chief engineer of Convair followed the codes of ethics up to a point; he did inform his employer of the danger of the blow-out of the cargo doors that would lead to the deaths of many innocent people, and he did attempt to persuade his company to correct the design. However, when his employer rejected his professional judgment, he should have informed the government agency responsible for aircraft safety at the time, the Federal Aviation Administration (FAA).

In conclusion, I hope that I have clearly illustrated the relevance of ethics to the practice of engineering and the importance of teaching it to engineering students. There is a broader context in which to view this. At Geneva College we are committed to educating students in the context of the liberal arts. Traditionally, the liberal arts address the question: what does it mean to be human? One answer to this question is that humans make decisions that have ethical implications.

Engineering is a human endeavor that, we believe, is best understood in the broader context of what it means to be human. Therefore, we require engineering students to take liberal arts courses. In a general way, this prepares them for my course in ethics. We also believe that it prepares them to be better human beings. Is it not a fine thing when education can achieve this?

Notes

[1]Unger, S. H. *Controlling Technology: Ethics and the Responsible Engineer* (New York, NY: Holt, Rinehart and Winston, 1982).

[2]Wikipedia, *McDonnell Douglass DC-10*. Retrieved May 23, 2019 from hhps://en.wikipedia.org/wiki/McDonnell_Douglas_DC-10. 2019a

[3]Wikipedia, 2019a.

[4]Wikipedia, 2019a.

[5]Wikipedia, *Volkswagen emissions scandal*. Retrieved May 23, 2019 from https://en.wikipedia.org/wiki/Volkswagen_emissions_scandal. 2019b.

[6]Wikipedia, *Defective device*. Retrieved May 2019 from https:/en.wikipedia.org/wiki/Defeat_device. 2019c.

[7]Wikipedia, 2019b.

[8]N. Bomey, Judge approves $15B Volkswagen settlement, *USA Today*. Retrieved May 21, 2019. https://www.usatoday.com/story/money/cars2016/10/25/volkswagen-settlement-approved/92719174/

[9]P. A. Vesilinid, Views on Teaching Ethics and Morals, *Journal of Professional Issues in Engineering Education and Practice, American Society of Civil Engineers*, 1991. Pp. 117, 2, 88–95.

[10]National Society of Professional Engineers (NPSE), *Code of Ethics*. Retrieved May 23, 2019 from https://nspe.org/resources/ethics/code-ethics, 2018.

[11]American Society of Civil Engineers (ASCE), *Code of Ethics*, 2017. Retrieved May 23, 2019 from https://asce.org/code-of-ethics/

[12]American Society of Mechanical Engineers (ASME), *Society Policy,*

Ethics: Code of Ethics of Engineers, 2012. Retrieved May 23, 2019 from https://www.asme.org/media/ResourceFiles/AboutASME/Get%20Involved/Advocacy/Policy-Publicaations/P-15-7-Ethics.pdf

[13]Illinois Institute of Technology: Center for the Study of Ethics in the Professions (IIT CSEP), *The Codes Collection (ECC): Engineering*, 2019. Retrieved May 23, 2019 from https: //etics.iit.edu/ecodes/ethics-area/10

[14]Accreditation Board for Engineering and Technology, *Criteria for Accrediting Engineering Programs, 2019–2020: Criterion 3: Student Outcomes*. Retrieved May 23, 2019 from https://www.abet.org/accrediation/accreditation-criteria/criteria-for-accreding-engineering-programs-2019-2020/#GC3

[15]R. A. Brooks, *Flesh and Machines* (New York, NY: Pantheon Books, 2002), 174.

[16]E. O. Wilson, *Consilience*. (New York, NY: Vintage Books, 1998), 130.

[17]Cornelius Van Til, *Christian Theistic Ethics* (Phillipsburg, NJ: Presbyterian and Reformed Publishing Company, 1980).

[18]1 Corinthians 13:13.

[19]Confucius, *The Analects (Lunyu)*, translation and commentary by Annping Chin (New York, NY: Penguin Books, 2014).

[20]Confucius, *Lunyu*, 4.4.

[21]Confucius, *Lunyu*, 2.14.

[22]Confucius, *Lunyu*, 12.2.

[23]Confucius, *Lunyu*, 5:12, 15:24.

[24]Luke 6:31 *English Standard Version* (ESV).

[25]Confucius, *Lunyu*, 12.22.

[26]Matthew 22:39 (ESV).

[27]Confucius, *Lunyu*, 12:18.

[28]C. M. Gayton, *Legal Aspects of Engineering*. 9th ed. (Dubuque, IA: Kendall Hunt Publishing Company, 2012).

[29]*Occupational Safety and Health Administration, OSHA Fact Sheet: Trenching and Excavation Safety*, Retrieved May 23, 2019 from https://www.osha.gov/OshDoc/data_Hurricane_Facts/trench_excavation_fs.pdf

[30]*ASCE*, 2017; *ASME*, 2012; *NSPE*, 2018; *IIT CSEP*, 2019.

References

ABET (Accreditation Board for Engineering and Technology) (2019). *Criteria for Accrediting Engineering Programs, 2019 – 2020: Criterion 3: Student Outcomes*. Retrieved May 23, 2019 from https://www.abet.org/accreditation/accreditation-criteria/criteria-for-accrediting-engineering-programs-2019–2020/#GC3

ASCE (American Society of Civil Engineers) (2017). *Code of Ethics*. Retrieved May 23, 2019, from https://www.asce.org/code-of-ethics/

ASME (American Society of Mechanical Engineers) (2012). *Society Policy, Ethics: Code of Ethics of Engineers*. Retrieved May 23, 2019, from https://www.asme.org/wwwasmeorg/media/ResourceFiles/AboutASME/Get%20Involved/Advocacy/Policy-Publications/P-15-7-Ethics.pdf

Bomey, N. (2016). Judge approves $15B Volkswagen settlement, *USA Today*. Retrieved May 21, 2019. https://www.usatoday.com/story/money/cars/2016/10/25/volkswagen-settlement-approved/92719174/

Brooks, R. A. (2002). *Flesh and Machines*, New York, NY, Pantheon Books.

Confucius (2014). *The Analects (Lunyu)*, translation and commentary by Annping Chin, New York, NY, Penguin Books.

Gayton, C. M. (2012). *Legal Aspects of Engineering*. 9th ed. Dubuque, IA, Kendall Hunt Publishing Company.

IIT CSEP (Illinois Institute of Technology: Center for the Study of Ethics in the Professions) (2019). *The Ethics Codes Collection (ECC): Engineering*. Retrieved May 23, 2019 from http://ethics.iit.edu/ecodes/ethics-area/10

James Bond Wiki (2019). *The World Is Not Enough (film)*. Retrieved may 23, 2019 from https://jamesbond.fandom.com/wiki/The_World_Is_Not_Enough_(film)

NSPE (National Society of Professional Engineers) (2018). *Code of Ethics*. Retrieved May 23, 2019, from https://www.nspe.org/resources/ethics/code-ethics

OSHA, Occupational Safety and Health Administration (2019). *OSHA Fact Sheet: Trenching and Excavation Safety*. Retrieved on May 23, 2019 from https://www.osha.gov/OshDoc/data_Hurricane_Facts/trench_excavation_fs.pdf

Unger, S. H. (1982). *Controlling Technology: Ethics and the Responsible Engineer*, New York, NY, Holt, Rinehart and Winston.

VanTil, C. (1980), *Christian Theistic Ethics*. Phillipsburg, NJ, Presbyterian and Reformed Publishing Company.

Vesilind, P. A. (1991). Views on Teaching Ethics and Morals, *Journal of Professional Issues in Engineering Education and Practice, American Society of Civil Engineers*, 117, 2, 88–95. https://doi.org/10.1061/(ASCE)1052-3928(1991)117:2(88)

Wikipedia (2019a). *McDonnell Douglas DC-10*. Retrieved May 23, 2019 from https://en.wikipedia.org/wiki/McDonnell_Douglas_DC-10

Wikipedia (2019b). *Volkswagen emissions scandal*. Retrieved May 23, 2019 from https://en.wikipedia.org/wiki/Volkswagen_emissions_scandal

Wikipedia (2019c). *Defeat device*. Retrieved May 23, 2019 from https://en.wikipedia.org/wiki/Defeat_device

Wilson, E. O. (1998). *Consilience*. New York, NY, Vintage Books.

About the Editors

Jonathan M. Watt, M.Div., M.A., Ph.D. serves as Professor of Biblical Studies at Geneva College (Beaver Falls, Pa.), Adjunct Professor of Biblical Studies at the Reformed Presbyterian Theological Seminary (Pittsburgh, Pa.), and pastor of the Tusca Area Reformed Presbyterian Church (RPCNA) in Beaver, Pa. He is the author of *Code-Switching in Luke and Acts* (Peter Lang), the forthcoming commentary on *Colossians-Philemon* in the Brill Exegetical Commentary Series, the forthcoming commentary on *Hebrews* in the New Testament Discourse Analysis Commentary Series (Wipf & Stock), the editor of *Pro Gloria Christi: Essays in Honor of Edward A. Robson* (Beaver Falls, PA), a co-editor of the forthcoming *Encyclopedia of Biblical Greek Language and Linguistics* (Baker), and author of numerous chapters, articles and papers mostly on Hellenistic Greek and linguistics.

Bruce R. Backensto, M.Div. is a retired Teaching Elder in the Reformed Presbyterian Church of North America, having served 42 years, beginning in Sterling, KS (1972-1980), church planting/organizing pastor in Colorado Springs, CO (1980-86), serving in Ridgefield Park, NJ (1989-1995) and finishing serving the First Reformed Presbyterian Church in Beaver Falls, PA. In 1995, he was installed minister in the Geneva RPC in Beaver Falls and helped effectuate the merger of that congregation with the First RPC congregation in Patterson Township, from which he retired in 2014 after serving 19 years. He serves as an Adjunct Professor of the Reformed Presbyterian Theological Seminary. He has a chapter in *The Church and Her Ministry* entitled "The Parity of Elders," and a chapter in the Festschrift in honor of Dr. Ed Robson, edited by Dr. Watt. He has articles published in *The Covenanter Witness* and *The Confessional Presbyterian*, "The Pepper Corn Controversy" as addressed by John Brown of Wamphray. He has served as the Book Review Editor for *The Covenanter Witness*. He was a member of the Geneva College Board of Trustees for several decades and is serving as a Corporator of the College presently. His wife, Kim, is the Development Assistant at the Reformed Presbyterian Theological Seminary. Together they have eight children and eight grandchildren.

About the Contributors

Karla Threadgill Byrd is the executive director of the Geneva College Pittsburgh, formerly known as the Center for Urban Biblical Ministry (CUBM), located at the Reformed Presbyterian Theology Seminary. When he was President of Geneva College in 1992, Jack White was a founding member of CUBM and still serves on the board of directors. Dr. White, always the role model of a servant leader, also spearheaded CUBM's collaborative partnerships in The Marriage Works and Two-Gether Pittsburgh grants. Both programs trained facilitators who then brought workshops and seminars on marriage enrichment and success throughout the five-county area of southwestern Pennsylvania.

Byron G. Curtis, Ph.D. is Professor of Biblical Studies at Geneva College in Beaver Falls, Pa., where he has taught Hebrew language, Old Testament Studies, and Christian theology since 1991. His published research focuses on the Minor Prophets and the history of biblical interpretation. He is the author of Up the Steep and Stony Road (Academia Biblica 25; Atlanta: Society of Biblical Literature, 2006), a study in the Hebrew text of Zechariah. He often serves the wider Church as preacher, teacher, and theological consultant. In 2011, he was Visiting Professor of Biblical Studies at Jerusalem University College, on Mount Zion, Israel. He previously served as Associate Pastor at Peace Presbyterian Church (PCA), Cary, NC; on the staff of the Reformed Presbyterian Church of North Hills (RPCNA), near Pittsburgh; and as Associate Campus Minister at LaRoche College, with the Coalition for Christian Outreach. His first "biblical" job came at age 20, when Dr. Jack White and Professor Joseph Hill hired him as a teaching assistant for freshmen Bible classes. He and his wife, Sue Ann, have two grown children, Nathan and Naomi, and one granddaughter, the ever-artful Psyche Ariel.

Robert M. Frazier, Ph.D. is Professor of Philosophy at Geneva College. He is the author of *Responsible Belief* (Pickwick Publicans) and has presented and published essays on Augustine, Kierkegaard, and Pittsburgh baseball. He has served as a pastor in congregations in Massachusetts, New York, and Pennsylvania, and as the Executive Presbyter of Beaver Butler Presbytery. Marina and Bob have known Jack since the early 1970s, soon after Bob came to faith in Jesus Christ, and he notes that Jack models many of the traits identified as a pastor/public intellectual – consistent with the chapter Bob has written for this volume.

Bradshaw Frey, Ph.D. is a graduate of Geneva College, where he has taught for the past 35 years. His doctoral work focused on segregation, re-segregation and bureaucratization of education. He is deeply engaged in linking college and community and, with two colleagues and two students as assistants, formed the Beaver Falls Community Development Corporation. He and his wife live in Beaver Falls, Pa. and have three adult children and five grandchildren.

James Gidley, Ph.D. has been Professor of Civil Engineering at Geneva College since 1990. He served as the chair of the Engineering Department from 1990-2000 and 2003-2019 and has taught ethics to virtually every student passing through the engineering program at Geneva College since 1994. He received a doctorate in engineering from Harvard University in 1981. He was ordained as a ruling elder in the Orthodox Presbyterian Church in 1985 and has served for more than 30 years on the OPC's Committee on Christian Education. He and his wife Betsy live across the river from the College, not far from the "G", and they have two grown sons, Jesse and Andrew, and one granddaughter, Madeline.

Esther Lightcap Meek, Ph.D. is Professor of Philosophy at Geneva College. She is a Makoto Fujimura Institute Scholar, and a member of the Michael Polanyi Society. Her books include *Longing to Know: The Philosophy of Knowledge for Ordinary People* (Brazos, 2003); *Loving to Know: Introducing Covenant Epistemology* (Cascade, 2011); *A Little Manual for Knowing* (Cascade, 2014); and *Contact with Reality: Michael Polanyi's Realism and Why It Matters* (Cascade, 2017). Esther enjoys talking with people in all walks of life about knowing and reality.

Edward A. Robson, Th.M., Ph.D. is Professor-Emeritus of New Testament Studies, Reformed Presbyterian Theological Seminary (1993–2005). He served as pastor of the Syracuse Reformed Presbyterian Church (RPCNA) from 1968–1992. He is the author of *Dear Young Shepherd: A Guide to the Gentle Use of a Pastor's Rod and Staff* (2007), and of a devotional commentary series on *Revelation: The Book of Blessing,* Volumes 1–7A*lB* (2010–18), along with *A Grammar of the Revelation* and *Appendices to the Grammar* (2019), and the forthcoming devotional commentary on *The Christology of the Book of Revelation.* Ed and Jack were classmates at RPTS (1958–61), and worked together at Community House Youth Center on the North Side of Pittsburgh during some of those years. The first wedding officiated by White was the marriage of Ed and Gretchen Robson in 1962, and they have been married more than 57 years.

Sharon L. Sampson, M.T.S. serves on the staff at the Reformed Presbyterian Theological Seminary, where she received her Master of Theological Studies degree with a concentration in biblical counseling. She enjoys teaching and speaking in a variety of settings and writes regularly for the Gentle Reformation blog. International travel is also an interest, and Sharon first met Jack White when they were part of the Calvin 500 Tour to Geneva, Switzerland, in 2009. This connection provided the rationale for Sharon's paper in this present work.

C. Scott Shidemantle, Ph.D. serves as Professor of Biblical Studies and Coordinator of the Bible Core at Geneva College, beginning his work at the College in 1997 during Dr. White's presidency. Dr. Shidemantle has interests in the Johannine literature of the New Testament (Gospel of John, the Epistles of John, and John's Revelation), with a special focus on how the redemptive-historical themes found in the Johannine literature inform a Christian understanding of the relationship between the Old and New Testaments. He is a frequent book review contributor in the area of Johannine studies for the *Journal of the Evangelical Theological Society* and member of both the Society of Biblical Literature and the Evangelical Theological Society. Dr. Shidemantle is a Ruling Elder in the PCA, the husband of Wendy Shidemantle (Associate Professor of Spanish at Geneva College), and proud dad of two sons (John and Luke).

Dean R. Smith, D. Min. came to faith in Christ at Geneva College in the fall of 1961, around the time Jack White became pastor of the College Hill R.P. Church and, subsequently, Dean's friend, mentor and pastor. He later succeeded Jack as pastor of that congregation, and later became chair of the Biblical Studies department at Geneva College (serving from 1991-2013), not long before Jack was to become college president. His areas of interest have included study of Luke/Acts, instruction in faith-based counseling, and development of the Community Ministry program in the college's Degree Completion Program. He has published or presented on the Scottish Covenanters, themes in Lukan writings, and he served on the Home Mission Board of the RPCNA for many years, and he was an active designer and implementer of growth programs for churches. Dean was listed in *Who's Who Among Teachers* (2002, 2003).

Kenneth G. Smith, a retired WWII navy veteran, was called to and pastored several churches, became director of Christian education for the Reformed Presbyterian Church of North America, then served as a missionary to the Island of Cyprus. He authored several practical books, married Floy Moody who gave birth to three sons, the eldest of whom was to serve as president of Geneva College. Ken is now living in the Reformed Presbyterian Home in Pittsburgh, Pa.

John Stanko, Ph.D. is a pastor, author, consultant, and publisher. He served as the assistant director and part-time faculty for Geneva's CUBM program and was also on the faculty of the Geneva College Masters of Science in Organizational Leadership program. When not in the States, John is usually involved in some project or program on the continent of Africa.

Jeffrey A Stivason, Ph.D. is pastor of Grace Reformed Presbyterian Church (RPCNA) in Gibsonia, Pa., and has recently been appointed Professor of New Testament Studies at the Reformed Presbyterian Theological Seminary (Pittsburgh, Pa). He is the author of *From Inscrutability to Concursus* (P&R), has contributed to *The Jonathan Edwards Encyclopedia* (Eerdmans), and is the Senior Editor of *Place for Truth*, an online magazine for the Alliance of Confessing Evangelicals.

Calvin L. Troup, Ph.D. is the twentieth president of Geneva College. After graduating from Geneva in 1983, he worked as a trend analyst for The Naisbitt Group (owned by its eponymous author of *Megatrends*), as congressional staff aide to U.S. Rep. Duncan Hunter, and as an executive for the National Association of Life Underwriters in Washington, D.C. In 1989, he returned to academia, earning a master's degree (1991) and a Ph.D. (1994) in Speech Communication from the Pennsylvania State University. He served on the faculties of Penn State, University Park, Pennsylvania, and Indiana University, Bloomington, Indiana, before moving to the Department of Communication & Rhetorical Studies at Duquesne University, Pittsburgh, Pa., where he directed the university's nationally-ranked Rhetoric Ph.D. program. His scholarly interests are in the rhetoric and philosophy of St. Augustine and the rhetoric of technology. His books include *Temporality, Eternity, and Wisdom: The Rhetoric of Augustine's Confessions* (Univ. of South Carolina Press, 1999) and *Augustine for the Philosophers: The Rhetor of Hippo, the Confessions* (Baylor University Press, 2014). He has edited the *Journal of Communication and Religion* and was president of the Religious Communication Association. He is the editor-elect of *Explorations in Media Ecology*, the international journal of the Media Ecology Association. Since returning to the Pittsburgh area, he has served on the Geneva College Board of Corporators and Board of Trustees, leading a number of college and board committees. He has been the Chair of the Board of Trustees' Education Committee for many years. Calvin and his wife Amy have four daughters, four sons-in-law, and three granddaughters.

Maureen O. Vanterpool, Ph.D. served as Professor of Leadership Studies at Geneva College from 2000 to 2014. White took a personal interest in connecting her with community organizations with which he was involved, including Family Guidance, Inc. (Pittsburgh), and the Morristown, Liberia School Project. Her writings have included a collection of puzzles and games for Bible study titled *Bible Goodies*, and she has written several articles for professional journals. She is the author of a February 2019 article published by Bible Advocate Press titled, "He Never Gave Up on Me," which is her testimony to God's faithfulness throughout her life.

Barry York, M.A.T., M.Div., D.Min. served more than two decades as a church planter and then pastor of Sycamore Reformed Presbyterian Church in Kokomo, In., before becoming the Professor of Pastoral Theology at the Reformed Presbyterian Theological Seminary. In 2018, he was appointed President of RPTS and, on behalf of the seminary, awarded Jack White the "Faithful Servant" award in 2019 for his many years of preaching, leadership, and service for the church. He is author of *Hitting the Marks: Restoring the Essential Identity of the Church*, writes regularly for the blog *Gentle Reformation*, co-hosts the podcast 3GT, and is general editor of the *Reformed Presbyterian Theological Journal.*

About Falls City Press

Established in 2014, Falls City Press is nestled in the Beaver River Valley in Western Pennsylvania.

In all of their work, the staff of Falls City Press is committed to the flourising of readers, writers, and their local communities.

www.fallscitypress.com

www.ingramcontent.com/pod-product-compliance
Lightning Source LLC
Chambersburg PA
CBHW032147080426
42735CB00008B/611
* 9 7 8 0 9 8 6 4 0 5 1 5 0 *